ISBN 978-1-333-30198-9
PIBN 10486211

1 MONTH OF
FREE
READING

at

www.ForgottenBooks.com

By purchasing this book you are eligible for one month membership to ForgottenBooks.com, giving you unlimited access to our entire collection of over 700,000 titles via our web site and mobile apps.

To claim your free month visit:
www.forgottenbooks.com/free486211

English
Français
Deutsche
Italiano
Español
Português

www.forgottenbooks.com

Mythology Photography **Fiction**
Fishing Christianity **Art** Cooking
Essays Buddhism Freemasonry
Medicine **Biology** Music **Ancient
Egypt** Evolution Carpentry Physics
Dance Geology **Mathematics** Fitness
Shakespeare **Folklore** Yoga Marketing
Confidence Immortality Biographies
Poetry **Psychology** Witchcraft
Electronics Chemistry History **Law**
Accounting **Philosophy** Anthropology
Alchemy Drama Quantum Mechanics
Atheism Sexual Health **Ancient History**
Entrepreneurship Languages Sport
Paleontology Needlework Islam
Metaphysics Investment Archaeology
Parenting Statistics Criminology
Motivational

WELD'S

ENGLISH GRAMMAR,

ILLUSTRATED BY EXERCISES IN

COMPOSITION, ANALYZING, AND PARSING.

BY ALLEN H. WELD, A. M.,

AUTHOR OF ANALYZING AND PARSING BOOK, LATIN LESSONS AND READER.

IMPROVED EDITION.

SANBORN & CARTER,
PORTLAND,
MAINE.

Entered according to Act of Congress, in the Year 1849, by
SANBORN AND CARTER,
In the Clerk's Office of the District Court of the District of Maine.

BOSTON:
Old Dickinson Office .... C. C. P. Moody, Stereotyper,
No. 52 Washington Street.

PREFACE.

As the plates from which the previous editions of this Work were printed were unfit for further use, and on that account it became necessary to stereotype a new set, the opportunity thus presented for a revision has been improved. In re-writing the book, full advantage has been taken of the unfriendly as well as the friendly strictures on former editions. From the past success of the Work, the Author has been much encouraged in this new labor, and has earnestly endeavored to make it more useful, and more acceptable to the hundreds of excellent teachers who have shown it continued favor and indulgence. He hopes his efforts will not be found to have been in vain.

No material alteration is made from the original plan; but the execution of it, in almost every part, is considerably modified. Much is added to the analytical, and also to the grammatical part of the Work; and, although its size is not enlarged, yet, by a more economical management of the type, it actually contains about one third more than any former edition.

The plan pursued necessarily requires some repetition; but this is avoided as much as is consistent with practical convenience. It is the design of the Part following Orthography, to explain and combine the elements of a simple sentence; but in doing this, the principles of Syntax are developed at every step. But these could not be fully illustrated in this Part, without diverting the mind of the learner from the chief end to be attained. It therefore seemed necessary to state principles as they were developed, and afterwards to illustrate them more fully in the Part devoted exclusively to Syntax. For a similar reason a separate Part was appropriated to Etymology. In this are contained tables, inflections and details, which must necessarily have a place in a Grammar for the purpose of reference. Had these been introduced in connection with the analytical process, they would have separated too widely from one another the explanations of the elementary parts of the sentence. It is confidently believed that in practice the arrangement adopted will be found convenient, and that the occasional repetitions and recapitulations will not be considered by the experienced teacher as a defect in the work.

While preparing the present edition, the author has had access to most of the principal works on Grammar, such as those of HARRIS, LOWTH, WARD, MURRAY, CROMBIE, DE SACY, CRAMP, and WEBSTER; and also to the articles on Grammar in the Edinburgh, Britannica, and Metropolitan Encyclopædias. In the analytical part much assistance has been derived from the Greek Grammars of BUTTMAN and KUNER, from the Latin Grammars of ZUMPT, and ANDREWS and STODDARD, and from the work of DE SACY on General Grammar.

The general plan and peculiar features of the Work, which distinguish it from others on the same subject, may be inferred from the "Synopsis of Grammatical Relations," found on pages 230 and 231.

BOSTON, *July*, 1849.

FAMILIAR INSTRUCTION FOR YOUNG BEGINNERS.

THE following introductory pages are prefixed to the work, mainly for the purpose of suggesting to the teacher a familiar and intelligible method of explaining to the learner the formation of words and sentences ; the terms employed in Grammar ; and the classification of words into what is called Parts of Speech.

Each lesson presents a subject for a familiar lecture, with a few illustrations which can be varied or extended at the discretion of the teacher.

LESSON I. (*Letters.*)

NOTE. — Let the class stand at the Blackboard, or be furnished with slates while practising these lessons ; or the teacher can do the writing on the Board for the class.

Write the marks or letters *a, e, i, o, u.* Sound or utter each separately.*

Write the letters *b, c, d, f, g, j, k, l, m, n, p, q, r, s, t, v.* Endeavor to sound each by itself, not using *a, e,* or *u* before or after them. Try to sound *b* and *d* in the word *bird, c* in the word *cat, f* in *faith, g* in *go, k* in *kind, s* in *sail, j* in *judge, t* in *toil.*

Sound *a* in the words *bate, bat, bar, ball.*

Sound *e* in *mete, met.*

Sound *i* in *pine, pin.*

Sound *o* in *note, not, move.*

Sound *u* in *tube, tub, full.*

What is the difference between the letters *a, e, i, o, u,* and the letters *b, c, d, f, g, h,* &c. ?

Ans. The letters *a, e, i, o, u,* can be sounded easily alone, and are called *vocals* or *vowels.* The other letters are not easily sounded without the aid of vowels, and are called *consonants.*

---

* Let the class practise simultaneously, on the different sound of these letters, with a full and distinct utterance.

1*

LESSON II. (*Words.*)

Put the letters *b, d, r, i,* together in such a way that they will call to mind something which you have seen.   In like manner place the letters *h, s, r, e, o ; d, g, o ; w, i, d, n ; r, n, i, a.*

When letters are put together so as to mean something, they form *words*. Before letters were invented, certain pictures or signs were used in writing, instead of words.

REMARK. — The whole number of words, consisting of about 40,000, is divided into *eight different* classes or sorts.

LESSON III. (*Classification of words.*) NOUNS, PRONOUNS.

One class of words consists of the *names* of things which we can see or think of.

Write or mention the names of the objects which you can see or think of.

Does every object have a name ?   *Ans.* A large number of objects of the same kind has a *common* name.   For example ; there is a great number of horses, and but one common name for all, viz. : *horse.*

Do any objects have a *particular* name which is applicable to no other object ?   *Ans.* Some objects are so important, that we wish to speak of them separately, and for convenience, we give them a particular name ; as, Washington, Boston, Amazon, James, Charles, &c.

Will you give particular names to some mountains ? cities ? rivers ? towns ? persons ?

Do trees, birds, fish, and stones, have particular names ?   Why not ?

Words which denote the names of objects and things are called NOUNS.

Write the words *I, thou, he, she, it, we, you, they, him, he, them, who, which.*

Are these words names of things ?   *Ans.* They are not names or nouns, but they stand in place of nouns, and are called *pronouns.*

EXAMPLE. — I heard from my brother yesterday ; *he* was well.   The word *he* is used to avoid repeating *brother.*

LESSON IV. (*Classification of words.*) VERBS.

Write the words *sings, runs, neighs.*

Do these words denote the names of objects ?   What do they denote ? *Ans.* They denote what something does.   *What* sings ?   *What* runs ? *What* neighs ?

Write other words which will denote what *a man, a horse, a lion, or a dog,* does.

How does the word *bird* differ from the word *sings?* *Ans.* The first is the name of a certain animal, the last denotes what the bird does.

What is the difference between the words *fox* and *runs?* *horse* and *neighs?* *dog* and *barks?* *sun* and *shines?* *wind* and *blows?*

Words which denote what any thing does, has done, or will do, are called VERBS.*

REMARK. — The two classes of words explained, viz.: *the noun* and the *verb*, comprise a large part of all the words in the English language.

LESSON V. (*Classification of words.*) ADJECTIVES.

Write the words *good, great, wise, prudent.*

Are these words nouns? Why not? Write each before the noun man. What do these words denote, when used before man? *Ans.* They denote *what kind* of a man, or the *quality* of a man.

Write words which will show what kind of a house you live in — what kind of a book you hold in your hand — what kind of a day it is.

These words which denote *what kind* or quality, are called ADJECTIVES.

NOTE — The words *an* or *a*, and *the* are generally called *articles*, but as they resemble in their office the words *one, this, that, &c.*, they are sometimes classed with adjectives which limit or restrict the meaning of nouns, and are called Definitive adjectives.

What is the difference between the words *horse* and *gray?* *Ans.* The word *horse* is the name of an animal, the word *gray* denotes the kind, or quality of something. What is the difference between the words *light* and *pleasant?* *boy* and *good?* *tree* and *high?* *house* and *large?*

Apply three adjectives to *man;* three to *child;* three to *day;* three to *night;* four to *horse;* five to *tree;* three to *sun.*

LESSON VI. (*Classification of words.*) ADVERBS.

Write the words *pleasantly, sweetly, cheerfully.*

Can these words be joined to nouns? In the expression, *the sun shines,* to which word can *pleasantly* be joined to make sense? What kind of a word is *shines?* "The bird sings *sweetly.*" Which word shows *how* the bird sings? "The night was very dark." Which word shows *how* dark the night was? What kind of a word is dark? "He came *yesterday.*" Which word denotes the time? With which word is *yesterday* connected?

* This is not designed as a complete definition of the verb. Oral explanation from the teacher, will be necessary to make the office of the verb intelligible to the learner.

Words which denote *manner, time, quantity,* &c., are called ADVERBS.

There are three other classes of words, termed PREPOSITIONS, see § 7; CONJUNCTIONS, see § 12; INTERJECTIONS, see § 14; these comprise but few words compared with the classes which have been explained above.

SUMMARY.

What is the number of words estimated to be in the English language?

Into what sorts or classes are these words divided, as explained in preceding lessons?

Name the Parts of Speech. *Ans.* THE NOUN, THE PRONOUN, THE ADJECTIVE, THE VERB, THE ADVERB, THE PREPOSITION, THE CONJUNCTION, and THE INTERJECTION.

LESSON VII. (*The sentence.*)

Write on the board or slate, in separate columns, the following *nouns* and *verbs.*

Nouns. — Wind, snow, stars.   *Verbs.* — Shine, flies, flows.

Place the nouns and the verbs together in such a way that they will make sense. How many things can be said with the six words above? Words put together in such a manner as to express an idea, form a SENTENCE; as, *The wind blows; the stars shine.* Write sentences, using the following words:

Water, ice, trees, sun, horse, grow, melts, freezes, shines, dogs, children, bark, play, walk, men, boys, ride, rolls, ball.

What parts of speech have you used in each sentence?

NOTE. — Every sentence contains at least one verb, and one noun, or something standing for a noun.

Write six sentences, using such nouns and verbs as you can recollect.

LESSON VIII. (*Modifications.*)

Join an *adjective* to each of the *nouns* in the following sentences to denote some quality; as, The oak falls; join an adjective to the noun *oak,* and the sentence will read, "The *sturdy* oak falls."

The — youth learns.   The — children obey.
The — sun shines.   The — child weeps.
The — bird sings.   The — water flows.

Join an *adverb* to each of the verbs in the sentences above; as, The youth learns *readily;* readily is an adverb joined to the verb learns. Point out the *adjectives, nouns, verbs,* and *adverbs,* in the following sentences.

Pine trees grow rapidly. The gentle wind blows softly. The little bird sings sweetly. The angry waves dash violently. The joyful tidings came to day. A wise man acts prudently.

LESSON IX. (*Formation of sentences.*)

Write in separate columns the following *adjectives, nouns, verbs,* and *adverbs.*

Adjectives. — Pleasant, kind, proud, dark.

Nouns. — Cloud, sun, parents, youth.

Verbs. — Shines, hangs, conducts, provide.

Adverbs. — Frowningly, brightly, carefully, unbecomingly.

Place four of the words above together, so as to form a sentence; as, The dark cloud hangs frowningly.

LESSON X. (*Object.*)

Write on the board or slate, " The wind shakes the leaves."

Which noun denotes the thing that acts ? *Ans.* Wind. Which noun denotes the thing acted upon ? *Ans.* Leaves. Which word expresses the action of the wind upon the leaves ? *Ans.* The verb *shakes.*

Point out the nouns which denote the actor, and the thing acted upon, in the following sentences.

The sun melts the snow.	The boy strikes the bell.
The wind drives the ship.	The hawk seizes the dove.
The frost swells the ground.	The rose perfumes the air.

In what condition or relation is the noun " sun," in the first sentence ? *Ans.* In the condition or relation which denotes the thing that acts. In what state or relation is the word " snow " ? *Ans.* In the state or relation to denote the thing acted upon.

The condition or relation of a noun in a sentence, is called its case.

The noun which denotes the doer or the thing spoken of, is in the *nominative case.*

The noun which denotes the thing acted upon, is in the *objective case.**

---

* The *subject* of a verb in the *passive form* is an exception to this remark.

Point out the nominative and objective cases in the sentences above. See § 18.

NOTE. — The cases of nouns need to be illustrated more fully than the limits of these first lessons will permit. But the teacher will be able by a little oral instruction, to make the subject intelligible to young learners. In this connection may be explained the difference between a *transitive* and an *intransitive* verb ; and also the *number* and *gender* of nouns.

LESSON XI. (*Prepositions, &c.*)

Write, " Rain falls — the clouds."

Place some word *before* " the clouds " to make sense.

They went — Boston — the cars.

Place a word before " Boston," and one before " the cars," to make sense.

The words which have been supplied are called PREPOSI-TIONS.   For further explanation and exercises, see §   6.

Write, " James — Charles — Thomas are brothers."   " George reads — writes."   What words should be supplied to connect James with Charles ? Charles with Thomas ?   reads with writes ?

He is happy *because* he is good.

What word connects *he is happy*, with *he is good ?*

The part of speech used to connect sentences or words, is called the CONJUNCTION.   See § 11.

INTERJECTIONS are exclamatory words ; as, O ! ah ! alas ! See § 14.

LESSON XII.

When the parts of speech and their offices are well understood, the learner can proceed to the exercise of forming sentences, gradually extending them by joining qualifying words to the principal parts, according to the following method.

SENTENCE.   The wind drives.

Join an adjective. — The *tempestuous* wind drives.

Join an objective case. — The tempestuous wind drives *the ship.*

Join an adverb. — The tempestuous wind drives the ship *violently.*

Join a preposition and a noun following.   { The tempestuous wind drives the ship violently *against the rocks.*

Extend the following sentences in a similar way.

The horse draws —	The scholar learns —
The sun warms —	Birds build —
The tree bears —	The tiger seizes —

Such exercises can be varied or extended at the pleasure of the teacher.

REMARK. — Exercises of this kind not only impart an interest to the study of Grammar, but also serve to facilitate the progress of the young learner, in acquiring a knowledge of the essential principles of language.

LESSONS FOR PARSING.

LESSON I.

Point out the nouns, verbs, and adjectives, in the lines below :

Cæsar, yesterday, shines, useful, dog, white, barks, runs, king, proper, rules, master, Cato, wise, sees, strives.

Point out the adjectives and the adverbs in the same lines.

DIRECTION. — The noun which denotes that of which something is said, is in the *nominative* case.

The bird sings. The dogs howl. Men labor. Time flies. The moon is bright. The stars twinkle.

LESSON II.

DIRECTION. — Some adjectives are joined to nouns, to qualify their meaning ; as, A *good* man ; *good* qualifies man.

Mention what the adjectives qualify in the following expressions :

Tall trees. Pale moon. Lurid sky. The day is long. A mild disposition. A rapid current. A florid countenance. The sky is blue. A fleet horse. A ferocious tiger. A stormy night. Time is short.

LESSON III.

DIRECTION. — A verb is used to assert something about that which its nominative denotes; as, The rain *falls ;* the verb *falls* is used to assert something about rain.

Point out the nominative case, and the word which is used to assert something.

Charles reads. James studies. The farmer ploughs. The fire burns. The coachman drives. The scholar learns. Sweet music charms. The tall tree bends.

LESSON IV.

DIRECTION. — The noun which follows a *transitive* * verb is in the *objective* case ; as, The miser loves *gold ;* gold is in the objective case.

---

* For an explanation of transitive verbs, See ∫ 3.

Point out the nouns in the objective case in the following sentences.

Charles reads his book. James studies his lesson. The farmer ploughs his ground. The fire burns the wood. The coachman drives his team. The scholar gains knowledge.

LESSON V.

DIRECTION. — Adverbs are joined to verbs, adjectives, and other adverbs, to modify their meaning.

NOTE. — Adverbs may be generally known by asking *how ? when !* or *how much ?* the word that answers is the adverb.

The bird flies, [*how ?*] *Ans.* Swiftly; swiftly is the adverb. He is very ill ; *how* ill ? the adverb answers.

Point out the adverbs in the following sentences, and show to what words they are joined.

The boat arrived to day. The ship was launched yesterday. I dislike his conduct exceedingly. I esteemed him too highly. He is very negligent. She sings sweetly.

LESSON VI.

DIRECTION. — A preposition connects the noun following it, in sense, to some word preceding it ; as, He returned *from* Boston ; from connects Boston with returned.

Mention what words the prepositions connect in the following sentences. For a list of prepositions, see § 7.

He dwells in the city. The ship has sailed for London. He was buried beneath the river. The boy stood on the burning deck. The soldiers were in the camp. The city was taken by the Americans. The hill slopes towards the East. The Mexicans were conquered in the battle.

LESSON VII.

Point out the different parts of speech and show their relation.

The Americans conquered the Mexicans in the battle at Palo Alto. The army under General Scott captured the fine city of Vera Cruz. The robin sings sweetly in the Spring. The flowers bloom in the meadow. The lambs skip over the hills. Spring is the most delightful season of the year.

GRAMMAR.

———

ENGLISH GRAMMAR is the science which teaches the principles of the English language.

GENERAL DIVISIONS AND TERMS.

1. ENGLISH GRAMMAR is generally divided into four parts, — *Orthography, Etymology, Syntax,* and *Prosody.*

2. ORTHOGRAPHY, (Greek *orthos,* "correct," and *grapho,* "to write,") treats of letters, and teaches their power and proper use.

3. ETYMOLOGY, (Greek *etumon,* "true and proper use," and *logos,* "a word,") treats of words, and teaches their derivation, classes, and variations.

4. SYNTAX, (Greek *suntaxis,* "the act of arranging,") treats of sentences, and teaches the proper construction of words in forming them.

5. PROSODY, (Greek *prosodia,*) treats of accent, quantity and versification.

NOTE. — This division of the subject is not strictly adhered to in this work.

2

PART I.

ORTHOGRAPHY.

LETTERS.

6. A letter is a character used in writing or printing, to represent an articulate sound.

7. Before letters were invented, pictures or symbols were employed in writing, called hieroglyphics.

8. The English alphabet consists of twenty-six letters, which are usually divided into two classes, called vowels and consonants.

> NOTE. — The word " Alphabet" is derived from *alpha*, *beta*, the names of the first two letters of the Greek Alphabet. The term has reference only to the arrangement of the letters; as, A, B, &c.

VOWELS.

9. Those letters which represent a free, uninterrupted sound, are called *vowels*, (Lat. *vocalis*, " that may be sounded ";) as *a, e, i, o, u ;* and *w* and *y,* when not occurring at the beginning of a word or a syllable.

EXERCISES.

1. Sound *a* in *all* without articulating the *ll;* sound *a* in *at* without articulating the *t;* also, *a* in *ape* without articulating the *p;* also, *a* in *arm* without articulating the *r*.

2. Sound the *a* in the following words ; first pronouncing the word, then omitting the letters which follow the *a*, then sounding the *a* alone.

1—*a*	2—*a*	3—*a*	4—*a.*
bate — ba — a	bat — ba — a	bar — ba — a	ball — ba — a
fate — fa — a	fat — fa — a	far — fa — a	fall — fa — a
mate — ma — a	mat — ma — a	mar — ma — a	wall — wa — a

Treat the other vowels in a similar manner, in the following words:

1—e	2—e	1—i	2—i.
eke — e	elk — e	ice — i	in — i
mete — me — e	met — me — e	mice — mi — i	mill — mi — i
deep — dee — e	set — se — e	pine — pi — i	pin — pi — i

1—o	2—o	3—o	*promiscuous.*
old – o	off – o	move – mo — o	fate, fall, far, fat.
hope – ho – o	not – no – o	prove – pro – o	me, met.

1—u	2—u	3—u	mite, did.
tube – tu — u	tub – tu – u	full – fu – u	note, nor, move.
lute – lu – u	mug – mu – u	pull – pu – u	tune, tun, full.

CONSONANTS.

10. Letters which are used only in connection with vowels for the purpose of articulation, are called *consonants.* (Lat. *consonans,* " sounding together.")

11. *B, c* (hard,) *g* (hard,) *k, p, t,* are called *mutes,* — they represent no audible sound.

12. *C* (soft,) *f, g* (soft.) *h, j, r, s, v, x, z,* are called *semivowels,* — they represent sounds obstructed by organs nearly closed.

13. *L, m, n, r,* are called liquids,— they easily coalesce with the sound of other letters with which they are associated.

EXERCISE.

Pronounce *ba, ka, pa, ta, ca, ga.*

Endeavor to sound b, k, p, t, c, g, without the *a.* What are these letters called ? Why ?

Pronounce *ef, ge, ja, re, se, ve, ex, ze.*

Sound f, g, h, j, r, s, v, x, z, without the *e.* Do these represent a full sound ? What are they called ? Why ?

Pronounce the following words; and as far as possible sound the consonants alone.

1. *mutes.*	2. *semivowels.*	3. *liquids.*
bat — b — t	sauce — s — c	lamp — l — m
cap — c — p	verge — v — g	nor — n — r
pat — p — t	sex — s — x	land — l — n
quake — q — k	jot — j — t	man — m — n

14. The consonants *b, p, m, w, v,* are called labials, (Lat. *labia,* " a lip,") because the lips are employed in articulating them.

15. The consonants *d, t, c* (soft,) *g* (soft,) *j, s,* and *z* (*sibilant* or *hissing,*) are called dentals, (Lat. *dens,* " a tooth,") — they are articulated by pressing the tongue upon the *teeth.*

16. The consonants *k, c* (hard,) *g* (hard,) and *y* (at the beginning of a syllable,) are called *palatals* — they are articulated by pressing the tongue against the *palate.*

17. *W* and *y* are consonants when they begin a word or a syllable.

SOUNDS OF THE VOWELS.*

A

18. The vowel *a* has four sounds peculiar to itself; as,

1. *a* in *fate,* 2. *a* in *fat,* 3. *a* in *far,* 4. *a* in *fall.*

It is also used to represent the sound of *e* in many, and *o* in what.

E

19. The vowel *e* has two sounds peculiar to itself; as,

1. *e* in *mete,* 2. *e* in *met.*

It is also used to represent the second sound of *a* in there; the second sound of *i* in England; and the second sound of *u* in her.

I

20. The vowel *i* has two sounds peculiar to itself; as,

1. *i* in *pine,* 2. *i* in *pin.*

It is also used to represent the first sound of *e* in machine and the second sound of *u* in bird.

---

* The analysis of the sounds of the vowels and consonants here given is taken by permission from a pamphlet by F. M. Thurston, A.M., just published. A chart ingeniously exhibiting the same analysis, and recently prepared by Mr. T., is commended to those who wish to see a concise and philosophical representation of the elements and sounds of the English Language.

O

21. The vowel *o* has three sounds peculiar to itself; as,

1. *o* in note, 2. *o* in not, 3. *o* in move.

It is also used to represent the second sound of *u* in dove, and the sound of *w* united with *u* in one.

U

22. The vowel *u* has three sounds peculiar to itself; as,

1. *u* in tube, 2. *u* in tub, 3. *u* in full.

It is also used to represent the second sound of *e* in bury; the second sound of *i* in busy; the sound of *w* in quoit, and the sound of *yu* in union.

EXERCISE.

Give the vowel sounds in the following words :

Ale, arm, law, cat, bat, lard, hard, ball, fall, what, wasp, wash.
Eel, me, elk, term, mild, mint, marine, brute, but, pull.

SOUNDS OF THE CONSONANTS.

23. Each of the following consonants and combinations of consonants has but one sound.

1. *b* as in bite, *k* as in kite, *p* as in pail, *l* as in late, *r* as in rate, *v* as in vain, *sh* as in shall, *zh* like *s* in pleasure, *ng* as in thing, *th* sharp as in thin, *th* flat as in thou, *j* as in joy, *m* as in man.

The consonant *h* is an aspirate, and has one sound as in hand.

In the word cupboard *p* has the sound of *b*.

In the word hallelujah *j* has the sound of *y*.

24. Each of the following consonants has one sound peculiar to itself, and is used to represent one or more of the sounds of other consonants, as follows :

d as in date,	and represents	*j* as in soldier.
f as in fan,	" "	*v* as in of.
g as in gave,	" "	*j* as gem.
n as in note,	" "	*ng* as in singular.
s as in sin,	" "	*z* as in his, *sh* as in sugar, and *zh* as in pleasure.
t as in time,	" "	*sh* as in nation, and *ch* as in nature.
w as in wave,	" "	*u* as in brown.
y as in yet,	" "	*i* as in tyrant.
z as in zone,	" "	*zh* as in azure.

Ch, also, has its own sound as in church, and represents the sound of *sh* as in machine, *k* as in chorus, and *kw* as in choir.

C and *G* are hard before *a, o, u, r, l,* and soft before *e, i,* and *y*.

2*

SUBSTITUTES, OR EQUIVALENTS.

CONSONANT SUBSTITUTES.

25. SUBSTITUTES are characters which have no sound peculiar to themselves, but are used to represent the sound of other letters.

EXAMPLES.

1. The character *c* represents *k* before *a, o, u, l, r;* and the sound of *s* before *e, i,* and *y;* the sound of *z* in sacrifice, and the sound of *sh* as in ocean.

     Q represents the sound of *k* as in liquid.

     X   "   "   *gz* as in exact, and *z* as in xanthus.

     Ph   "   "   *f* as in phlegm, and *v* as in Stephen.

     Gh   "   "   *f* as in cough, and *k* as in hough.

VOWEL SUBSTITUTES.*

     A a represents   *a* as in Baalam.

     A e   "   long *e* as in Caesar, and short *e* as in diaeresis.

     A i   "   *a* as in plaid, *e* as in again, *i* long as in aisle, *i* short, as in villain, and *u* short, as in Britain.

2. *Ao* represents the first sound of *a* as in gaol, and the second sound of *o* as in extraordinary.

3. *Au* represents the second sound of *a* as in draught, and the first sound of *a* as in gauge, the third sound of *a* as in aunt, the fourth sound of *a* as in caught, the first sound of *o* as in hautboy, and the second sound of *o*, (or the fourth sound of *a*) as in laurel.

4. *Aw* represents *a* as in law   *Ay* represents the first sound of *a* as in day and the second sound of *e* as in says.

5. *Ea* represents the first sound of *a* as in steak, the third sound of *a* as in heart, the first sound of *e* as in tea, the second sound of *e* as in head, and the second sound of *u* as in vengeance.

6. *Ee* represents the first sound of *e* as in tree, and the second sound of *i* as in been.

7. *Eï* represents the first sound of *a* as in veil, the second sound of *a* as in their, the first sound of *e* as in deceit, the second sound of *e* as in heifer, the first sound of *i* as in height, and the second sound of *i* as in forfeit.

8. *Eo* represents the first sound of *e* as in people, the second sound of *e* as in leopard, the first sound of *o* as in yeoman, the second sound of *o* as in George, and the second sound of *u* as in dungeon.

---

* The compounds here termed *substitutes* are usually called *diphthongs*, or *digraphs*, when composed of two vowels; *triphthongs*, when composed of three vowels.

9. *Eu* represents the first sound of *u* as in de*u*ce, and the third sound of *u* as in rh*eu*m.

10. *Ew* represents the first sound of *o* as in s*ew*, and the first sound of *u* as in d*ew*.

11. *Ey* represents the first sound of *a* as in pr*ey*, and the first sound of *e* as in k*ey*.

12. *Ia* represents the second sound of *a* as in part*ia*l, and the second sound of *i* as in marr*ia*ge.

13. *Ie* represents the first sound of *e* as in gr*ie*f, the second sound of *e* as in quot*ie*nt, the first sound of *i* as in d*ie*, and the second sound of *i* as in s*ie*ve.

14. *Ii* represents the first sound of *i* as in Pompe*ii*.

15. *Io* represents the second sound *u* as in nat*io*n.

16. *Iu* represents the second sound of *u* as in Luc*iu*s.

17. *Oa* represents the fourth sound of *a* as in br*oa*d, and the first sound of *o* as in b*oa*t.

18. *Oe* represents the first sound of *e* as in ant*oe*ci, the second sound of *e* as in f*oe*tid, the first sound of *o* as in d*oe*, and the third sound of *o* as in sh*oe*.

19. *Oi* represents the first sound of *i* as in ch*oi*r, and the second sound of *i* as in tort*oi*se.

20. *Oo* represents the first sound of *o* as in d*oo*r, the third sound of *o* as in f*oo*l, the second sound of *u* as in fl*oo*d, and the third sound of *u* as in g*oo*d.

21. *Ou* represents the fourth sound of *a* as in *ou*ght, the first sound of *o* as in th*ou*gh, the second sound of *o* as in c*ou*gh, and the third sound of *o* as in s*ou*p, the second sound of *u* as in r*ou*gh, and the third sound of *u* as in c*ou*ld.

22. *Ow* represents the first sound of *o* as in kn*ow*.

23. *Ua* represents the second sound of *a* as in g*ua*rantee, the third sound of *a* as in g*ua*rd, and the first sound of *u* as in mant*ua*maker.

24. *Ue* represents the second sound of *e* as in g*ue*st, the third sound of *u* as in tr*ue*, the first sound of *u* as in bl*ue*, and the second sound of *u* as in conq*ue*r.

25. *Ui* represents the first sound of *i* as in g*ui*de, the second sound of *i* as in g*ui*lt, the third sound of *u* as in fr*ui*t, and the first sound of *u* as in j*ui*ce.

26. *Uo* represents the second sound of *u* as in liq*uo*r.

27. *Uy* represents the first sound of *i* as in b*uy*.

28. *Awe* represents the fourth sound of *a* as in *awe*.

29. *Aye* represents the first sound of *a* as in *aye*.

30. *Eau* represents the first sound of *o* as in b*eau*, and the first sound of *u* as in b*eau*ty.

31. *Eou* represents the second sound of *u* as in herbac*eou*s.

32. *Eye* represents the first sound of *i* as in *eye*.

33. *Ieu* represents the first sound of *u* as in ad*ieu*.

34. *Iou* represents the second sound of *u* as in grac*iou*s.

35. *Iew* represents the first sound of *u* as in v*iew*.

36. *Oeu* represents the first sound of *u* as in man*oeu*vre.

37. *Owe* represents the first sound of *o* as in *owe*.

DIPHTHONGS.

26. A diphthong is a union of two vowel sounds in the same syllable.   There are three diphthongs in the language, viz: *ay*, the adverb of affirmation ; *oi* or *oy*, and *ou* or *ow*.

In the first, *a* has its third sound, and *y* represents the first sound of *e*.   In the second, *o* has its second sound, and *i* or *y* the first sound of *e*, as heard in the words *toil, joy*.   In the third, *o* has its second sound, and *u* or *w* has the third sound of *u*, as heard in *bound, town*.

NOTE. — The *i* and the *y* in the diphthongs, represent the first sound of *e* somewhat clipped ; still it is the element of *e* as heard in *me*.

WORDS.

27. A *word* consists of one or more letters, and is used as the sign of an idea.

28. A *syllable* is a word, or such a part of a word as is uttered by one articulation.

29. A word of one syllable is termed a *monosyllable ;* of two syllables a *dissyllable ;* of three syllables, a *trisyllable ;* of more than three syllables, a *polysyllable*.

DIRECTIONS FOR THE USE OF CAPITAL LETTERS.

It was formerly the custom to begin every noun with a capital ; but as this practice was troublesome, and gave the writing or printing a crowded and confused appearance, it has been discontinued.   It is, however, very proper to begin with a capital, in the following instances, viz :

30. The first word of every book, chapter, letter, note, or any other piece of writing.

31. The first word after a period ; and if the two sentences are *independent*, after a note of interrogation or exclamation.

32. The appellations of the Deity.

EXAMPLES.

"God, Jehovah, the Almighty, the Supreme Being, the Lord, Providence, the Messiah, the Holy Spirit."

33. Proper names of persons, places, streets, mountains, rivers, ships, and common nouns personified.

EXAMPLES.

" George, York, the Strand, the Alps, the Thames, the Sea-horse."

34. All titles of honor, professions, or callings; also the names of religious sects, courts, societies, and public bodies of men.

EXAMPLES.

" Governor, Judge, Esquire, Baptists, Friends, Congress, the Supreme Judicial Court."

35. Names of months and the days of the week.

36. Adjectives derived from the proper names of places; as, " Grecian, Roman, English, French, and Italian."

37. The first word of a quotation, introduced after a colon, or when it is in a direct form.

EXAMPLES.

" Always remember this ancient maxim: 'Know thyself.'" " Our great Lawgiver says, 'Take up thy cross daily, and follow me.'"

But when a quotation is brought in indirectly after a comma, a capital is unnecessary: as, " Solomon observes, 'that pride goes before destruction.'"

The first word of an example may also very properly begin with a capital; as, "Temptation proves our virtue."

38. Every noun and principal word in the titles of books.

EXAMPLES.

" Johnson's Dictionary of the English Language;" " Thomson's Seasons;" " Rollin's Ancient History."

39. The first word of every line in poetry.

40. The pronoun *I*, and the interjection *O*, are written in capitals; as, "I write;" " Hear, O earth!"

41. Other words, besides the preceding, may begin with capitals, when they are remarkably emphatical, or the principal subject of the composition.

RULES FOR SPELLING.

NOTE.— A few rules are given as a guide in the important art of spelling, but these are so general, that they apply to only a small part of the words of our language; and even these rules admit of exceptions.

42. Monosyllables ending with *f, l,* or *s,* preceded by a single vowel, double the final consonant; as, *staff, mill, pass.*

The exceptions are *of, if, as, is, has, was, yes, his, this, us,* and *thus.*

43. Words ending with *y* preceded by a consonant, commonly change *y* into *i,* on assuming an additional syllable beginning with a consonant; as, hap*py,* happ*ily,* happ*iness.*

44. The final *y* preceded by a consonant is generally changed into *i* before the endings *es, er, est,* and *ed;* as, spy, spi*es;* carry, carri*est,* carri*er,* carri*ed;* happy, happi*er,* happi*est.*

45. Monosyllables, and words accented on the last syllable, ending with a single consonant preceded by a single vowel, commonly double that consonant, when they take another syllable beginning with a vowel; as, wi*t,* wi*tty;* thin, thin*nish;* regre*t,* regre*tted;* begin, begi*nning.*

46. But if a diphthong precedes, or the accent is not on the last syllable, the consonant remains single.

47. With respect to most of the words ending in *l,* which are not accented on the last syllable, usage is not uniform. According to Perry and Webster, the *l* in such words should not be doubled.

The prevailing usage, however, is in favor of doubling the *l;* as, travel, *travelling;* cancel, *cancelling;* libel, *libeller;* duel, *duelling, dueller, duellist.*

The words *kidnap* and *worship* also, according to general usage, double the *p;* as, *kidnapping, worshipping.*

48. Words ending with any double letter, except double *l,* preserve the letter double on assuming the ending *ness, less, ly* or *ful;* as, *harmlessness, carelessly, successful.*

But words ending in double *l,* commonly drop one *l* on receiving the syllables *ness, less,* &c.

49. Silent *e* is usually dropped in the following instances:

1. Before the terminations *able* or *ible*; as, blame, blam*able*; except when preceded by *c* or *g* soft; as, peace*able*, change*able*.

2. Before *ing, ish, ed, er,* or *est*; as, plac*ing,* slav*ish;* love, lov*ed;* pale, pal*er,* pal*est.*

50. Silent *e* is usually retained in the following instances:

1. Before the endings *ness, less, ly* and *ful;* as, pale*ness,* close*ly,* peace*ful.*

2. Before the ending *ment*; as, abate*ment,* chastise*ment,* &c.

The words judgment, abridgment, and acknowledgment, are commonly written without the silent *e.*

PART II.

—

ETYMOLOGY AND SYNTAX.

SECTION I.

ANALYSIS OF SENTENCES.

51. Language consists of signs used to communicate ideas. These signs in spoken and written language are called *words.*

52. Words suitably arranged to make a complete sense, form a sentence.

53. Sentences are simple or compound. A simple sentence consists of one proposition. A compound sentence consists of two or more propositions connected.

54. The *subject* is that of which something is affirmed.

55. The *predicate* is that which is affirmed.

For example: "Trees grow;" "trees" is the subject; "grow" is the predicate.

56. The *analysis* of a sentence consists in dividing it into the parts of which it is composed, and pointing out their relations. Thus:

SENTENCE.　*Trees grow.*

Analyzed. "Trees" is the subject, because it is that of which something is affirmed.

"Grow" is the predicate; because it is that which is affirmed of trees.

57. The subject explained, described, or limited, by one or more words, is called the *modified* or *logical* subject; as, "Large trees of the forest grow." The subject "trees" is described, 1. by "large;" 2. by "of the forest." *Large trees of the forest* is the modified subject.

58. The predicate modified by any word, phrase, or clause, is called the *modified* or *logical* predicate; as, "Large trees of the forest grow *rapidly in summer.*" "Rapidly" and "in summer" modify the predicate "grow."

59. An attribute is a word or expression forming a part of the predicate, and denoting some quality, state or office of the subject; as, "Glass is *brittle.*" "The sea is *in commotion.*" "Franklin was a *philosopher.*"

60. A phrase is an expression that consists of two or more words not forming a complete sentence.

61. The simple propositions that form a compound sentence, are termed *clauses.*

EXERCISE IN ANALYSIS.

Model I.

SENTENCE.　*Time flies.*

Analyzed. It is a simple sentence, because it consists of but one proposition.

"Time" is the subject, because it is that of which the action "flies" is affirmed.

"Flies" is the predicate, because it is the action affirmed of "time."

NOTE.—In this sentence the subject and predicate are both unmodified. See 57.

Model II.

SENTENCE. *Life is short.*

It is a simple sentence. (Why?)

"Life" is the subject. (Why?) See 54.

"Is short" is the predicate, because it is a property affirmed of "life."

In this sentence, two words constitute the predicate, viz: "is" and "short." The word "short" denotes a property, or *attribute*, and the word "is" denotes that this attribute belongs to life. Hence is," is termed the *copula* (band,) because it unites the attribute and the subject.

A few examples will illustrate this more clearly.

Snow is white. "Is white" is the predicate. "White" is an *attribute* of snow. "Is" is the *copula*, because it unites the subject "snow" and the attribute "white."

The sun is rising. "Is" is the copula, "rising" is the attribute, and "is rising" is the predicate.

62. The copula is commonly the word *be*, some of the forms of which are *am, is, are, was, were*, &c. A single word very often constitutes the predicate, which comprises in itself the *copula* and the *attribute*; as, The wind *blows*, i. e. *is blowing.*

SENTENCES TO BE ANALYZED.

Vice is degrading. Virtue is ennobling. Ships sail. Ships are sailing. James writes. James is writing. Boys play. Boys are playing. Stars twinkle. Stars are twinkling.

Model III.

This model is designed to show how the predicate which comprises the copula and *attribute* in a single word, may be analyzed.*

SENTENCE. *Water flows,* [customarily or continually.]

Analyzed. "Water" is the subject, because it is that of which something is affirmed.

"Flows" is the predicate, because it is the action affirmed.

---

* The verb (except the substantive verb used as the copula,) is a mixed word, being resolvable into the *copula* and *predicate* [attribute,] to which it is equivalent; as, The Romans conquered; equivalent to the Romans were *victorious.*— *Whately.* See also *Watts, De Sacy,* and *Cramp.*

Predicate Analyzed. "Flows," i. e. "is flowing."
"Is" is the copula; "flowing" is the attribute.
The copula unites the subject "water" and the attribute "flowing."

SENTENCES TO BE ANALYZED.

Water runs. Ravens croak. Horses neigh. Bees hum.
Flowers bloom. James reads. Charles works. Wine intoxi-
cates. He studies. They smile. We sing.

Model IV.

Sentences which express command or entreaty.

SENTENCES. *Depart thou. Come.*

Analyzed. "Thou" is the subject, because it denotes the person com-
manded.
"Depart" is the predicate, because it expresses a command.
"Come" is a word expressing command. The subject "Thou" or "ye"
is omitted.
"Come" is the predicate.
"Thou" or "ye" understood is the subject.
Predicate Analyzed. "Depart," i. e. "be departing." "Be" is the copula;
"departing" is the attribute.
[In sentences expressing command the subject is commonly omitted.]

SENTENCES TO BE ANALYZED.

Give thou. Do thou. Speak ye. Hasten. Send. Obey.
Believe. Read. Write. Study.

Model V.

Sentences in which questions are asked.

SENTENCE. *Is he alive?*

"He" is the subject, because it denotes the person concerning whom the in-
quiry is made.
"Is alive" is the predicate, because it expresses the inquiry.
"Is" is the copula; "alive" the attribute.

SENTENCES TO BE ANALYZED.

Is he dead? Are animals intelligent? Is honor sacred?
Is friendship enduring? Is levity becoming? Is theft for-
bidden?

CLASSIFICATION OF SENTENCES.

63. Simple sentences or clauses may be divided into three classes; viz. *declarative*, *imperative*, and *interrogative*.

64. A declarative sentence is one in which something is directly affirmed or denied; as, The ships sail.

65. An imperative sentence is one which expresses a command, exhortation, or entreaty; as, Obey; let your moderation be known unto all men; do come.

66. An interrogative sentence is one in which a question is asked; as, Whence art thou?

To these classes several others are sometimes added, such as *exclamatory*, *conditional*, &c. But these are modifications of the first class mentioned above.

NOTE.— In the progress of the work, the sentence, the principal elements of which have been explained, will be gradually extended by joining to these elements modifying words and phrases. In connection with this, the parts of speech will be presented in what is deemed to be the natural order of their union in the structure of language.

SECTION II.

PARTS OF SPEECH.

67. The different sorts of words, of which language is composed, are called PARTS OF SPEECH. For example; in the sentence "large trees grow rapidly in summer," "trees" and "summer" are called *nouns*; "grow" is called a *verb*; "large" an *adjective*, and "rapidly" an *adverb*. The following are names given to the *parts of speech*;

NOUN.	VERB.
PRONOUN.	ADVERB.
ADJECTIVE.	PREPOSITION.

CONJUNCTION.

INTERJECTION.

THE NOUN.

68. A Noun is the name of an object; as, George, Manchester, tree.

1. The word noun is derived from the Latin *nomen*, which signifies "name." The noun can be easily known by inquiring whether the word in question is the name of any thing that can be thought of, or spoken of.

2. We can think of *virtue, vice, goodness, time, light, darkness,*— these words, being names of objects of thought, are therefore called nouns.

3. We can think of *persons, places, rivers, mountains,* &c. The words that designate these, are likewise called nouns.

4. We can think of a *word, letter,* or *figure* employed merely as a term, independently of its usual signification; as, *me* is a pronoun; *a* has four sounds; *by* is a preposition; *and* is a conjunction. Words, letters, or figures thus used are nouns.

5. A *clause* or a *phrase,* expressing some event, action, or state, is often used as a noun; as, *To see the sun* is pleasant; *How he escaped* is not known.

EXERCISE.

To be written on a Black Board or Slate.

Write the *names* of the objects in a school room.

Write the *names* of animals in a farm yard.

Write the *names* of flowers in a garden.

Write the *names* of trees in the forest.

Write the *names* of the five senses; as, *Hearing, &c.*

Write the *names* of the metals; as, *Gold, &c.*

Write the *names* of the persons, places, and things, which you can see or think of.

What part of speech has been used to denote the objects whose names have been written? Why?

Place a noun *before* each of the following predicates.

Model

is hard.		— is steep.	
The flint is *hard*.		The hill is *steep*.	
—is pleasant.	— is kind.	— is dark.	— runs.
— walks.	— reads.	— writes.	— mows.
— is high.	— studies.	— studies.	— shines.

69. The names of individual persons or things are called *proper nouns;* as, Charles, Boston, April.

70. Names given to whole classes are called *common nouns;* as, animal, man, boy.

[For a more particular classification, see 167, 168, &c.]

NOTE.— Sections XV, and XVI, may be studied in connection with this section, if thought desirable. But it is recommended to study Part III, in connection with a review of Part II.

PRONOUNS. PERSON.

71. A pronoun is a word used instead of a noun; as, *He* reads. *She* writes. *I* study.

72. *I, thou, he, she, it,* and their plurals *we, you, they,* are called *personal pronouns,* because they are used to denote the relation of a person or thing in discourse. See 180.

73. *I* is of the first person, because it denotes the speaker.

74. *Thou* or *you* is of the second person, because it denotes the one spoken to.

75. *He, she, it,* are of the third person, because they denote that which is spoken of.

76. Most nouns are of the third person. When the speaker names himself, as, I, *Paul;* or names the person spoken to, as, You, my *brother;* then the nouns agree in person with the pronouns. *Paul* is in the first person, *brother* in the second.

See Sections XVI, XVII, and XVIII.

NUMBER. GENDER. CASE.

77. A noun or a pronoun which denotes but one person or thing is of the *singular number;* if it denotes more than one, it is of the *plural number.*

78. The plural number of nouns is generally formed by adding *s* or *es* to the singular; as *bird* (singular,) *birds* (plural.)

[For variations from this rule, see Section XVI, 187 — 208.]

79. The plural of *pronouns* is represented by a different word from the singular. The plural of *I* is *we;* the plural of *thou* is *you* or *ye;* the plural of *he, she, it,* is *they.*

80. Gender denotes a distinction in sex.

81. *The masculine gender* denotes objects of the male kind.

3*

82. *The feminine gender* denotes objects of the female kind.

83. *The neuter gender* denotes things which are neither male nor female. See 208, 209, 210.

84. Case denotes the relation of a noun or pronoun to some other word in a sentence. See 217, 218, 219.

85. There are three principal cases; *Nominative, Possessive,* and *Objective.*

86. The *nominative case* denotes the subject of a proposition. For other offices of the nominative, see 218, 1, 2, 3.

87. The *possessive case* denotes that to which something belongs.

88. The *objective case* denotes the object of a transitive verb or preposition. See 92.

To these principal cases may be added the case independent. See 224.

Nouns or pronouns which have no relation to the subject or predicate of a sentence, are properly said to be in the case independent or absolute.

EXERCISE.

[Mention the nouns and pronouns in the following sentences, and give the number, gender, and case of each.]

Planets revolve.   Soldiers march.   Leopards are spotted. Death is approaching.   Civility is pleasing.   Thomas is obedient; he works; he reads; he is diligent.   You eat; you drink; you sleep.   Locusts are destructive.   Labor fatigues.

For the Board or Slate.

[Write a noun or pronoun in the plural number before each of the following expressions:]

— are good.	— are pleasant.	— walk.	— sleep.
— neigh.	— plough.	— reap.	— grow.
— bloom.	— are ripe.	— are sweet.	— rule.
— are indolent.	— disobedient.		

REVIEW.

Mention the parts of speech. Define a noun. What nouns are called proper? Common? Define a pronoun. What does a noun or pronoun in the singular number denote? In the plural? How is the plural of nouns generally formed? What is the plural of the pronoun I? Thou? He, she, it? What does gender denote? What do the different genders denote? What does case denote? Mention the cases, and what each denotes.

Section III.

THE VERB.

89. Verb, from the Latin *verbum*, signifies "a word," "or the word;" so termed from its importance in speech.

90. A verb is a word by means of which something is affirmed.

EXAMPLES.

The horse runs. Which word is used to affirm the action of the horse, or to express what the horse does?

The bird flies. Which word is used to affirm the action of the bird?

The worm creeps. Which is the verb? Why?

The wolf howls. Which word denotes the thing that acts, or the actor?

The bee hums. Which word denotes the actor? Which is used to affirm the action?

EXERCISE.

[Write a verb after each of the following nouns to affirm something.]

Model.

The wind
The wind *blows*.

The horse
The horse *neighs*.

The waves —	The sun —	The dog —	The rain —
The day —	Birds —	The lion —	The ships —
Fire —	Flowers —	Trees —	Stars —

[Point out the verb in the following expressions.]

The moon rises.

The child reads his book.

The loud thunder peals.

The sun sets.

The sword kills.

The waves dash violently.

91. Verbs may be divided into two general classes, *transitive* and *intransitive*. See 232 — 238.

92. A transitive verb is one which requires an object to complete the sense.

EXAMPLES.

The sun warms the earth. If we should say *the sun warms*, the sense would be incomplete. To complete the assertion, it is necessary to supply some word to limit the meaning of the verb. The word proper to be supplied is termed the object. "The sun warms" (what?) the *earth*.

" The wind drives " (what ?) *the snow*.

" Heat melts " (what ?) *wax*.   What is the object ?

" Fire consumes " (what ?) *wood*.   What kind of a verb is consumes ?

EXERCISE.

[Supply a transitive verb in each of the blank places.]

Subjects.	Objects.	Subjects.	Objects.	Subjects.	Objects.
George —— play.	Trees —— fruit.	Children —— books.
Water —— thirst.	Food —— hunger.	Eyes —— light.
Teeth —— food.	Diamond —— glass.	Water —— fire.

93. An intransitive verb is one that does not require an object to complete the sense; as, " Waves dash." " Ships sail." " He sleeps."

94. Verbs have various forms; 1, to denote the manner of asserting, called *mode ;* 2, to express the time of an action, called *tense ;* 3, to denote the *number* or *person* of the subject. These are explained in Part III.   See Sections XXI and XXII.

NOTE. — In the exercises of Part II only one *mode* of the verb occurs, called the *indicative*, because it is used to indicate or declare something. Two tense forms only are used in this part. 1, The *present tense*, which denotes the present time of an action or event; as, *I write*. 2, The *imperfect tense*, which denotes the past time of an action or event; as, *I wrote*. The person of the verb corresponds with the person of its subject.

Example of Forms of the Verb used in Part I.

INDICATIVE MODE.

PRESENT TENSE.

	Singular.	*Plural.*
1st person,	I write.	We write.
2d "	Thou writest.	Ye or you write.
3d "	He writes.	They write.

IMPERFECT

	Singular.
1st person,	I wrote.
2d "	Thou wrotest.
3d "	He wrote.

NOTE. — *She* or *it*, or any noun of the   in place
of HE, in conjugating the verb.

Forms of the Verb BE *in the Present and Imperfect Tenses of the Indicative Mode.*

PRESENT TENSE.

	Singular.	*Plural.*
1st person,	I am.	We are.
2d "	Thou art.	Ye or you are.
3d "	He is.	They are.

IMPERFECT TENSE.

	Singular.	*Plural.*
1st person,	I was.	We were.
2d "	Thou wast.	Ye or you were.
3d "	He was.	They were.

95. A verb in the *infinitive mode* is preceded by the word *to ;* as, *to be ; to write ; to love ; to begin,* &c.

96. A verb in any form, but that of the infinitive mode, is called a *finite verb.*

97. The subject of a finite verb is the same as the subject of the proposition in which it stands; as, "*Soldiers march;*" soldiers is the subject of the verb march; it is also the subject of the proposition.

SECTION IV.

THE PROPOSITION.

98. The principal elements of every proposition are the *subject* and *predicate.*

SUBJECT.

See 54, Sec. I.

99. The subject is a noun, or some word or expression used as a noun.

100. Number, person, gender, and case, belong to the subject in common with other nouns.

NOTE.—The grammatical relation of the subject is indicated by the following Rule.

RULE I.

101. The subject of a finite verb must be in the nominative case. See 218.

EXAMPLES. — "*Flowers* bloom." "Flowers" is the subject of the propo sition, and also the grammatical subject of the *finite verb* bloom. See 96, 97.

"*To lie* is base." The subject is the infinitive, "to lie," used as a noun in the nominative case.

ANALYSIS AND PARSING.

Sentences should be analyzed before parsing the words.

The following questions may serve as a guide in parsing nouns. 1. Why called a noun? 2. Proper or common? Why? 3. What person? 4. What number? Why? 5. What gender? Why? 6. What case? Why?

Model of Parsing a Noun in the Nominative Case.

SENTENCE. *Leaves shake.*

Analyzed. It is a simple proposition. "Leaves" is the subject, because it is that of which something is affirmed.

"Shake" is the predicate, because it is the action affirmed.

Predicate analyzed. "Shake," i. e. "are shaking." "Are" is the copula, and "shaking" is the attribute. See Model II. Sec. I.

The Noun Parsed. "Leaves" is a noun, because it is the name of something — *common*, because it is the name given to a class of objects — *of the third person*, because it denotes that which is spoken of — *of the plural number*, because it denotes more than one — *in the nominative case*, because it denotes the subject. Rule I.

SENTENCES.

Children play. Foxes bark. Masters teach. Cæsar con quered. Pompey fled. Water runs. Air invigorates. Ice melts. Gold glitters. Kings rule. I teach. They learn.

THE PREDICATE.

See 55, Sec. I.

102. The predicate is a verb, or some form of the verb BE, (called *copula*,) and an attribute.

EXAMPLES. — *Grass grows.* "Grows" is the predicate, because it is the action affirmed.

The day is pleasant. "Is pleasant" is the predicate, because it is that which is affirmed of day. The verb "is" is the *copula*, and "pleasant" is the attribute.

103. When the attribute is a noun it is in the same case as the subject; as, "Cicero was an orator;" *orator* is in the same case as *Cicero.*

104. If the subject is in the nominative case it is called the *subject nominative ;* and the noun that is the attribute of it is called the *predicate nominative.*

EXAMPLES. "Newton was a philosopher." "Newton" is the *subject nominative,* and "philosopher" is the *predicate nominative.*

"David was king of Israel." "King" is the *predicate nominative.*

ANALYSIS AND PARSING.

RULE II.

105. A noun in the predicate after an intransitive verb is in the same case as the subject when both words refer to the same person or thing ; as " Paul was an *apostle.*"

"Apostle" stands in the predicate, and denotes the same person as "Paul," the subject. It is therefore in the same case. See Rule II, *Syntax.*

Model of Parsing a Predicate Nominative.

SENTENCE. — *Milton was a poet.*

Analyzed. "Milton" is the subject. "Was a poet," is the predicate, "Poet" is the predicate nominative.

Predicate Nominative Parsed. "Poet" is a common noun, third person, singular, masculine gender, and the *predicate nominative,* because it denotes the same person as Milton. RULE. — "A noun in the predicate," &c.

SENTENCES.

Venus is a planet. Orion is a constellation. Washington was a statesman. Arnold was a traitor. Lycurgus was a lawgiver. Virgil was a poet. Learning is a treasure.

NOTE. — The grammatical relation of a finite verb is expressed in the following Rule.

ANALYSIS AND PARSING.

RULE III.

106. A finite verb must agree with its *subject nominative* in number and person ; as, *I write ; he writes.*

The verb *write* is of the first person singular, because *I,* its subject, is of the first person singular. *Writes* has the ending *s* to agree with its subject *he,* which is of the third person, and singular number. See Rule IV, *Syntax.*

Model of Parsing a Finite Verb.

SENTENCE.—*Children love play.*

Analyzed. "Children" is the subject; "love" is the predicate; "play" is the object of the verb "love."

Verb Parsed. "Love" is a *transitive* verb, because it requires an object; in the *indicative mode*, because it is used to indicate or declare something; in the present tense, because it denotes the present time of an action; third person, plural, because its subject, *children*, is in the third person, plural. Rule.

SENTENCES.

The tempest raged. The storm ceases. The beasts fled. The morning comes. The day dawns. The sun appears. The wind subsides. Gold is a metal. War is a calamity. Peace is a blessing. Cæsar conquered. Pompey fled.

EXAMPLES TO BE CORRECTED BY RULE III.

[Give the reason in each instance why the example is wrong.]

I goes; I walks; I is; I art. Thou loves; thou write; thou hate; thou trembles. He, she or it desire; he commend; she dress; it rain. We finds; we sees the clouds; we dreadeth the cold. Ye or you studies; you ploweth the field; you runs fast. They playeth; they strikes the ball; they sells corn.

A soft answer turn away wrath. The pupils loves study. Evil communications corrupts good manners. The smiles of a hypocrite hides his wickedness. These boxes weighs thirty pounds. A mixture of salt and vinegar make a good bath. Adjectives belongs to nouns.

COMPOSITION.

DIRECTION.—Write the composition in a plain neat hand, leaving a wide margin on the left side of the page. Make a period at the close of every complete sentence.

Write six predicates to each of the following *subjects.*

Model.

Subject—sun—

The sun shines.   The sun gives light.

The sun warms the earth.   The sun melts the snow.
The sun dries the ground.   The sun is eclipsed by the moon.

A man.   A bird.   A boy.   A child.

REVIEW.

What does "verb" signify? Into what two general classes are verbs divided? What is a transitive verb? Give an example of a transitive verb. What is an intrahsitive verb? Give an example. What is the form of the verb to denote manner called? To denote time? Give the forms of "write," in the indicative mode, present tense. In the imperfect tense. Give the forms of the verb *be* in the present and imperfect tenses. How is a verb in the infinitive mode known? What is understood by finite verb? What are the principal elements of a proposition? What part of speech is generally used as the subject of a proposition? What is Rule I? What part of speech generally forms the predicate? What must be used with the verb *be* to form a predicate? What case is a noun in, when used as an attribute of the subject? What case is the subject generally in? What is this case called? What is the case of the attribute called? Give Rule II. Give Rule III.

Section V.

MODIFIED SUBJECT.

NOTE.—If the learner has gained a clear idea of the principal elements of a sentence, viz., the subject and predicate, he is now prepared to advance another step in the construction of a sentence. He will find that each element can be extended by the addition of words, to limit or modify its meaning. As he will often meet with the word "modify," it is important that he should have a clear understanding of its meaning. As used in this book, *to modify* signifies "to restrict," "to qualify," "to limit," "to describe," "to explain." It has reference to the influence which a word or phrase has on the meaning of some other word with which it is connected.

107. The subject explained, described or limited by one or more words, is called the *modified* or *logical subject*.

I. The Subject modified by Adjectives.

THE ADJECTIVE.

108. An adjective is a word joined to a noun or pronoun, to qualify, describe, or limit its signification.

109. Adjectives may be divided into two general classes, DESCRIPTIVE and DEFINITIVE.

110. A descriptive adjective is one that expresses a quality of an object.

4

EXAMPLES. — *Good* is an adjective; it expresses a quality of every person or thing to which it is applied; as,

Good men.	Good friends.	Good fruit.
Good houses.	Good scholars.	Good farms.

Why is good an adjective? *Ans.* It denotes the quality or character of men, fruit, &c.

EXERCISE.

Join the adjective *bad* to such nouns as you can recollect; also the adjectives,

Sweet —	Bitter —	Idle —
Hard —	Small — .	Selfish —
Great —	Round —	Hungry —

Join three adjectives to each of the following nouns.

Model.

—sun.

Bright sun.	*Glorious* sun.	*Cloudless* sun.
— moon.	— parents.	— tree.
— home.	— rose.	— house.

Point out the descriptive adjectives in the following expressions.

The lofty sky.	The silver moon.
The silent orb.	The dark cloud.
The shaggy brow.	The turbid stream.
The auburn locks.	The dashing waves.
The impetuous temper.	The rosy morn.

111. Definitive adjectives are those which serve to *define* or *limit* the meaning of nouns or pronouns.

112. These are *an* or *a, the, one, two, three,* &c., *this, that, these, those, both, each, every, either, neither, some, other, any, one, all, such, much, many, none, same, few.*

NOTE. — 1. *An* or *a* and *the*, are called ARTICLES, and in parsing may be regarded as such. *An* is from a Saxon word which signifies *one.*

2. *An* is used before words beginning with a vowel sound. *A* is used before words beginning with a consonant sound; as, *An* industrious man, *a* man, *an* hour, *a* union. Union begins with the sound of *y.*

EXERCISES.

Point out the *definitive* adjectives in the following expressions, and desig
nate those which are called articles.

A tree.	This watch.	Every hour.
An apple.	This gold watch.	Every good man.
A high tree.	That monster.	Those tyrants.
The world.	That bloody man.	All lions.
The good man.	Each day.	Another evil.

COMPOSITION.

Let each sentence contain at least one descriptive adjective.

Model.

Theme. The rose.

The fragrant rose perfumes the air. It is opening its *sweet* flower to *the morning* sun. Will the mower cut down *the fair* rose? The *pale* rose withers and dies.

Themes.

The kite. The hawk. The bird. The morning.

REMARK. — An adjective used with the copula, to form a predicate, is called a *predicate adjective.* See Model II, Sect. I.

EXAMPLES. — "The sea *is rough*." "Rough," with the copula "is," forms the predicate; it is, therefore, called a predicate adjective.

"The wind is *cold*." "Cold" is the predicate adjective, and describes "wind."

ANALYSIS AND PARSING.

The following questions may serve as a guide in parsing the adjectives. Why called an adjective? Is it a descriptive, definitive, or predicate adjective? What does it describe or limit?

RULE IV.

113. An adjective belongs to the noun or pronoun which it qualifies or defines. See Rule XV, *Syntax.*

Model.

SENTENCE. — *Gentle manners are pleasing.*

Analyzed. "Manners" is the subject; "gentle manners" is the modified subject, because "manners" is described by the adjective "gentle." "Are

pleasing" is the predicate. "Are" is the copula; "pleasing" is the attri
bute.

Adjectives Parsed. "Gentle" is a descriptive adjective, because it qualifies "manners," to which it belongs according to the Rule. "Pleasing" is a
predicate adjective, because it forms with the copula "are" the predicate. It
is a descriptive adjective, and belongs to "manners."

SENTENCES.

The cool breeze is refreshing. The morning sun was cloud-
ed. The loud thunder pealed. The red lightning flashed. The
blooming rose is fragrant. That tall tree bends. A little learning is dangerous. These men are angry.

NOTE.—The modification of nouns and pronouns, by participles, is explained in Part III, Sec. XXIV.

REVIEW.

What is the modified subject? What is the first modifier of the subject?
Define the adjective. Into what classes are adjectives divided? What is a
descriptive adjective? What is a definitive adjective? Which of the definitive adjectives are called *articles?* What is a predicate adjective? Repeat
Rule IV.

SECTION VI.

II. The Subject modified by a Noun or Pronoun in Apposition.

114. The subject may be modified in the second place by a
noun or pronoun, used as an explanatory term.

EXAMPLES.— "Milton, the poet, was blind." "The poet" modifies "Milton," by indicating the individual and his office or rank. The noun so used is
said to be in apposition. A clause in apposition sometimes does the same
office; as, The question, *how the injury can be repaired,* is now to be considered.

ANALYSIS AND PARSING.

RULE V.

115. A noun or pronoun, limiting another noun and signifying the same person or thing, is put by apposition in the
same case. See Rule I, *Syntax.*

Model.

SENTENCE. — *Cæsar, a Roman general, was victorious.*

Analyzed. "Cæsar" is the subject. "Cæsar, a Roman general," is the
modified subject. "General" is an explanatory term, denoting the office of
Cæsar, and is limited by the adjectives "a," and "Roman.". "Was victorious,"
is the predicate.

Parsed. " General " is a common noun, third person, singular, masculine gender, nominative case, and in apposition with Cæsar by Rule V.

SENTENCES.

Marius, a Roman, was courageous.   Themistocles, an Athenian, was sagacious.   Dionysius, the tyrant, was cruel.   The emperor Napoleon was ambitious.   Homer, the celebrated poet, was blind.

III. The subject modified by a Noun or Pronoun, in the possessive case.

116. The subject may be modified by a noun or pronoun in the possessive case; as, "*The giant's arm* prevailed." " Giant's " limits " arm," by denoting whose arm is referred to.   The arm prevailed.   Whose arm?   Answer, the giant's.   " Giant's " is in the possessive case.

117. The possessive case is commonly formed by adding an apostrophe (') and the letter *s;* as "*Virtue's* reward."

118. Plural nouns ending in *s,* omit the *s* after the apostrophe ; as, "*Eagles'* wings."

119. The possessive case of the personal pronouns is as follows :

SINGULAR.

Nominative.	I	Thou	He	She	It
Possessive.	my	thy	his	her	its

PLURAL.

Nominative.	We	Ye or you	They
Possessive.	our	your	their

ANALYSIS AND PARSING.

RULE VI.

120. The possessive case limits the noun which denotes the object possessed.   See Rule VIII, *Syntax.*

Model.

SENTENCE. — *My courage failed.*

Analyzed. " Courage " is the subject, limited by " my." " My courage " is the modified subject. " Failed ' is the predicate.

Possessive Case Parsed. "My" is a personal pronoun, in the possessive case, and limits "courage," by Rule VI.

SENTENCES.

The earth's orbit is elliptical. Saturn's ring is wonderful. The ship's crew mutinied. The gentleman's servant absconded. His hard heart relented. My good friend Davis was unfortunate.

COMPOSITON.

Sentences to be written, each of which shall include one of the following nouns, in the possessive case.

Model. — Cicero.

All admire Cicero's orations.

Washington. Franklin. Milton. Columbus. Birds. Eagles. Lion. The sun. A miser. Boys. Children. Men.

The learner can change the form of the sentence written by using the preposition *of*, instead of the possessive case, and not alter the sense ; as, "All admire the orations *of Cicero*," instead of " Cicero's orations."

REVIEW.

What is the second modifier of the subject? (114.) Give an example. Repeat Rule V. What is the third modifier of the subject? (116.) How is the possessive case formed? How is the possessive of plural nouns ending in *s*, formed? Repeat Rule VI.

Section VII.

IV. Subject modified by an Adjunct.

121. The subject may be limited by a noun or pronoun connected with it by a preposition.

THE PREPOSITION.

Note. — Preposition signifies "a placing before," or "a place before," (Latin, *præ,* "before," and *positio* "a placing," or a "place.")

122. The preposition is a part of speech commonly used before a word, to connect it in sense with some other word or expression.

Examples. — " *The snow lies — the ground.*" The word which should stand *before* ground, to connect it *in sense* with *lies*, is called a preposition. The snow lies *on* the ground.

" *He went — England — Cork.*" England may be connected with *went* by the preposition *from*. Cork may be connected with *went* by *to*. He went *from* England *to* Cork.

123. The following is a list of words usually considered prepositions.

LIST OF PREPOSITIONS.

Above.	Below.	From.	Throughout.
About.	Beneath.	In.	
Across.	Beside, *or*	Into.	
After.	Besides.	Notwithstanding.	
Against.	Between, *or*	Of.	
Along.	Betwixt.		
Amid, *or*	Beyond.		
Amidst.	By.		
Among, *or*	Concerning.		
Amongst.	Down.		
Around.	During.		
At.	Ere.		With.
Athwart.	Except.		Within.
Before.	Excepting.		Without.
Behind.	For.	Through.	Worth.

124. Other words and combinations of words are sometimes used as prepositions; such as, *as to, according to,* &c.

125. The word that immediately follows a preposition is called its object; as, Above *the earth.*

126. A preposition with its object, is called the *adjunct* * of the word to which it is joined in sense, and serves to limit a noun in various ways; some of which are as follows:

1. By expressing *quality* or *state;* as, A man *of piety;* a state *of bliss;* habits *of industry.* In such instances, the adjunct is equivalent to an adjective, and one may be used for the other without affecting the sense; as, A man of piety, or a *pious* man; a state of bliss, or a *blissful* state; industrious habits, or habits *of industry.*

2. By denoting *place;* as, Plants *in the garden* blossom earlier than plants *in the field;* waters *under the earth;* a storm *at sea.*

3. By denoting the *state* or *condition* of an object; as, A nation *in debt;* a person *in distress;* a ship *under sail.*

4. By denoting *possession;* as, The trials *of life;* that is, *life's* trials; the sons of *Aaron.* The adjunct of possession is generally equivalent to a noun in the possessive case.

---

* The term adjunct is also applied to a verb in the infinitive mode.

ADDITIONAL EXAMPLES.—"A man *of sorrow;*" "a man *in affliction.*" The adjuncts "of sorrow," and "in affliction," modify man; that is, they describe the condition of a man. They are equivalent to the adjectives, *sorrowful, afflicted.*

"The prisoner *at the bar.*" The adjunct "at the bar" modifies prisoner.

"An *army* on the march." How is *army* modified? What does the adjunct denote?

"A house *with green window-blinds;*" house is modified by the adjunct, "with green window-blinds," and "window-blinds" is modified by "green."

"Spring is the time *to sow.*" The infinitive "to sow" is the adjunct of "time."

RULE VII.

127. Prepositions connect words and show the relation between them.

RULE VIII.

128. The object of a preposition must be in the objective case. See Rule XXIII, *Syntax.*

ANALYSIS AND PARSING.

Model.

SENTENCE.— *Thomson's description of a storm is admirable.*

Analyzed.—"Description" is the subject, modified—1, by "Thomson's," (a noun in the possessive case,) and 2, by the adjunct "of a storm." "Thomson's description of a storm" is the modified subject. "Is admirable" is the predicate, consisting of the copula "is," and the attribute "admirable."

The Preposition parsed. "Of" is a preposition. It is placed before the noun "storm," to show its relation to "description." It, therefore, connects "storm" and "description." Rule VII.

Object of the Preposition parsed. "Storm" is a noun, third person, singular, neuter, objective case, by Rule VIII.

SENTENCES.

The learner should be particular to point out the adjunct in each sentence, and explain its use, before parsing the preposition.

The landscape before us is delightful. The black clouds above our heads are terrific. Death in a good cause is honorable. The orations of Demosthenes, the Grecian orator, are inimitable. The sun's light at mid-day is dazzling. He has a strong desire to see his friend. Have you a wish to come? See Model V, Sect. I.

V. The Subject modified by a Clause.

129. The subject is often modified by a Clause, which serves —1, to express *quality;* or, 2, to denote a *state* or *condition;* or, 3, to restrict the meaning of the subject to some particular person, place, time, or thing.

NOTE.— The limiting clause is often equivalent to an adjective, an adjunct, or a noun.

EXAMPLES. — " The tree *which bears sweet apples,* is decaying." The subject " tree " is modified by the clause " which bears," &c. The whole expression, " The tree which bears sweet apples," is equivalent to the phrase, " the sweet apple tree."

" The man *who lives contented,* is happy." The clause " who lives," &c. denotes a condition of the subject " man." It is nearly equivalent to the expression, " The contented man is happy," or to the expression, " If a man lives contented, he is happy."

" The question, *who goes there?* was often repeated by the sentinel." The clause " who goes there ? " serves to restrict the meaning of the subject " question," and stands in apposition with it.

" The bridge, *which the army crossed,* was afterwards destroyed." The clause " which," &c., restricts the subject to a particular bridge.

" The time *when Lafayette visited this country,* is remembered with much interest." How is the subject " time " limited?

COMPOSITION.

Supply adjuncts, or clauses, to fill the blank places.

Model.

The terror   —   —   —   overpowered his faculties.
The terror *of an eternal judgment,* overpowered his faculties.

He,   —   —   —   —   should build his house upon a rock.
He, *who would act like a wise man,* should build his house upon a rock.

Washington	—	—	died in the year 1799.
Columbus	—	—	was a native of Genoa.
Youth	—	—	often find an early grave.
The pleasures	—	—	are transient.
The man	—	—	will be esteemed.
The counsel	—	—	should be respected.

REVIEW.

What is the fourth modifier of the subject? What is a preposition? What is the word following a preposition called? What is a preposition with its object called? To what else is the term adjunct applied in this work? What is the fifth modifier of the subject called?

Section VIII.

MODIFIED PREDICATE.

NOTE.—The learner has seen how the subject of a sentence is capable of being extended by modifying words, clauses, and phrases. He is now to attend to the other equally important division of a sentence, viz., the *predicate.*

130. The predicate modified by any word, phrase, or clause, is called the *modified* or *logical* predicate.

EXAMPLES.—" The husbandman *tills the ground.*" " Tills " is the predicate; but the expression " The husbandman tills," would be incomplete without the addition of some other word. Tills *what?* Answer, " the ground." " Ground " is, therefore, the modifying word, and is the object of the transitive verb " tills."

" The swallow *flies swiftly through the air.*" " Flies " is the predicate in its simple form. By adding " swiftly," it is denoted how or in what manner the swallow flies. By adding " through the air," the place where the swallow flies is indicated.

" The news *came yesterday.*" " Yesterday " modifies " came," by denoting the time when the news came.

" Swiftly " and " yesterday " are called *adverbs,* and " through the air " is an adjunct of " flies."

I. The Predicate modified by an Object.

131. When the Predicate is a *transitive* verb, it is modified by an *object* expressed or understood.

EXAMPLES. — " Bees produce *honey.*" " Honey " is the object of the verb " produce," and limits its meaning by denoting *what* is produced.

" Worms destroy *plants.*" The predicate " destroy " is modified by " plants."

" Destroy " and " produce " are transitive verbs, because they do not complete an affirmation without the addition of an object. Produce (what?) honey. Destroy (what?) plants.

EXERCISE.

Complete the predicate by adding an object.

Sickness causes —	God created —
The king conquered —	The tree yields —
The wolf followed —	Hunters pursue —
Perseverance overcomes —	Bees collect —
The gentleman has —	Knowledge enlarges —
Worms destroy —	Snow covers —

ANALYSIS AND PARSING.

RULE IX.

132. The object of a transitive verb must be in the objective case.

133. The form of the objective case of nouns is the same as that of the nominative.

134. The objective case of pronouns is as follows:

	SINGULAR.					PLURAL.	
Nominative.	I	Thou	He	She	It	We	Ye or you	They
Objective.	me	thee	him	her	it	us	you	them

Model.

SENTENCE. — *Alonzo, a youth of great promise, found an early grave.*

Analyzed. "Alonzo" is the subject, modified by the noun "youth" in apposition with it. "Youth" is modified by the definitive adjective "a," and by the adjunct "of great promise." "Promise" is modified by the adjective "great."

"Alonzo, a youth of great promise," is the modified subject.   "Found" is the predicate limited by the object "grave."   "Grave" is described by the adjectives "an" and "early."

"Found an early grave," is the modified predicate.

The Object parsed. "Grave" is a common noun, third person, singular, neuter, and in the *objective case.* It is the object of the transitive verb "found."

SENTENCES.

The sharp point of a diamond cuts glass. The prisoner in chains made his escape. The prince obeys the king's command. The youth's extraordinary diligence deserves praise. The rays of the sun disperse darkness. Obey the laws. Govern your passions. They bound him. They tortured him. A guilty conscience tormented him. Fear God. Forgive your enemies. Seek peace. See Model IV, Section I.

COMPOSITION.

Sentences to be written, each including one of the following words, in the objective case, after a transitive verb.

Model.

America.   Go.a.   Air.

Columbus *discovered America.* Misers *hoard gold.* Rain *cools the air.*

Steam. Ship. Freight. Sails. Carriage. Horses. Grass. Hay. Money. Time. Books. House. Trees. Grain. Food.

SECTION IX.

II. The Predicate modified by Adverbs.

135. The predicate may be modified by words which denote *how, how much, how often, when, where,* &c. Such words are called *adverbs.*

EXAMPLES.—"He studies *diligently.*" "Diligently" modifies the predicate, by denoting *how* he studies.

"I admire him *exceedingly.*" "Exceedingly" modifies the predicate "admire." It denotes *how much* I admire.

"The boat arrived *yesterday.*" "Yesterday" modifies "arrived," in respect to time.

ADVERBS.

136. An adverb is a word joined to a verb, adjective, or to another adverb, to modify its meaning.

137. Some adverbs are joined to verbs to denote *manner;* as, "The youth studies *diligently.*" "Diligently" denotes *in what manner,* or *how* the youth studies.

EXERCISE.

Write two adverbs after each of the following verbs, to denote manner.

Model.

The water flows—
The water flows *smoothly.*
The water flows *rapidly.*

The pupil writes—   The fire burns—   The child talks —
The sun shines —   The lion roars—   The bird sings —

How are the verbs which you have written modified?

2. Place a noun and a verb before each of the following adverbs;

—proudly.   —ill.   —well.   —foolishly.
—correctly.   —cruelly.   —unwisely.   —justly.

138. Some adverbs denote *time;* as, "*Now* I will go." *Now* is an adverb.

Point out the adverbs of time, and the verbs which they modify.

The boat arrived yesterday.   He is coming soon.

When did his brother arrive? I never saw him.

I heard the news before.   He formerly lived in Boston.

139. Some adverbs denote *place ;* as, "I am *here ;*" "you are *there ;*" that is, in *this place,* in *that place.*

140. Some adverbs denote *assent, denial, doubt ;* as, *Yes, no, not, undoubtedly, truly, perhaps, probably, possibly.*

141. Some adverbs denote *comparison, quantity ;* as, *More, most, very, much, enough.*

142. Most adverbs answer to the questions, *how? when?* or *how often?* as, The prattler talks—*how?* Ans. *Foolishly.* The boat arrived — *when?* Ans. *To-day.* You come to town — *how often?* Ans. *Frequently.*

143. Adverbs are often joined to adjectives, to modify their meaning; as, *More* pleasing; *most* fanciful; *very* true.

144. Adverbs sometimes modify the meaning of other adverbs; as, *Very* soon; *most* assuredly.

145. Adverbs rarely modify prepositions; as, *Almost* to; *directly* under.

COMPOSITION.

Sentences to be written; each of which may include one of the following adverbs:

Diligently.	Rapidly.	Assuredly.	Pleasantly.
Undoubtedly.	Possibly.	Probably.	Cheerfully.
Truly.	To-day.	To-morrow.	Often.
Yes.	Not.	More.	Most.

ANALYSIS AND PARSING.

RULE X.

146. Adverbs generally modify verbs, adjectives, or other adverbs.

Model.

SENTENCE. — *Time flies swiftly.*

Analyzed. "Time" is the subject. "Flies" is the predicate, modified by swiftly." "Flies swiftly," is the modified predicate.

5

Adverb Parsed. "Swiftly," is an adverb and modifies "flies." Rule.

SENTENCES.

A generous man bestows his favors seasonably.

The old ship Constitution arrived yesterday.

A large army encamped here.

Each member performed his part cheerfully.

Where is my friend? (My friend is where?)

Quite small children sometimes read very well.

Study diligently. Labor patiently. How often is he absent?

REVIEW.

What is the first modifier of the predicate? (131) In what case is the object of a transitive verb? What is the form of the objective case of nouns? Of pronouns? What is the second modifier of the predicate? (135) What is an adverb? Mention what some of the different classes of adverbs denote. Repeat Rule IX, (132) and Rule X, (146).

SECTION X.

III. The Predicate modified by Adjuncts.

147. The Predicate may be modified by an adjunct denoting *time, place, quantity, cause, manner, means, instrument,* or *accompaniment.*

NOTE. — The adjunct of the predicate should receive very careful attention. By means of this we may give almost endless variety in the expression of thoughts. This adjunct consists of a preposition and its object, and may be used frequently in place of an adverb.

EXAMPLES. "I work *at home, in the field, in the morning, on a farm, with diligence, with a friend," &c.* Either of the adjuncts may modify the predicate "work," to denote *time, place,* &c.

"The snow falls, (where?) on the ground, (when?) in the winter, (how much?) in great abundance."

"He lives, (where?) in London, (how?) in poverty."

"The ship sailed (whence?) from Boston, (to what place?) to Liverpool."

Supply an adjunct to modify

He lived ——   ——

They cast him ——

He fell ——   ——

They walked ——

They sailed —	Birds build their nests —
His brethren cast Joseph —	The prodigal wasted his sub-
Joseph ruled —	stance —
The rain descends —	Bees collect honey —
The rain fell —	

ANALYSIS AND PARSING.

In analyzing the following sentences particular attention should be given to the adjuncts of the predicate.

Peter wept bitterly for his sin.

He recited the lesson imperfectly in the morning.

They divided the inheritance among them.

Rivers flow into the ocean.

The sailors abstained from intoxicating drinks.

They made preparations for the funeral.

They bore the body to the church on the Sabbath following.

The sun gives light by day.

The ships sail over the boisterous deep.

IV. The Predicate modified by Clauses.

148. The predicate may be modified by clauses which express *time, place, cause, &c.*

EXAMPLES. — "I fled *when I saw the enemy.*" The predicate "fled" is modified by the clause "when," &c., which denotes both the time and cause of fleeing.

"I fled *because I was afraid.*" The predicate "fled" is modified by the clause "because," &c., which denotes the cause.

"He dwells *where his father dwelt.*" The predicate "dwells" is modified by the clause "where," &c., which denotes the place of dwelling.

EXERCISES.

Show how the predicates are modified in the following sentences.

The building shakes when the wind blows.

We were present when General Lafayette embarked at Havre for New York.

You sleep while I write. You are idle while I labor.

They persevered as long as there was a prospect of success.

I saw him as soon as he arrived.

He finished his work before he departed.

REVIEW.

How is the predicate modified in the third place? (147) Give an example of a predicate modified by an adjunct? How is the predicate modified in the fourth place? (148) In how many different ways may a predicate be modified? In how many different ways may a subject be modified? What are these ways?

Section XI.

GENERAL EXERCISE IN ANALYSIS AND PARSING.

Note 1. The models already given will be a sufficient guide in the following exercise.

2. In analyzing, the learner will first look for the subject, and then for the words or adjuncts which modify it. Then he will point out the predicate and its modifications. In the foregoing pages he will find a model for parsing any part of speech occurring in the sentences that follow.

SENTENCES.

Good breeding consists in a respectful behavior to all.

The early natives of the country fell into the hands of the Romans.

The patient ox submits quietly to the yoke.

The angry waves dash violently against the rocks.

The affecting story of the crucifixion often melts hard hearts into penitence.

The memory of Washington is fresh in the hearts of his countrymen.

The sun sank in the western horizon, in clouds of foreboding darkness.

I heard the crashing of the pointed rocks through the bottom of the ship.

COMPOSITION.

Supply *modified predicates* for the following modified subjects.

Model.

Modified subject.	Modified predicate.
Many enemies of public liberty —	
Many enemies of public liberty, *have been distinguished by their private virtues.*	

A contented mind —.   Idleness in the season of youth—.

Industrious habits —.   Great advantage —.

The trees of the forest —.   The duties of children at school –

The flowers of the field —.   The darkness of the night —.

Children who are obedient to their parents —.

The world which we live upon —.

NOTE. — Some other modifications of the predicate will be explained in Parts III, and IV.

SECTION XII.

MODIFICATION OF WORDS.

149. The meaning of any noun or pronoun, may be modified in the same manner as the subject.

1. By an adjective; as, "*A good* farm."

2. By a noun or pronoun in apposition; as, " Cicero, *the orator.*"

3. By a noun or pronoun in the possessive case; as, "*Cowper's* poems."

4. By an adjunct; as, " The prayer *of faith.*"

5. By a clause; as, " I abhor the man *who deceives.*"

150. The meaning of a verb, in any form, may be modified in the same manner as the predicate.

1. If transitive, by an object; as, "I love *to see the sun.*"

2. By an adverb; as, " He strives *to live contentedly.*"

3. By an adjunct; as, " He is ambitious *to excel in learning.*"

4. By a clause, denoting *time, place, cause,* &c.

151. An adjective is often modified,

1. By an adverb; as, " He is *quite* industrious."

2. By an adjunct; as, " He is *capable of understanding.*"

152. An adverb may be modified,

1. By another adverb; as, " He *conducted quite improperly.*"

2. By an adjunct; as, " Agreeably *to your wishes.*"

ANALYSIS AND PARSING.

The doctrines *of* the gospel are practical principles.

The immense quantity *of* matter *in* the universe, presents a most striking display *of* Almighty power.

5*

The rapid motions *of* the great bodies *of* the universe, display the infinite power *of* the Creator.

I mentioned the unexpected meeting *with* my friend, *in* a distant spot. [*In* connects spot and meeting.]

He directed my eye *with* his finger *over* another landscape.

Medical science first struck its root in .Grecian soil.

Homer is the fountain-head of European poetry.

Confusion in speech leads to confusion in morals.

COMPOSITION.

Exercise in forming Sentences.
Model.

Subject.	Predicate.
Washington —	— commanded.

Washington commanded.   (The simplest, that is, the unmodified form.)

Modified subject.	Modified predicate.
The illustrious Washington	*bravely* commanded.

The illustrious Washington bravely commanded.

The illustrious Washington, the son of a Virginian planter, { bravely commanded the American army in the revolutionary war.

NOTE. — It will be seen that a simple sentence consists of two parts, viz : a *subject* and a *predicate*, or a *modified subject* and a *modified predicate*.

Sentences may now be formed after the model above.

Subjects.	Predicates.
Columbus	discovered.
Trees	grow.
Ship	sails.
Fire	consumes.

SECTION XIII.

CONJUNCTIONS.

153. A Conjunction is a part of speech used to connect *words*, *adjuncts*, or *clauses*.

EXAMPLES. — " Charles *and* James are brothers." "And," the conjunction, connects " Charles " and " James ; " that is, it denotes that they are spoken of together.

"I walked *in the fields* and *in the groves.*" The adjuncts "in the fields" and "in the groves," are connected by *and.*

" *I love him* because *he is good.*" The clauses "I love him," and "he is good," are connected by the conjunction *because.*

154. The following is a list of the principal conjunctions :

And, although, as,	Or,
Because, both, but,	Since, same,
Either,	Than, that, therefore, though,
For,	Unless,
If,	Wherefore, whether,
Lest,	Yet.
Neither, nor, notwithstanding,	

NOTE. — Several of the words in the list above, are used in other offices as well as that of a connective. See *Syntax*, under Rule XXIV.

EXERCISE.

Supply conjunctions to connect the words or sentences separated by the blank spaces.

He reads — writes.   He neither reads — studies.
I neither command — forbid.   He is despised — he is poor.
He is either a knave — a dunce. I ask — you believe it to be true.
             The wind subsides — the clouds disperse.

COMPOSITION.

Write sentences, each of which shall include one of the following conjunctions.

NOTE. — *Nor* must be used after *neither ;* or after *either.*

And,	Whether,	Than,	Unless,
Because,	Neither,	Or,	Either,
If,	Though,	But,	That.

SECTION XIV.

COMPOUND SUBJECT.

155. The Compound Subject consists of two or more simple subjects connected in one proposition.

EXAMPLES. — " *Pompey* and *Cæsar* were Roman generals." " Pompey and Cæsar " is the compound subject. This proposition may be resolved into two distinct propositions; as, "Cæsar was a Roman general, and Pompey was a Roman general." In the former case, the conjunction *and* connects the nouns *Pompey* and *Cæsar;* in the latter, it connects the two propositions.

"*James or Charles* is in fault." "James or Charles" is the compound subject. This sentence may also be resolved as follows: "James is in fault, or Charles is in fault."

156. A proposition containing a compound subject may be resolved into as many propositions as there are simple subjects. This is not true, however, when the predicate is not applicable to the subjects taken separately; as, "Two and three make five." This sentence cannot be resolved like the examples above. In propositions of this kind, the subject may be regarded as *simple*, although in *form* it is compound.

157. When three or more subjects stand connected, the conjunction is frequently omitted except before the last; as, "James, Charles and John are brothers."

ANALYSIS AND PARSING.

In this Exercise, the learner may analyze the sentence having a compound subject as a whole, and then resolve it into as many separate propositions as there are simple subjects.

The moon and stars are shining.

The rain and snow fell in great abundance last season.

The Scribes and Pharisees came to Jesus.

Moses and Aaron spake to the children of Israel.

Moses, Aaron, and Hur went up to the top of the hill.

Spring, summer, or autumn, is preferable to winter.

COMPOUND PREDICATE.

158. The Compound Predicate contains two or more simple predicates that are applicable to one subject.

EXAMPLE. — "He *writes and studies.*" "Writes and studies" is the compound predicate. The sentence may be resolved into two simple propositions, by repeating the subject; as, "He writes," *and* "he studies." In the former case, the conjunction connects the verbs *writes* and *studies;* in the latter, it connects the two propositions.

159. Sentences having a compound predicate may be resolved into as many propositions as there are simple predicates.

160. When three or more predicates stand connected, the conjunction is often omitted, except before the last; as, "James reads, writes and ciphers."

ANALYSIS AND PARSING.

Let the sentence be analyzed as a whole, and then be resolved into separate propositions.

The husbandman ploughs, sows, reaps, and gathers into his storehouse.

Peaches are agreeable to the taste, delight the smell, and charm the sight.

Ducks swim in the water, fly in the air, or walk on the land.

Hear counsel, and receive instruction.

Forsake the foolish, and live; and go in the way of understanding.

INTERJECTIONS.

161. An Interjection is a word used in giving utterance to some sudden or strong emotion; as, *O! Alas!*

The following are the principal interjections: O! oh! ah! alas! ho! halloo! hurrah! huzza! pish! poh! tush! fie! 'lo!

162. Certain verbs are often used as interjections; as, *Behold! look! hark! hail! welcome!*

NOTE. — Some other parts of speech are occasionally used in exclamations of wonder or surprise; as, *Strange! what! mercy,* &c.

PART III.

—

CLASSES, VARIATIONS, AND INFLECTIONS.

SECTION XV.

CLASSIFICATION OF NOUNS.

163. A single *name* is often applicable to a great number of objects; as, *Animal, plant, river, stone, mountain.*

164. The name *animal* is applicable to every living being. The name *man* is applicable to each of a certain class of living beings. So likewise each of the names, *bird, fish, reptile, quadruped,* is applicable to a whole class of beings and to every individual of a class. The names *robin, thrush, lark, eagle,* and *raven,* denote distinct classes of birds, and each of them is the common term applicable to every individual of its own class.

165. Sometimes a *particular* name is given to an individual of a certain class, to distinguish it from the rest; as, *Adam, Homer, Bucephalus, Amazon, Andes.*

166. NOUNS are divided into two general classes; *Common* and *Proper.* See 69, 70.

167. Common nouns are divided into *collective, abstract, participial* or *verbal, compound,* and *complex.*

168. A *collective* noun is the name of a body or collection of individuals; as, *People, flock, council, assembly.*

169. An *abstract* noun is the name of some quality; as, *Cheerfulness, vanity, goodness, frailty.*

170. A *participial* or *verbal* noun is the name of some action, or state of being; as, "The *cheering* of the multitude." "The *singing* of birds."

NOTE. — Such nouns are called *verbal,* because they are derived from verbs; *participial,* from having the form of the participle.

171. A *compound* noun is a name composed of two or more words, which are generally separated by a hyphen; as, *Rail-road, will-with-the-wisp,*

172. A *complex* noun is a name with some distinguishing or complimentary title added to it; as, *Mr. James White, Judge Wild, Dr. E. Smith.*

173. A common noun often becomes proper when it denotes an inanimate object or an abstract quality personified; as, "O *Time!* how few thy value weigh."

174. A common noun becomes proper when, with the article *the,* it distinguishes some particular place, object or event, as remarkable above others of

the same name; as, *The Bar, the Park, the Common, the Tempest, the Dark Day, the Deluge.*

175. A proper noun becomes common, when applied to a class of individuals, to designate in them some character or quality of the person or object to which the name was originally given; as, " He is *the Cicero* of his age." " He will never become *a Washington.*"

176. Proper names generally become common when they comprehend two or more individuals; as, *The Smiths, Two Roberts.* But this is not the case with names that designate a whole people; as, *The Americans, the Russians, the Indians.* But when such nouns are applicable to individuals, or to any part of the people thus designated, they become common; as, *Americans, Russians, Indians.*

ANALYSIS AND PARSING.

Particular attention should be given to the different classes of nouns that have been before described. If the learner meets with difficulty in analyzing and parsing, he can turn back for assistance to the *Models* in Part I.

SENTENCES.

Columbus, a native of Genoa, discovered America.

Cambyses, the son of Cyrus, led an army against Amasis.

The Thebans commenced hostilities with the Athenians.

The thoughts of the diligent tend only to plenteousness.

Slothfulness casteth into a deep sleep.

Genius and learning walk in the train of virtue.

In reason and in fact character goes before scholarship.

Professing regard and acting indifferently discover a base mind.

ORAL EXERCISE.

Questions like these contained in the oral exercises should be multiplied until the learner is perfectly familiar with the subject under examination.

Are there as many names in the English language as objects which can be described ? Give some examples of names, each of which is applicable to a number of objects.

Which name is applicable to the largest number of objects, animal or man ? Animal or bird ? Bird or robin ? Bird or lark ? Reptile or worm ? Tree or maple ? Plant or tree ?

Mention the names of as many animals as you can recollect. Is each of the names given applicable to more than one animal ?

What kind of nouns are those which you have mentioned ? Why so called ? Define a common noun.

Which noun is the more general or common, mountain or Alps ? river or Amazon ? man or Washington ? boy or Charles ? Why ?

What kind of nouns are those which designate individuals of a class? Why?

What is an abstract noun? A collective noun? A participial noun? A compound noun?

SECTION XVI.

PROPERTIES OF NOUNS AND PRONOUNS.

177. It is the nature of a noun to represent to the mind an object, together with some quality or relation pertaining to it. For example, the noun "man," denotes a being, together with the sex. The noun "houses," represents an object together with the idea of plurality.

178. This quality or attribute of representing number, sex, and certain relations, is called a *property* of the noun.

179. The properties of nouns and pronouns are *person*, *number*, *gender*, and *case*.

PERSON.

180. Person is the property that indicates the relation of a noun or pronoun to the speaker.

181. There are three persons, called *first*, *second*, and *third*.

1. The speaker, or first person, may speak of himself; or, 2, he may speak of the person whom he addresses, called the second person; or, 8, he may speak of some other person.

182. As each person may include one or more, it may be singular or plural. See declension of nouns and pronouns, 225. See also, 72, 78, 74, 75, 76.

NUMBER.

188. Number is the property that distinguishes one from more than one. See 77.

184. There are two numbers, *singular* and *plural*.

Forms of the Plural Number.

185. The plural of nouns is generally formed by adding *s* to the singular; as, Road, *roads* ; mountain, *mountains*.

186. The plural ending often makes an additional syllable. This is the case when the *s* does not unite in sound with the word or syllable to which it is added ; thus, the plurals of *horse, house, page, rose, voice*, have two syllables; as, *hor-ses, hou-ses*, &c.

187. Nouns ending in *x*, *z*, *ss*, *sh*, or *ch* soft, form their plurals by adding *es ;* as, Fox, *foxes*, glass, *glasses*, adz, *adzes*, lash, *lashes*, church, *churches*.

NOTE. — The insertion of the *e* is necessary in such words to give the sound of *s* in the plural form.

188. Most nouns ending in *f* or *fe*, form their plural in *ves ;* as, Wife, *wives*, loaf, *loaves*.

189. The following nouns and their compounds form their plurals regularly; *strife, fife, safe, brief, chief, grief, kerchief, mischief, dwarf, scarf, turf, surf, gulf, roof, proof, hoof*, and such as end in *ff*, except *staff*, which has *staves*. Staff as a military term has *staffs* in the plural.

190. Nouns ending in *y* after a *consonant*, change the *y* into *ies*, to form the plural ; as, Body, *bodies ;* lady, *ladies*. But nouns ending in *y* after a *vowel*, have their plural regular ; as, Valley, *valleys ;* boy, *boys;* day, *days.**

191. Nouns ending in *o*, preceded by a consonant, form their plural by adding *es* to the singular ; as, Hero, *heroes ;* except *junto, canto, tyro, grotto, portico, solo*, and *quarto*, which have *s* only, added for the plural.

192. Nouns ending in a vowel preceded by another vowel, form their plurals regularly ; as, Folio, *folios.*

193. The plural of the following nouns is irregularly formed :

Singular.	*Plural.*	*Singular.*	*Plural.*
Man	men	Tooth	teeth
Child	children	Louse	lice
Woman	women	Goose	geese
Ox	oxen	Mouse	mice.

194. The following nouns have two forms in the plural, with different significations.

Singular.	*Plural.*	*Plural.*
Brother	brothers (of one family)	brethren (of one society.)
Die	dies (for coining)	dice for gaming.
Penny	pennies } distinct	pence } applied to
Pea	peas } objects.	pease } a mass.
Cow	cows	kine
Genius	geniuses, persons of genius.	genii, a kind of aerial spirits.

195. The compounds of *man* form the plural in the same manner as the simple word ; as, Alderman, *aldermen ;* statesman, *statesmen.*

196. Some words ending in *man*, as *Turcoman, talisman*, are not compounds of this word, and form their plural regularly.

---

* Formerly, the singular number of this class of words ended in *ie* ; as *Glorie, vanitie.*

The Plural of Foreign Words.

197. Nouns whose plurals are formed according to the analogy of the languages from which they are derived.

Singular.	Plural.	Singular.
Alumnus,	alumni.	Gymnasium, {
Amanuensis,	amanuenses.	
Analysis,	analyses.	Hypothesis,
Animalculûm,	animalcula.	Ignis fatuus,
Antithesis,	antitheses.	Index,
Apex,	{ apices, apexes.	
Appendix,	{ appendices, appendixes.	Index,
Automaton,	{ automata, automatons.	
Axis,	axes.	Lamina,
Arcanum,	arcana.	Lava,
Bandit,	{ banditti, bandits.	Medium, { {
Basis,	bases.	
Beau,	beaux.	
Calix,	{ calices, calixes.	
Cherub,	{ cherubim, cherubs.	
Chrysalis,	chrysalides.	
Datum,	data.	
Desideratum,	desiderata.	
Diæresis,	diæreses.	
Dogma,	{ dogmas, dogmata.	
Effluvium,	effluvia.	radii.
Ellipsis,	ellipses.	Scoria,
Emphasis,	emphases.	Scholium, { {
Ephemeris,	ephemerides.	
Encomium,	{ encomiums. encomia.	
Erratum,	errata.	{ seraphim, seraph.
Focus,	foci.	specula.
Formula,	{ formulas, formulæ.	theses.
Fungus,	{ fungi, funguses.	vortices.
Genus,	genera.	

198. Some nouns, from the nature of the things which they denote, have the singular form only ; as, *Wheat, pitch, gold, sloth,* &c. Some words of this class, when used to denote different kinds of the substances or qualities which they represent, admit of a plural form ; as, *Wine, wines; vice, vices.*

199. Some nouns have the same form in both numbers ; as, *Mathematics, ethics, means, species, series, deer, sheep.*

The singular *mean* is used to signify the middle between two extremes.

200. *News,* which was formerly used both in the singular and plural, is now regarded as singular only.

201. The words *cannon, shot, sail;* also the words *horse, foot, infantry,* and *cavalry,* comprehending bodies of soldiers, are used as plural nouns ; as, " Several *shot* being fired ;" "several *sail* of ships." The word *fish* has a plural, but is used in the plural sense without a change of form.

202. To express the plural of a proper noun with a title prefixed, the title only is usually varied in writing, to express the plural ; as, " The Messrs Harper ;" "the Misses Young." But in regard to the plural of such complex nouns, usage is not uniform. Some good writers vary the name and not the title, and in conversation this usage is more common ; as, " The Miss Youngs." With the title of *Mrs.,* or the numerals *two* or *three* prefixed, the name only is varied to express the plural.

203. Compounds, in which the principal word is put first, vary the principal word to form their plurals ; as, *Father*-in-law ; plural, *Fathers*-in-law. *Court*-martial ; plural, *Courts*-martial. Compounds ending in *ful,* and all those in which the principal word is put last, have the regular plural form ; as, *Spoonfuls, man-traps.*

204. Proper names, generally, do not admit of a plural form, except the names of *nations, societies, chains of mountains,* and *groups of islands ;* as, *The Apennines, the Friends, the English, the West-Indies.*

205. The following nouns are used only in the plural.

Annals.	Drawers, (an article of	Lees.	Snuffers.
Antipodes.	dress.)	Lungs.	Scissors.
Archives.	Dregs.	Letters, (literature.)	Shears.
Ashes.	Embers.	Measles.	Shambles.
Assets.	Entrails.	Minutiæ.	Tidings.
Billiards.	Goods.	Manners.	Tongs.
Bitters.	Hatches.	Morals.	Thanks.
Bowels.	Hose, (stockings.)	Nippers.	Vespers.
Breeches.	Hysterics.	Nones.	Vitals.
Clothes.	Ides.	Pincers.	Victuals.
Calends.	Literati.	Pleiads.	Wages.

Add to these the names of things consisting of two parts only ; as, *Bellows, scissors, tongs,* &c.

NOTE. — Words, figures, and letters, used merely as nouns, without regard to their appropriate signification, form their plural with an apostrophe and the letter *s* ; as, the *if's* and *and's;* the *but's* and *wherefore's;* the 8's and the 9's; the *a's* and the *b's.*

EXERCISE.

Give the plurals of the following nouns.

Tax; brush; gas; monkey; attorney; valley; fly; lady;
destiny; liberty; city; berry; prodigy; hero; negro; portico;
motto; potato; tyro; elf; wolf; leaf; half; thief; life; knife;
staff; flagstaff; brother; foot; emphasis; handful; spoonful;
penny; genus; index; mother-in-law; brother-in-law; genius;
alderman; statesman.

SECTION XVII.

GENDER.

206. Gender is a property of the noun or pronoun to distinguish sex.   See 80, 81, 82, 83.

There are three different ways of distinguishing sex,—1. by
the use of different words; as, Father, *mother;* 2. by difference
of termination; as, Actor, *actress;* 3. by prefixing or annexing
another word; as, Land*lord,* land*lady.*

207.   By different words.

Masculine.	Feminine.	Masculine.	Feminine.	Masculine.	Feminine.
Beau,	belle.	Gentleman,	lady.	Man,	
Boy,	girl.	Hart,	roe.	Master,	
Brother,	sister.	Horse,	mare.	Master,	
Buck,	doe.	Husband,	wife.	Nephew,	
Drake,	duck.	King,	queen.	Papa,	
Earl,	countess.	Lad,	lass.	Son,	
Father,	mother.	Landlord,	landlady.	Stag,	
Friar *or* monk,	nun.	Lord,	lady.	Uncle,	
Gander,	goose.	Male,	female.	Wizard,	witch.

208. By difference of termination.

Masculine.	Feminine.	Masculine.	Feminine.
Abbot,	abbess.	Instructor,	instructress.
Actor,	actress.	Jew,	Jewess.
Administrator,	administratrix.	Landgrave,	landgravine.
Adulterer,	adulteress.	Lion,	lioness.
Ambassador,	ambassadress.	Marquis,	marchioness.
Arbiter,	arbitress.	Margrave,	margravine.
Author,	authoress.	Negro,	negress.

Masculine.	Feminine.	Masculine.	Feminine.
Baron,	baroness.		
Bridegroom,	bride.		
Benefactor,	benefactress.		
Caterer,	cateress.		
Chanter,	chantress.		
Conductor,	conductress.		
Count,	countess.		
Czar,	czarina.		
Dauphin,	dauphiness.		
Deacon,	deaconess.		
Duke,	duchess.		
Emperor,	empress.		
Enchanter,	enchantress.		
Executor,	executrix.		testatrix.
Governor,	governess.		tigress.
Heir,	heiress.	Tutor,	tutoress.
Hero,	heroine.	Viscount,	viscountess.
Host,	hostess.	Votary,	votaress.
Hunter,	huntress.	Widower,	widow.

209. By prefixing or annexing another word; as,

Land*lord*,	land*lady*.	*Man*-servant,	*maid*-servant.
Gentle*man*,	gentle*woman*.	*Cock*-sparrow,	*hen*-sparrow.
Pea*cock*,	pea*hen*.	*Male* child,	*female* child.
He-goat,	*she*-goat.		

210. Some nouns denote objects which are either male or female; as, *Child, parent, neighbor.* Such nouns, when used in a general way, without particular reference to some individual of the class,* are said to be of the COMMON GENDER.

211. Things without life are sometimes figuratively represented as having the attributes of living beings; to such the distinction of sex is applied; as, when we say of a ship, *she* sails well, or of the sun, *he* is rising. Things remarkable for power, size, &c., are spoken of as masculine. Things beautiful, amiable, or productive, as feminine.

212. When we speak in a general manner of a species; as, the dog, the cat, &c., to the species which is remarkable for boldness, strength, or generosity, the male sex is generally attributed; to animals of opposite qualities the female sex is attributed; as, "The dog is remarkable for *his* sagacity." "The cat, as *she* beholds the light, contracts the pupil of *her* eye."

213. The masculine gender has a general meaning, expressing both male and female, and is always employed when the office, occupation, or profession,

---

* The term *common* does not refer to any distinction in sex, but is applied to a certain class of nouns, which, from their form, are indeterminate in respect to gender; but when the context determines to which sex they are to be referred, they are not to be considered of the *common gender.*

and not the sex, of the individual is chiefly to be expressed. In the following sentence, both male and female writers are included. "The poets of this age are distinguished more by correctness of taste than sublimity of conception." But if it is intended to designate the sex of the individual spoken of, the appropriate form of the word must be used.*

214. In speaking of an animal, whose sex is not known or not important to be regarded, it is often considered without sex; as, "If a man steal an ox or sheep and sell *it*," &c.

ORAL EXERCISE.

How many does the word river denote? Change the form so that it shall denote more than one. Change the following nouns to the plural form; *knife, strife, wife, chief, fox, glass, brush, vanity, money, child, emphasis, analysis, memorandum, gymnasium.*

What is that property of a noun called, which distinguishes one from more than one?

How is the plural number formed? What are some of the variations from the general rule?

What is gender? What does the masculine gender denote? feminine? neuter? Mention the different ways of distinguishing sex. To what object is the term *common gender* applicable? Is the distinction of sex ever applied to things without life?

SECTION XVIII.

CASE.

215. The term Case (Latin, *casus*, "a fall," "an end," or "a close,") is strictly applicable to the ending of declinable words. But in the English language the relations of words are not generally determined by syllables annexed or prefixed.

216. In every sentence there is one word which denotes the person or thing of which an assertion is made, called the *subject*. This relation is easily determined, and is called the *nominative case*. The predicate expresses some action or state of the subject. This action sometimes relates only to the subject itself; as, "The bird *sings*," "a man *sleeps*," and sometimes extends beyond itself to some object which is controlled, produced, possessed, or in some way affected by it. This object is denoted by a noun or pronoun, in quite a different relation from that of the nominative, and is said to be in the *objective case*.

217. The objective case may be easily known, from its being the direct limitation of a *transitive* verb or *preposition*. As the relation of property or ownership is indicated by a certain termination of the noun, the case, called

---

* See Crombie's Etymology and Syntax. Also, Cramp's Philosophy of Language.

the *possessive*, occasions no difficulty to the learner. There are, therefore, three distinct relations of nouns and pronouns in a sentence, called, in grammar, *nominative, possessive*, and *objective* cases. See 84.

218. The nominative case is used to denote the following relations. See 85, 86, 87.

1. Of the subject of a proposition; as, " *The sun* is the source of heat."

2. Of a noun, pronoun, or clause, in apposition with the subject; as, "Cicero, *the orator;* " "the question, *how he should succeed,* was not considered."

3. Of a noun in the predicate referring to the *subject nominative;* as, "Cicero, the orator, was a great *statesman*." · *Cicero, orator,* and *statesman,* are in the nominative case.

219. The possessive case of nouns is generally formed by annexing *s* with an apostrophe; as, "*Swift's* journal;" "*Spencer's* anecdotes;" "*men's* shoes;" "*children's* toys."

220. The possessive case plural, ending in *s*, is formed by adding the apostrophe without the *s;* as, "*Boys'* tops;" "*eagles'* wings."

221. To a noun in the singular number, ending in *s* or *z*, the apostrophe is sometimes added without the *s*, when its use would occasion a disagreeable harshness; as, " Moses' disciples;" " righteousness' sake."

222. When the letter *s* added as a sign of the possessive will not coalesce with the noun, it adds a syllable to it ; as, Thomas's book; church's property, pronounced Thomas-is, church-is.

NOTE. — The possessive case of pronouns has no regular formation.

223. The objective case denotes the object of a transitive verb or preposition.

224. Nouns and pronouns are often used absolutely ; that is, they form no part of a regular sentence ; such nouns are said to be in the *independent case.**

NOTE. — As the form of this case is generally like that of the nominative, it is not given in the declension. The objective form of the pronoun is sometimes in this case.

---

* The term *nominative independent* or *absolute*, seems to be inconsistent both with the true definition of the nominative, and with the rules which govern its construction with the verb. Besides, pronouns in the *objective* case are sometimes used in this way; as, *Me! miserable.* Such words might be termed *independent* or *absolute*, without the appendage of " *case*."

Section XIX.

225. Declension of nouns and pronouns.

NOUNS.		PRONOUNS.	
REGULAR.		**FIRST PERSON.**	
Singular.	*Plural.*	*Singular.*	*Plural.*
Nom. King,	kings.	Nom. I,	we.
Poss. King's,	kings'.	Poss. My, mine,	our.
Obj. King,	kings.	Obj. Me,	us.
REGULAR.		**SECOND PERSON.**	
Fox,	foxes.	Thou,	You, ye.
Fox's,	foxes'.	Thy, thine,	your.
Fox,	foxes.	Thee,	you.
IRREGULAR.		**THIRD PERSON, (MAS.)**	
Man,	men	He,	they.
Man's,	men's.	His,	their.
Men,	men.	Him,	them.
PROPER NOUNS.		**THIRD PERSON, (FEM.)**	
George,	———	She,	they.
George's,	———	Her,	their.
George,	———	Her,	them.
ABSTRACT.		**THIRD PERSON, (NEUT.)**	
Virtue,	———	It,	they.
Virtue's,	———	It's,	their.
Virtue,	———	It,	them.

226. *Mine* and *thine* were formerly used before nouns beginning with vowels, instead of my and thy. But this use is no longer retained, except in grave or formal style.

227. *Ours, yours, theirs, hers,* and generally *mine* and *thine*, are possessive pronouns, used in either the nominative or objective case.

As pronouns they represent both the possessor and the thing possessed.

EXAMPLES. — "*Your* house is on the plain, *ours* is on the hill;" "ours" standing in place of "our house," is in the nominative case. " *Yours* is just received;" that is, your letter. "Yours" is the subject of "is." *

* See *Webster, S. S. Greene, Wells,* &c.

228. In most Grammars these words are treated as pronouns in the posses-sive case. But as they are invariably used in the place of a noun and pronoun, and cannot be used before nouns either expressed or understood, they have a better claim to the rank of *subject* or *object* than several other words called compound pronouns.

229. The pronoun *you*, although plural in form, represents nouns in either number. *Thou* and *thee* are seldom used except in grave or formal style. *You*, therefore, is the only pronoun *of the second person* in common use, to represent nouns in the singular or plural number.

ANALYSIS AND PARSING.

Particular attention should be given to the nouns and pronouns in the different cases. The rules given in Part I, should be applied here.

The earth revolves swiftly. The boat glides rapidly down the stream. Fragrant flowers bloom in the garden. The lark mounts high in the air.

Youth's joys depart. Edward's courage failed, in view of the difficulties before him. Joseph's father mourned for him. Washington's army suffered. The ship's crew mutinied. Bona-parte's soldiers conquered.

The prince obeys the king's command. Arnold's treason dis-graced his name. The eagle's talons seized the prey. George studies Colburn's arithmetic. The sun's rays disperse the dark-ness. The youth's diligence deserves praise. They took Jo-seph's coat, and killed a kid of the goats, and dipped the coat in the blood.

We compel them. I hear your request. She fears him. Thou rulest us. You believe me. Thine is the kingdom. They hate me. You see me. He fears my anger. It is his book. They care for you. We lost ours. You took mine. You have his book. He bought my watch. I received yours. We injured theirs. They came to our house. They wasted their property.

ORAL EXERCISE.

1. What does case denote ? How many principal cases ? What relations does the nominative case denote ? When the nominative denotes the subject, what is it called ? *Ans.* Subject nominative. When a nominative occurs in the predicate, what is it termed ? *Ans.* The predicate nominative. In the sentence " Time is money," which is the subject nominative ? Which the predicate nominative ?

2. What does the possessive case denote ? How is it generally formed ? What does the objective case denote ? Decline "king," "fox," "man," and the pronouns, "I," "thou," "he," "she," "it." What is said of "mine," and "thine ?" Of "ours," "yours," "theirs," &c. ? Can they stand before nouns ? In what case are these words considered to be by most grammarians ? What is an objection to their being considered in the possessive case ?

SECTION XX.

VERBS.

230. A Verb is a word by means of which something is affirmed.*

NOTE. — The word "affirm" is intended to apply to the office of the verb in direct and indirect assertions; also in expressing command, entreaty, and inquiry.

CLASSES.

231. Verbs are divided into two general classes, namely: TRANSITIVE and INTRANSITIVE; and into five subordinate classes, namely: *regular*, *irregular*, *auxiliary*, *defective*, and *impersonal*.

TRANSITIVE VERBS.

232. A *Transitive Verb* is one that requires an object to complete the sense; as, "Fire *consumes*," (what?); the addition of an object is required to complete the sense. See 92.

NOTE. — The term "transitive" is applicable to the active form only of this class of verbs. See 239.

233. The object is sometimes omitted, when it is suggested by the connection, or when the verb expresses a customary act; as, "The husbandman *ploughs, sows,* and *reaps.*" The object of each of these verbs is naturally suggested; as, "Ploughs *the ground,* sows *the seed,* and reaps *the grain.*"

---

* The chief characteristics of this important part of speech, appearing in the numerous definitions of it, have been its necessity to every sentence of *affirmation*, energy, action, suffering, being, time, number, and person. Every verb, whilst it implies time, *predicates* or connects an attribute, or expresses action. — *Dr. Wilson.*

Assertion or affirmation is the act peculiar to the verb, being never performed by any word which grammarians have referred to a different part of speech. — *Edinburgh Encyclopædia,* Art. GRAM.

234.　Transitive verbs express an action which an agent or doer exerts upon, or in reference to, some person or thing; and it is called *transitive* from its appearing to be the means of passing over or transferring this action. It is a convenient term, but calculated to mislead the learner in regard to the real nature of the verb. The verb has no agency in either exerting or transferring the action, but stands simply as the sign of an action, or as the medium which the writer or speaker employs in affirming the action.

INTRANSITIVE VERBS.

235. An intransitive verb is one that does not require an object to complete the sense; as, I *stand;* he *sits.*

236.　Some verbs of this class are transitive in relation to an object that has a meaning similar to their own; as, "To dream *a dream;*" "to run *a race;*" "to live *a life,*" &c.

237.　It is to be understood that the term *object,* used in connection with transitive and intransitive verbs, usually has reference to a noun or pronoun in the objective case, used immediately after a verb, without a preposition expressed or understood.

238.　It frequently happens, however, that verbs called "intransitive" express action as exerted upon an object in the strongest manner, through the medium of a preposition; as, "He stamped *upon the ground;*" "they fell *upon the enemy.*" In such instances the preposition seems to combine with the verb, and together they form a compound expression, equivalent to a transitive verb.

VOICE.

239. Verbs used transitively have two forms, called *active* and *passive voices.*

240. In the *active voice* the subject of the verb is represented as acting upon an object; as, "*The sun* warms *the earth.*"

241. In the *passive voice* the subject of the verb is represented as being acted upon; as, "*The earth* is warmed by the sun." *

242.　In both of these examples the sense is the same, but the form of the expression is entirely changed. The object "earth," in the *active form,* has become the *subject* in the *passive,* while the agent "sun" appears in the passive form as the object of the preposition *by.*

NOTE. — As a convenient mode of expression, the term *passive verb* is sometimes applied to the passive form of a *transitive verb.*

---

* When a nominative is the name of an agent, the verb is said to be active. When it is the name of an object, it is said to be passive. This mode of expression is illogical, for it is the noun that becomes active in one instance and passive in the other. — *Edinburgh Encyclopædia.*

EXERCISE.

Change the verbs in the following expressions to the passive form.

The hunter kills the fox.	The wind shakes the trees.
The farmer tills the ground.	The sun melts the snow.
The waves toss the ship.	The wood-cutter fells trees.

243. A few intransitive verbs are used in the passive form by reputable writers. The following expressions occur in Gray's Letters : "I *am* this night *arrived* here." "I *am to-day just returned* from Alba." So in Shakspeare: "He *is not yet arrived;*" "Who 't is that *is arrived?*" Such usage with these verbs, however, is not general among good writers. It should be, "I have arrived;" "I have returned," &c. But a passive form of the verbs *come, go, become, rise, set, fall, grow,* and some others, is in common use. "*Is* Hector arrived and *gone?*"—*Troilus.* "My lord, your loving nephew now *is come.*" "Richard, my friend, *is he come?*"—*King Henry VI.* "The sun *is risen.*" "Christ *is risen* indeed." "The park that surrounded the house *was all. run* wild, and the trees *were grown* out of shape."—*Irving.*[*]

NOTE.—Some verbs are used transitively and intransitively in the same form ; as, "They *cut* the tree." "The fir *cuts* more easily than the oak."[†]

ORAL EXERCISE.

Into what two general classes are verbs divided? What is a transitive verb? an intransitive? The "bird flies." What kind of a verb is flies? Why? "The husbandman tills the ground." What kind of a verb is tills? Why? What is its object? Is the object ever omitted? Give an example.

Do intransitive verbs ever have an object? Do intransitive verbs ever express action? What forms have transitive verbs? How is the subject represented in the active form? in the passive form? Give examples of

---

[*] The neuter [intransitive] admits in many instances a passive form, retaining still the neuter signification; chiefly in such verbs as signify some sort of motion, or change of place or condition; as, "I *am come;*" "I *was gone;*" "I *am grown;*" "I *was fallen.*" I doubt much the propriety of the following examples; "We *are swerved.*" *Tillotson.* "The obligation *was ceased.*" *Ib.* "Whose number *was amounted.*" *Swift. — Lowth.*

[†] Transitive verbs in English are sometimes used without an objective case, in a sense between the active and passive voices; as, "I *taste* the apple;" "the apple *is tasted* by me;" "the apple *tastes* sweet;" "the field *ploughs* well." — *Hart.*

both forms. Do any intransitive verbs admit of a passive form? Give an example. Are the expressions, "is arrived," "is returned," strictly proper? Why is the expression, "is perished," improper? What should it be?

SECTION XXI.

MODES.

244. Mode (Latin, *modus*, "manner,") is a form of the verb which expresses the manner in which something is affirmed.

245. Some of the different modes in which the verb is used are as follows:

1. We say, the flower *blooms*, the flower *bloomed*, the flower *will bloom*, the flower *has bloomed*, or *has the flower bloomed?*

This manner of asserting or inquiring is called the INDICATIVE mode.

NOTE. — *Indicative* means "showing," or "declaring."

2. We say, the child *may learn, can learn, must learn, could learn, should learn*, or *can he learn? must he learn? &c.*

This manner of asserting or inquiring is called the POTENTIAL mode.

NOTE. — *Potential* (Latin, *potens*, "able," "having power,") signifies *having power* or *ability.*

3. We say, *learn thou, obey ye, do, go.*

This manner of speaking is called the IMPERATIVE mode or manner.

NOTE. — *Imperative* signifies "commanding."

4. We say, *to read, to have read.*

This manner of speaking is called the INFINITIVE mode.

NOTE. — *Infinitive* (Latin, *infinitus*, "unlimited,") signifies "in an unlimited manner."

5. We say, *if it rains, suppose it should rain, lest it should rain, unless it rains.*

This manner of speaking is called the SUBJUNCTIVE mode.*

---

* The following are appellations given to modes of assertion by different writers.

Personative, impersonative, the indicative, declarative, definitive, the rogative, interrogative, requisitive, percontative, assertative, enunciative, vocative,

NOTE.— *Subjunctive* (Latin, *subjungo*, " to subjoin,") signifies subjoined to. This mode is called subjunctive, because the clause in which it occurs must be " subjoined to," or connected with some other clause to make complete sense ; as, " If it rains," expresses only a supposition ; but when subjoined to " I cannot work," the sense is complete.

ORAL EXERCISE.

' In what mode are the following assertions : " I love," " I have loved," " I will love," " I loved." Why ?

In what mode are the following assertions : " I may love," " I might love," " I can love," " I must love." Why ? *Ans.* They imply power, ability, necessity, or obligation.

In what mode are the following expressions : " See thou," " see," " see ye," ' believe him," " obey your rulers." Why ?

In what mode are the following expressions : " To do," " to learn," " to speak," " to have seen." Why ?

In what mode are the following expressions : " If I love," " unless you hear."

How many modes have been mentioned ? What are they ?

EXERCISE.

Put each of the following verbs in all the different modes.

Model.

Verb—MAKE. INDICATIVE. —I make, I made, I have made, I shall make.

POTENTIAL. — I may or can make, I might make, I may have made.
SUBJUNCTIVE. — If I make, lest I make, unless I make.
IMPERATIVE. — Make, make thou, make ye, do make.
INFINITIVE. — To make, to have made.

VERBS.

Command.	Deny.	Praise.
Obey.	Forgive.	Blame.
Speak.	Turn.	Walk.

246. As the verb is the only medium of expressing an assertion or affirmation, the different ways of asserting are called the modes of the verb. Of these, there are commonly reckoned five, namely : the *indicative*, the *potential*, the *subjunctive*, the *imperative*, and the *infinitive*.

NOTE. — Several grammarians of high authority consider the participle a mode of the verb, which they call the *participial mode*.

---

precative, deprecative, responsive, concessive, permissive, promissive, adhortative, optative, dubitative, imperative, mandative, conjunctive, subjunctive, adjunctive, potential, participial, infinitive, &c.

MODES OF THE VERB.

247. The *Indicative Mode* is the form of the verb used simply to affirm or declare something; as, " He *writes*." " He *will come*."

248. The *Potential Mode* is the form used to affirm something as *possible, obligatory*, or *necessary ;* as, " He *may write*." " He *can write*." " He *should write*." " He *must write*."

249. This mode may be known by the sign *may, can, must, might, could, would*, or *should*.

NOTE. — As the peculiar import of this mode depends upon the signification of the auxiliaries *may, can*, &c., the learner is referred to the explanation of these verbs in 318, 1, 2, 3, &c.

250. Both the potential and indicative modes, are used in asking questions of an import corresponding to their different significations.*

251. The *Subjunctive Mode* is the form used to represent something as *uncertain, conditional*, or *contingent* ; as, "*If it is* true, it is unaccountable."

252. The subjunctive mode may be known generally by the signs *if, though, except, unless, whether, lest, suppose*, or any other word that implies uncertainty, condition, or supposition.

253. The sign, however, is often omitted, especially before the verbs WERE, HAD, COULD, and SHOULD as, "*Were* I," "*Had* I the wings of a dove," for "If I were," "If I had," &c.

254. The *Imperative Mode* is used *to command, entreat, exhort*, or *permit ;* as, "*Go*," "*Come thou*," "*Obey*."

255. The *Infinitive Mode* is used to express an action, or state, in an unlimited manner; as, " *To live*," " *To know*," " *To have known*."

It is known by the sign *to*, which precedes the verb.

256. A verb in the infinitive has properties in common both with the noun and the verb. Like a verb, when transitive, it is limited by an object. It also expresses an action, or a state of being, and in some of its relations implies time ; and like the verb, when transitive, it admits of an active and a passive form.

---

* The interrogative form is no other than the indicative, with such accentuation or transposition of words as to show the doubt of the speaker, and sometimes with an interrogative particle prefixed. — *Edinb. Enc.*

Like the noun, it is used in the *nominative case* both as *subject* and *attribute*, and in the *objective case* as the *object* of a transitive verb. It does not take an adjective *before* it, but when used as the subject of a proposition, it may have a *predicate adjective* belonging to it.

EXERCISE.

Mention the *mode* and the class of the verbs, or answer the questions, what kind of verb, *transitive* or *intransitive?* In what *mode?* Why?

The sun warms the earth. James should love his book. I will walk in the field. George must not kill the bird. If sinners entice thee, consent thou not. Love justice. Speak the truth. He wished he could learn. He might learn if he would. I must go. Suppose it should rain. If it should rain I shall not go. He should strive to improve. Go and do likewise. Seek peace and pursue it. Does he believe the rumor? Must I go?

REVIEW.

How many modes have verbs? Name them. What is the office of the indicative mode? What does the potential mode imply? The subjunctive mode? How may the potential mode be known? What words are signs of the subjunctive mode? Is the sign ever omitted? Give an example. How is the imperative mode used? What does the infinitive mode express? How may the infinitive be known? In what respects is the *infinitive* mode like a noun? In what respects is it like a verb?

Section XXII.

TENSE.

257. Tense signifies " time." (French, *temps*, or Latin, *tempus*, " time.")

We speak of actions or events as taking place in *different times*.

1, We say "the flowers bloom," in the *present time;* — 2, "the flower bloomed," in *past time;* — 3, "the flower will bloom," in *future time*.

ORAL EXERCISE.

How many kinds of time have been mentioned? Put the verb *love* in the present, past and future time. Put the verb *to study* in the present, past and future time or tense. *I walk;* is the verb walk in the present or past time or tense? *I walked,* in what time? What is the future time or tense of the verb walk?

Use the following verbs to express something in the present, past and future time The pronouns *I, we* and *they,* may be used.

Strike. Learn. Talk. Hear. See. Work. Look. Hides. Believe.

258. Besides the three general divisions of time mentioned, there are some subordinate divisions.

1. We say, "the flower had bloomed;" that is, before some other occurrence had taken place; as, "Before I came the flower had bloomed." This is a division of past time.

2. We say, "the flowers have bloomed;" that is, at a time before the present, but it is not certain whether it bloomed a moment ago, or at a period considerably distant.
This is also a division of *past time.*

3. We say, "The flower will have bloomed;" that is, at or before some other occurrence will take place; as, "The flower *will have bloomed* before we shall return." This is a division of *future time.*

ORAL EXERCISE.

I love, I loved, I have loved, I had loved, I shall or will love, I shall have loved.

In how many different times is the verb *love* used?

Put the verb *play* in the different times or tenses; also the verbs *hate, destroy, praise* and *blame.*

How many divisions of time have been made? Ans. *Six.*

How many divisions of *past* time has the verb? Ans. *Three,* called the *Imperfect* or *Past* tense; as, I loved; the *Perfect* tense; as, I have loved, and the *Pluperfect* tense; as, I had loved.

How many divisions of *future* time has the verb? Ans. *Two,* the *First Future* tense; as, I shall or will love; and the *Second Future* tense; as, I shall have loved.

TENSES OF THE VERB.

259. Tense is the distinction of time. There are six tenses, called the *Present,* the *Imperfect* or *Past,* the *Per-*

fect, the *Pluperfect*, the *First Future* and the *Second Future*.

260. Verbs have two forms in each tense, called *Simple* and *Progressive*. I *write, wrote, have written, shall or will write*, or *shall have written*, are simple forms, and mark time by themselves with less precision than the progressive forms.

261. The *Progressive Form* consists of the participle in *ing*, and some form of the verb *be*. It denotes an action or event going on at the time specified; as, I *am writing, was writing, have been writing, shall be writing*, &c.

TENSES OF THE INDICATIVE MODE.

THE PRESENT TENSE.

262. The Present Tense denotes the present time of an action or event; as, "I *am writing*." "I *write*."

263. The *simple form* expresses what is customary or what is always true; as, "The sun rises and sets." "God *is* eternal."

It embraces any extension of time, a portion of which is included in the present; as, "Caligula *is justly abhorred* for his cruelty;" that is, *was* and still *is* abhorred.

This form is sometimes used in the narration of past events, to impart spirit and vivacity to the style; as, "He *fights, conquers*, and *takes* an immense booty which he *divides* among his soldiers and *returns* home."

264. This form sometimes refers to future time, especially when preceded by the words *when, before, after, as soon as*, &c.; as, "When he arrives he will hear the news. Mr. Coleman goes off for Boston to-morrow."—*J. Adams; Let. CXLVIII.*

265. The *progressive form* of this tense expresses what is passing in the present moment; as, "He *is reading*."

THE IMPERFECT TENSE.

266. The Imperfect Tense denotes simply the past time of an action or event; as, "I *wrote*." "I *was writing*."

267. The *simple form* expresses an action or event as completed in past time; as, "The ship *sailed* yesterday."

268. The *progressive form* of this tense expresses an action or event as going on at some specified past time; as, "I *was writing* yesterday, when you called to me."

269. This tense is called by some writers the *past* or *preterit* tense. The term *imperfect* is not strictly applicable, except to the *progressive form*.

THE PERFECT TENSE.

270. The Perfect Tense denotes past time with some reference to the present; as, "I *have written*," "I *have been writing*."

The sign of this tense is *have*.

271. The *simple form* of a verb in this tense expresses an action or event that took place at any period of past time, together with the idea of continuance to some period of time up to the present moment; as, "Philosophers *have made* great discoveries in the present century." Here the action spoken of is past, but still the idea of continuance to the present time is distinctly implied in the expression "present century."

272. This form expresses also an action or event as just finished; as, "I *have spoken* freely what I had to say."*

273. The *progressive form* of this tense expresses an action or event as *going on* in past time, but *continuing* to the present; as, "I *have been waiting* a day, a month, or a year," &c. The duration of the action is determined by some limiting word or adjunct.

274. A verb in this tense sometimes denotes a future action or event, if preceded by *when, before, as soon as*, &c.; as, "We will go *as soon as* we *have completed* our work."

NOTE. — This tense is termed *completive present* by Harris; by Lowth, Ward, &c., *present perfect*; by Murray, Webster, &c., *perfect.*

PLUPERFECT TENSE.

275. The Pluperfect Tense denotes time past at or before some other specified past time; as, "I *had finished* my letter

---

*This is also called the present perfect tense, as it denotes actions done in three degrees or distinctions of time, all terminating with the present; that is, either without any time intervening between their being done and the present time; or within some compass, or certain portion of time extending to the present. Thus in the first degree we say, "I have now written my letter;" which intimates that no space of time intervened between the action and the time of speaking.

In the second degree we say, "I have written a letter this morning;" when nothing is determined, but that the action was done within that space of time. Wherefore in speaking of the same action in the afternoon, it is proper to say, "I wrote a letter this morning," not "I have written," &c. In the third degree we may say, "Cicero has written three books of offices," or "moral duties;" where, notwithstanding these books were written many ages since, yet as the expression is general and no intimation given of any intermediate space, we use this tense. See *Essays on Language, by John Ward.*

before he arrived." "Had finished," is in the pluperfect
tense.

This tense may be known by its sign "had."

276. This tense has the same relation to the imperfect as the perfect has to
the present. A verb in this tense expresses something anterior to the imper
fect, but extending to it in some relation; as, "Many discoveries *had been
made* in the arts and sciences before the days of Bacon."

FIRST FUTURE TENSE.

277. The First Future Tense denotes simply future time ;
as, " I *shall write,*" or " *shall be* writing."

The sign of this tense is *shall* or *will.*

SECOND FUTURE.

278. The Second Future Tense denotes time that will be
past at or before some future time specified; as, " They
will have finished their work by the appointed time."

279. This tense may be known by the sign, *shall have.*

NOTE. — Various other distinctions in time are denoted by *adverbs, adjuncts,*
and *modifying clauses*

REVIEW.

What is tense ? How many tenses ? What two forms in each tense have
verbs ? What does the present tense denote ? What does the *simple form* of
a verb in this tense express ? Is the present ever used in the narration of
past events ? For what purpose ? When does this tense denote future time ?
How does the progressive form of this tense express an action or event ?

What does the imperfect tense denote ? How does the simple form express
an action ? The progressive form ? By what other terms is this tense sometimes called ?

What does the perfect tense denote ? What is the sign of this tense ? How
does this tense differ from the imperfect ? Does a verb in this tense ever denote a future action ?

What does the pluperfect tense denote ? What is its sign ? What relation
does this tense have to the imperfect ? What does the first future tense denote ? What is its sign ? What does the second future denote ? What is its
sign ?

ANALYSIS AND PARSING.

In this exercise the learner should be particular to specify the class, mode,
and tense of the verb, or to answer the following questions in parsing it.
Why a verb ? transitive or intransitive ? why ? In what mode ? why ? In
what tense ? why ?

We have dismal accounts from Europe of the preparations
against us.

The summer will be very important to us.

We shall have a severe trial of our patience, fortitude, and perseverance.

Mr. Reed, formerly General Washington's Secretary, goes with Mr. Dickinson. (How is the present tense used in this sentence?)

Education makes a great difference between man and man.

This morning * I received your two letters.

I have this morning * been out of town with Generals Washington, Lee, and Schuyler.

I am reading history. He has been reading poetry

TO BE CORRECTED.

I have attended church last sabbath. This year I saved my wages. I have expected a letter a month ago. I see him yesterday. I have seen him last week. We escaped many dangers through life. I see a wagon yesterday drawn by four elephants. I had pleasing intelligence to-day. I never see such a sight before.

Section XXIII.

TENSES OF THE POTENTIAL MODE.

280. This Mode has four tenses, viz., *the present, the imperfect, the perfect,* and *the pluperfect.*

281. The present and imperfect tenses of this mode are less definite in regard to time than the same tenses of the indicative mode. For example, *I may go, he may go, I can go,* are forms of the *present tense,* potential mode, but by themselves they mark no precise time.

282. *I might go, I could go, he should go,* &c., are forms of the imperfect tense, but alone they imply no definite time.

283. These tenses seldom mark time definitely, except when some limiting word, phrase, or clause is added; as, I *may go* to-morrow, I *would like* to go to-day, he *should go* instantly, he said *he would* go to-morrow.

TENSES OF THE SUBJUNCTIVE MODE.

284. The Subjunctive Mode has all the tenses of the indicative, but is more commonly employed in the *present, imperfect,*

---

* See Rule X, Part IV.

and *perfect* tenses; as, If I go, if he would come, if we have sinned, &c.

285. The present tense generally expresses a condition on which something future is asserted; as, "*If I justify* myself, mine own mouth shall condemn me;" "*If I be* wicked, woe unto me."

286. The imperfect is frequently used without marking any precise period of time, and may refer to the *present, past,* or *future;* as, "Though all men should be offended because of thee, yet will I never be offended."

287. In a negative sentence the subjunctive mode often implies an affirmation; as, "I would take a walk *if it did not* rain;" implying that it does rain; and on the other hand, in an affirmative sentence the subjunctive form often implies a negation; as, "I would contribute liberally *if I had* the means;" implying that I have not the means.

288. This is especially true of the verb *be,* in one of its forms in the subjunctive; as, "*If it were possible,* they shall deceive the very elect;" "to seduce, *if it were possible,* even the elect;" "*if it were* not so I would have told you."

Section XXIV.

PARTICIPLES.

289. A Participle is a word that partakes of the properties of a verb and an adjective.*

290. A verb has three participles; a *present,* a *perfect,* and a *compound participle.*

291. The *present participle* ends in *ing,* and implies continuance of action; as, *Loving, having, standing, being.*

292. This participle is sometimes called the *imperfect* participle, because it denotes action going on, but not completed.

293. The present participle implies time present, in relation to the time denoted by the verb of the sentence in which it stands.

294. The *perfect participle* denotes action or state *completed;* as, *Loved, been, stood.*

295. The perfect participle of a regular verb always ends in *ed.* For perfect participles of irregular verbs, see table of irregular verbs.

---

* Every complete verb is expressive of an attribute, of time, and of assertion. Now if we take away the assertion, and thus destroy the verb, there will remain the *attribute* and the *time,* which make the essence of a participle.— *Harris, Hermes, Chap. X.*

296. The *compound participle*, formed of the verb *have* and a perfect participle, denotes *action* or *state* completed, before some other action or event; as, *Having loved, having been*.

297. A participle sometimes performs the office of a noun; and is then called a *participial* or *verbal noun*; as, "The general's *having failed* in this enterprise, occasioned his disgrace."

298. The present participle of a transitive verb, though generally active in its signification, is sometimes used passively; as, "The book *is printing;*" "the house *is building.*" *

REGULAR VERBS.

299. A Regular Verb is one which forms its imperfect tense and perfect participle by adding *ed* to the present; as, Borrow, imp. borrow*ed*, perf. part. borrow*ed*.

NOTE. — This rule is applicable only to the common form in the active voice.

300. When a regular verb ends in silent *e*, it drops the *e* on receiving *ed;* as, Love, lov-*ed*. Regular verbs ending in *y*, preceded by a consonant, change the *y* into *i* before the *ed* is added; as, present, *rarify*, perfect, *rarified*, perfect participle, *rarified*. See 44.

301. Certain regular verbs double the final consonant before receiving the termination *ed;* as, Fit, fit*ted*; plan, plan*ned*; regret, regret*ted*; drop, drop*ped*. See 45.

302. An Irregular Verb is one which does not form its imperfect tense and perfect participle by adding *ed* or *d* to the present; as, *Go*, imp. *went*, perf. part. *gone*.

EXAMPLES OF REGULAR VERBS.

Indic. Present, or root.	Indic. Imperfect.	Perf. Participle.
Love,	loved,	loved.
Labor,	labored,	labored.
Move,	moved,	moved.

---

* The form of expression, "*is being* built," "*is being* committed," &c., is almost universally condemned by grammarians, but it is sometimes met with in respectable writers. — *Worcester.*

"The grammar is printing;" "the brass is forging." This is in my opinion a vicious expression, probably corrupted from a phrase more pure, but now somewhat obsolete; "the book is *a* printing;" "the brass is *a* forging;" *a* being properly *at*, and "printing" and "forging" verbal nouns, signifying action." — *Dr. Johnson.*

Indic. Present, or root.	Indic. Imperfect.	Perf. Participle.
Relate,	related,	related.
Conceal,	concealed,	concealed.
Fatigue,	fatigued,	fatigued.
Rest,	rested,	rested.
Perform,	performed,	performed.

NOTE. — The present participle is formed by annexing *ing* to the root. The silent *e* of the verbs ending with that letter is, with one or two exceptions, dropped before receiving *ing;* as, love, lov*ing;* move, mov*ing.* See rules of spelling.

EXAMPLES OF IRREGULAR VERBS.

Indic. Present, or root.	Indic. Imperfect.	Perf. Participle.
Have,	had,	had.
Know,	knew,	known.
Stand,	stood,	stood.
Behold,	beheld,	beheld.
Bring,	brought,	brought.
Sting,	stung,	stung.
Lay,	laid,	laid.
Lie,	lay,	lain.

EXERCISE.

Write the present, perfect and compound participles of the following verbs.

Labor. Open. Fatigue. Stand. Move. Prove. Have. Know. Perform. Regret. Transfer. Plan. Lay. Bring. Lie. Create. Command. Complain. Relate. Rest. Deceive. Improve.

ANALYSIS AND PARSING.

RULE XI.

303. Participles belong to nouns, which they limit or explain.

304. Present and compound participles of transitive verbs in the active form, govern* the objective case.

Model.

SENTENCE. — *The past participle signifies action finished.*

Analyze. "Participle" is the subject, modified by "past." The "past participle" is the modified subject. "Signifies" is the predicate. "Signifies

* Government, in grammar, is the power of one word in determining the mode, tense or case of another.

action finished," the modified predicate. " Finished," the participle, modifies action

Participle Parsed. " Finished " is a perfect participle of the regular verb *finish,* and belongs to " action." *Rule.*

SENTENCES.

He had a poniard *concealed* under his coat.

However *fatigued,* he always returned in spirits.

Having rested, we descended the hill.

After *having performed* the ceremony, he returned.

Jesus *knowing* their thoughts, rebuked them.

I saw him *laboring* in the field.

The Most High dwelleth not in temples *made* with hands.

I see the heavens *opened,* and the Son of man *standing* on the right hand of God.

PERSON. — NUMBER.

305. The verb receives certain endings to agree with the different numbers and persons of its subject.

These endings denote two *numbers,* and *three persons.*

PRESENT TENSE.

EXAMPLES.

1st person singular.	*2d person singular.*	*3d person singular.*
I love	Thou love*st*	He love*s.*
1st person plural.	*2d person plural.*	*3d person plural.*
We love	Ye or you love	They love.

306. The ending *st* or *est,* denotes that the pronoun *thou* of the second person singular, is the subject, and the ending *s* or *es* denotes that some noun or pronoun of the third person singular is the subject. These are the only variations in the present tense, from the simple form of the verb. Formerly, the third person singular of the *present indicative,* ended in *eth ;* as, He loveth.

IMPERFECT TENSE.

1st person sing.	*2d person sing.*	*3d person sing.*
I loved	Thou loved*st*	He loved.

8

1st person plural.	*2d person plural.*	*3d person plural.*
We loved	Ye or you loved	They loved.

307. The only variation in the imperfect tense, on account of number and person, is in the second person singular. The ending of *st* or *est*, is added to agree with *thou.*

308. The pronoun *thou* and the termination *st* or *est* are not much used, except in grave and formal style.

309. The pronoun *you* is generally employed now to represent nouns of the second person in both numbers, although it requires a verb in the plural form.＊

310. In the subjunctive present, the personal terminations were formerly omitted; as, If *thou love,* if *he love.* This form is still retained to express *future contingency,* and is by some grammarians termed the *elliptical form,* used for if thou *shall love,* if he *shall love.*

311. In all other cases the forms of the indicative mode are used in the subjunctive throughout all the tenses, except in the second and third persons of the second future, and except also in the *present* and *imperfect tenses* of the verb *be,* which have each two forms.

312. The imperative mode is commonly used only in the second person; as, Come *thou;* go *ye.*

313. There are expressions, however, in which the form of the imperative mode is used with the third person; as, "Be *it* enacted;" "blessed be *he* that cometh;" "fall *he* that must."

314. The first person is rarely used with the imperative; as, "Well, march *we* on — meet *we* the medicine of the sickly weal; and with him pour *we in* our country's purge, each drop of us." — *Shakspeare.*

EXERCISE.

Mention the class, number, person, mode, and tense of each of the following verbs.

They labor. They labored. I have labored. I shall labor. He will labor. It moves. It moved. It will move. We know. We knew. We shall know. We have known. The bees sting. The bees stung. The bees will sting. The bees may sting. They can sting. They might sting. You have. You had. You have had. You will have. You might have. You may have.

＊ Thou in polite, and even in familiar style, is disused, and the plural *you* is employed instead of it; we say *you have,* not *you hast.* Though in this case we apply " you " to a single person, yet the verb too must agree with it in the plural number. " *You was,*" is a solecism, and yet authors of the first rank have inadvertently fallen into it. "Knowing that *you was* my old master's good friend." — *Addison. Lowth's Introd.* p. 48.

Section XXV.

CONJUGATION.

315. Conjugation is the inflection of a verb in the different modes, tenses, numbers, and persons.

Inflection of the verb May in the Indicative Mode, Present Tense.

Singular.

I may, first person, singular, because the pronoun *I* is of the first person singular.

Thou mayst, second person, singular, because *thou* is of the second person singular.

He, she, or *it, may*, third person, singular, because *he* and *she* and *it*, are of the third person, singular.

Plural.

We may, first person, plural, because *we* is of the first person, plural.

Ye or *you may*, second person, plural, because *ye* and *you* are of the second person plural.

They may, third person, plural, because the nominative *they* is of the third person, plural.

The Principal Parts of a verb are, the *Present Indicative*, the *Imperfect Indicative*, and the *Perfect Participle*.

AUXILIARY VERBS.

316. Auxiliary verbs are such as are used to form some of the modes and tenses of other verbs. They are *may, can, must, shall, will, have, do, be.*

317. *Will, have, do, be*, are also used as principal verbs.

May, can, shall, and *will* (when auxiliaries) have only the present and imperfect tenses.

Conjugation of MAY, CAN, SHALL, and WILL.

PRESENT TENSE.

Singular.

	1. I may	I can	I will	I shall
PERSON.	2. Thou mayst	Thou canst	Thou wilt	Thou shalt
	3. He may	He can	He will	He shall

Plural.

1. We may	We can	We will	We shall
2. You may	You can	You will	You shall
3. They may	They can	They will	They shall

IMPERFECT, OR PAST.

Singular.

1. I might	I could	I would	I should
2. Thou mightst	Thou couldst	Thou wouldst	Thou shouldst
3. He might	He could	He would	He should

Plural.

1. We might	We could	We would	We should
2. You might	You could	You would	You should
3. They might	They could	They would	They should

NATURE OF THE AUXILIARIES.

MAY, CAN, MUST.

May, } Derived from the Saxon word *magan,* "to be able,"
Might. }   "to avail."

Can, } From the Saxon *cennan,* "to know," "to contain," "to
Could. }   be able."

318. *May* and *can* are used as auxiliaries in forming the *potential present* of other verbs. They were once used as principal verbs and were followed by an infinitive; as, "*I can* to go," "I *may* to go;" that is, "I am able to go."

MAY in its present use implies,

1. *Possibility;* as, "Something *may* happen to defeat our plans." "He *may* complete his task if he is diligent."

2. *Ability;* as, "What he *may* do is of two kinds; what he *may* do as just, and what he *may* do as possible."

3. *Liberty,* or *permission;* as, "A man *may* do what the laws permit." "Thou *mayst* be no longer steward." "He *may* go, if he wishes."

4. *Wish* or *desire;* as, "*May* prosperity attend you."

5. The expressions, *may be, it may be,* are equivalent to *perhaps,* or by chance; as, "*May be* I will go," or, "it *may be,* that," &c.

6. *May* is sometimes used to soften the harshness of command; as, "You *may give* my compliments to Mr. B."

7. *Might,* the past tense of *may,* implies also possibility, power, liberty, &c., and is sometimes used instead of "may," to soften the expression; as, "O that Ishmael *might* live before thee."

CAN implies *power, skill, permission, possibility,* or *will.*

EXAMPLES. "*Can* faith save him?" [power.] "He *can* go to-morrow." "The Jews *could not* eat certain kinds of animals," [permission.] "An astronomer *can* calculate an eclipse," [skill.] "I *cannot* rise and give thee; yet because of his importunity, he will rise and give him" [will.]

MUST implies necessity, certainty, or obligation, and has no variation to express time, person or number.

Section XXVI.

SHALL, WILL.

Shall, ⎫ From the Saxon *scealan* "to be obliged,"
Should. ⎬ formerly used as a principal verb, and fol-
          ⎭ lowed by an infinitive mode.

Will,   ⎫ From the Saxon *willa,* " to will," used still as
Would. ⎬ a principal verb, but more commonly as an
          ⎭ auxiliary.

319. These verbs are now used as auxiliaries to other verbs, and are signs of the future tense. The following are some of the various shades of meaning which they admit of.

1. *Shall* in the first person foretells or declares what will take place, or expresses the decision of the speaker in reference to some future action, or state; as, " I *shall* go to morrow;" sometimes contingently; as, " I *shall* go to-morrow with your leave, or if the weather permit."

2. When uttered with emphasis, "shall" in the *first person*, denotes the determination of the speaker; as, " I *shall go* to-morrow, whether I obtain your leave or not."

3. *Shall* in the *second* and *third persons* generally expresses the *will, decision, permission, promise,* or *command* of the speaker in reference to some other person or thing; as, " He *shall* go;" [it is my will to compel him to go.] " Then *shall* ye return, saith the Lord of hosts," [promise.] " Thou *shalt* not kill," [command.] " It is a mind that *shall* remain."

> "—————— *Shall* remain !
> Hear you this triton of the minnows? Mark you,
> His absolute *shall !* " — *Shakspeare.*

4. After another verb, *shall* in the *third person* simply foretells; as, " He thinks he *shall* succeed well."

5. In questions, *shall* in the *first person* is used to ask permission, direction, or intention; as, " *Shall* I go?" " *Shall* I suffer such injustice?" " What *shall* I do?" " Whither *shall* I fly?" [direction.] " *Shall* he be punished?" " *Shall* you go to-morrow?" [intention.]

6. *Shall* in all the persons, denotes simply futurity after *if,* and some other words which express a condition; as, " If I, we, you, or he, *shall* go."

7. *Should* in all the persons commonly expresses obligation, but after *if, though, unless,* and other signs of the subjunctive, it expresses future contingency; as, " If it *should* happen," " though all *should* deny thee."

8. WILL in the *first person* expresses the promise or decision of the speaker; as, " I *will* go," " I *will* reward you."

9. In the *second person, will* simply denotes a future event; as, " You *will* go." In questions it asks consent, or inquires for the intention of the subject; as, " *Will* you go?" " *Will* you resist?"

10. In the *third person*, *will* in most instances simply denotes futurity, but sometimes it expresses strong determination of the subject; as, " He *will* not listen," i. e., he is determined not to listen.

11. *Should* in the *second* and *third persons*, is also used to express an event, under a condition or supposition; as, " He *would* be censured, if he should remain longer."

12. The difference between *shall* and *will* may be expressed in a general way as follows:

Will in the *first person*, and *shall* in the *second* and *third*, signify resolution. Simple futurity is expressed by *shall* in the *first*, and *will* in the *two others*.

Simple future.

I shall,	thou wilt,	he will.
We shall,	ye will,	they will.

The future of determination.

I will,	thou shalt,	he shall.
We will,	ye shall,	they shall.

13. *Would* implies will, desire, or resolution, under a *condition* or *supposition ;* * as, " I *would* if I could." " I could if I *would*." " *Would* God we had died in Egypt."

Section XXVII.

320. *Do,* { *Do*, as an auxiliary, is often used in the following
Did. { offices : —

1. In negative and interrogative sentences; as, " *Do* you see ?" *Do* is the auxiliary of " see. " " *Does* he expect to come ?" " I *do* not know."

2. To express emphasis; as, " I *do* hate him, but will not wrong him."

3. In the imperative mode, to express an urgent request or command; as, " *Do* help me ;" " make haste, *do*."

4. To save the repetition of another verb; as, " I shall come, but if *I do* not, go away;" that is, " if I come not."

Note. — Other auxiliaries are used in a similar manner; as, " *Will* you come ?" " *I will* ;" that is, I *will come*.

5. *Do* is sometimes used expletively; as, " I *do* love," for " I love." " Expletives, their feeble aid *do* join." — *Pope*.

6. *Did* is sometimes used to express opposition ; as, " I *did* honor him, but now despise him."

---

* The condition implied in " would " is not always expressed. " By pleasure and pain *I would be understood* to mean what delights or molests us ;" that is, if it should be asked what I mean by pleasure and pain, *I would thus explain* what I wish to have understood. In this form of expression, which is very common, there seems to be implied an allusion to an inquiry, or to the supposition of something not expressed. — *Webster*.

7. *Do*, when used before a verb, except in the imperative mode, is the sign of the present tense.

8. *Did*, when used before a verb, is the sign of the *imperfect tense.*

THE VERB BE.

321. The common use of the verb *to be* is to assert a connection between a subject and an attribute of it ; as, " Gold *is* a metal." A connection between gold and metal is asserted to exist by the copula *is*.

322. This verb with a participle in *ing* constitutes the *progressive form* in each tense of every other verb ; as, " I am writing," " I was writing," &c.

323. It is also used with a past participle of the transitive verb, to form the passive voice ; as, " He *is* moved ; " " he *will be* moved," &c.

324. The important office of this verb in asserting or indicating a connection between a subject and its attribute, will appear by omitting the verb, and thus bringing the noun and the attribute together ; as, "He wr.ting."

325. The juxtaposition of the words might denote that writing is an attribute of *he*, but in order to assert positively the fact of writing, the copula must be inserted.

326. This verb sometimes expresses simply existence ; as, " Whatever *is*, is right." The first *is* expresses simply existence, and is synonymous with the verb *exists*.

327. This verb is irregular in its conjugation, as well as in the formation of its imperfect tense and perfect participle.

NOTE. — *Were* is sometimes used instead of the imperfect potential, for *would be* ; as, " It *were* useless to attempt it ; " " It *were* unwise to pursue any other course."

EXERCISE.

Point out the auxiliaries to the following verbs, and mention the mode and tense of each principal verb.

I have moved. They had called. We shall move. I will write. They have elected. He has read. They will come. They will have learned. I may go. May he go ? Can he go ? He must go. They cannot go. They might go. They could succeed. They would learn, if they would try. They must have been informed. I did not know. You might have known.

NOTE. — The auxiliary is often separated from the principal verb by one or more intervening words ; as, " The accused *will* certainly *be convicted*."

SECTION XXVIII.

328. *Conjugation of the verb-Have.*

PRINCIPAL PARTS.

Present or root.	Imperfect.	Perfect participle.
Have.	Had.	Had.

INFINITIVE MODE.

Present. Have.   *Perfect.* To have had.

PARTICIPLES.

Present. Having.   *Perfect.* Had.   *Compound.* Having had.

INDICATIVE MODE.

Present tense.

Singular.	Plural.
1. I have.	1. We have.
2. Thou hast.	2. You * have.
3. He has.	3. They have.

Imperfect tense.

Singular.
1. I had.
2. Thou hadst.
3. He had.

Singular.
1. I have had.
2. Thou hast had.
3. He has had.

Pluperfect tense.

Singular.
1. I had had.
2. Thou hadst had.
3. He had had.

First Future. Sign — *shall* or *will.*

Singular.	*Plural.*
1. I shall or will have.	1. We shall or will have.
2. Thou shalt or wilt have.	2. You shall or will have.
3. He shall or will have.	3. They shall or will have.

Second Future. Sign — *shall or will have.*

Singular.	*Plural.*
1. I shall have had.	1. We shall have had.
2. Thou shalt or wilt have had.	2. You shall or will have had.
3. He shall or will have had.	3. They shall or will have had.

POTENTIAL MODE.

Present tense. Sign — *may, can,* or *must have.*

Singular.	*Plural.*
1. I may * have.	1. We may have.
2. Thou mayst have.	2. You may have.
3. He may or can have.	3. They may have.

Imperfect tense. Sign *might, could, would,* or *should.*

Singular.	*Plural.*
1. I might have.	1. We might have.
2. Thou mightst have.	2. You might have.
3. He might have.	

Perfect tense. Sign —

Singular.

1. I may have had.
2. Thou mayst have had.
3. He may have had.

Pluperfect tense.

Sign — *might, could, would,* or *should have.*

Singular.	*Plural.*
1. I might have had.	1. We might have had.
2. Thou mightst have had.	2. You might have had.
3. He might have had.	3. They might have had.

---

* The verb may be conjugated with either auxiliary: as, I *may* have, or I *can* have, or I *must* have.

IMPERATIVE MODE.

Have thou.   Have ye.

SUBJUNCTIVE MODE.

Present tense.

Singular.   *Plural.*

1. If I have or may have. *
2. If thou hast or mayst have.
3. If he has or may have.

Or thus ;

Singular.

1. If I have.
2. If thou have.
3. If he have.

Imperfect

Singular.   *Plural.*

1. If I had or could have.   1. If we have or could have.
2. If thou hadst, &c.   2. If you have, &c.
3. If he had, &c.   3. If they have, &c.

Singular.   *Plural.*

1. Had I or could I have.   1. Had we or could we have.
2. Hadst thou, &c.   2. Had you, &c.
3. Had he, &c.   3. Had they, &c.

NOTE. — The other tenses of the subjunctive are conjugated like the corresponding tenses of the *indicative* and *potential* modes, by prefixing the subjunctive sign, except the second and third persons of the second future, which
require *shall* instead of *will*, (311)

SECTION XXIX.

329. CONJUGATION OF THE VERB BE.

PRINCIPAL PARTS.

Present or root.	*Imperfect.*	*Perfect participle.*
Am or be.	Was.	Been.

INFINITIVE MODE.

Present. To be.   *Perfect.* To have been.

---

* The subjunctive mode differs not in the least from the indicative, and to
form it, the learner has only to prefix a sign of condition ; as, *if, though, unless,* &c., to the indicative, in its several tenses ; with this exception, however,
that in the future tense the auxiliary may be, and often is, suppressed. Thus,
instead of *If I shall love,* &c., authors write, *If I love,* &c. — *Webster.*

PARTICIPLES.

Present. Being.   *Perfect.* Been.   *Compound.* Having been.

INDICATIVE MODE.

Present tense. *

Singular.	Plural.
1. I am.	1. We are.
2. Thou art.	2. You are.
3. He is.	3. They are

PERSON.

Imperfect tense.

Singular.	Plural.
1. I was.	1. We were.
2. Thou wast.	2. You were.
3 He was.	3. They were.

Perfect tense. Sign — have.

Singular.	Plural.
1. I have been.	1. We have been.
2. Thou hast been.	2. You have been.
3. He has been.	3. They have been.

Pluperfect tense. Sign — had.

Singular.	Plural.
1. I had been.	1. We had been.
2. Thou hadst been.	2. You had been.
3. He had been.	3. They had been.

First Future tense. Sign — shall or will.

Singular.	Plural.
1. I shall or will be.	1. We shall or will be.
2. Thou shalt or wilt be.	2. You shall or will be.
3. He shall or will be.	3. They shall or will be.

Second Future. Sign — shall have.

Singular.	Plural.
1. I shall have been.	1. We shall have been.
2. Thou shalt or wilt, &c.	2. You shall or will have been.
3. He shall or will, &c.	3. They shall or will have been.

* *I be, thou beest, we be,* &c., is an ancient form, and nearly obsolete.

POTENTIAL MODE.

Present tense. Sign — may.

Singular.	*Plural.*
1. I may be.	1. We may be.
2. Thou mayst be.	2. You may be.
3. He may be.	3. They may be.

Imperfect tense. Sign — might, could, would, or should.

Singular.	*Plural.*
1. I might be.	1. We might be.
2. Thou mightst be.	2. You might be.
3. He might be.

Perfect tense. Sign —

Singular.

1. I may have been.
2. Thou mayst have been.
3. He may have been.

Pluperfect tense.

Sign — might, could, would, or should have.

Singular.	*Plural.*
1. I might have been.	1. We might have been.
2. Thou mightst have been.	2. You might have been.
3. He might have been.	3. They might have been.

IMPERATIVE MODE.

Singular.	*Plural.*
Be thou.	Be you.

SUBJUNCTIVE MODE.

Present tense.

Singular.	*Plural.*
1. If I am.	1. If we are.
2. If thou art.	2. If you are.
3. If he is.	3. If they are.

Or Thus:

Singular.	*Plural.*
1. If I be.*	1. If we be.
2. If thou be.	2. If you be.
3. If he be.	3. If they be.

Imperfect tense.

Singular.	*Plural.*
1. If I was.	1. If we were.
2. If thou wast.	2. If you were.
3. If he was.	3. If they were.

Or thus:

Singular.	*Plural.*
1. If I were or were I,* (288.)	1. If we were or were we.
2. If thou wert or wert thou.	2. If you were or were you.
3. If he were or were he.	3. If they were or were they.

NOTE. — Conjugate throughout like the indicative, except as stated in Note under the subjunctive mode in the conjugation of *Have.*

EXERCISE.

The learner may point out the mode, tense, number and person of the verbs *have* and *be.*

I have had. I had been. I shall be. I shall have been. I can be. He may have. He may be. May he be? May he have? We must have. We must be. We may have been. We must have been. I might be. I might have. They could have. They should have. He would have been. He might have been. You were. You have been. You might be. You could be. You should be. They were. He was. We are. We have. We had. You had. They have been.

TO BE CORRECTED.

You was. They has been. When was you there? There has been men who disbelieved the existence of God. There is

---

* The form, *If I be*, sometimes called the elliptical form, from its being used as a conditional future for *shall be*, is often employed instead of the more common form, *If I am*, &c. The form *If I were*, or *Were I*, is also elliptical, and used in the sense of "could be."

some sweet flowers.   We was ten days on our journey.   There
was men, women and children in the assembly.   I be contented.
They be robbers.   We be true men.   Was* you there?

COMPOSITION.

Let each sentence include one of the following expressions.
Have. Has. Am. Was. Were. Has been. Have been.
Would be. Shall be. Was. Were. Might have. Could have.

Section XXX.

380. Conjugation of the regular Verb Love.

ACTIVE VOICE.

PRINCIPAL PARTS.

Present, or root.	Imperfect.	Perfect Participle.
Love.	Loved.	Loved.

INFINITIVE MODE.

Present. To love.   *Perfect.* To have loved.

PARTICIPLES.

Present. Loving.   *Perfect.* Loved.   *Compound.* Having loved

INDICATIVE MODE.

Present Tense.

Singular.	Plural.
1. I love.	1. We love.
2. Thou lovest.	2. You love.
3. He loves.	3. They love.

* This use of "was" with the pronoun *you*, is defended by some grammarians, on account of its frequent occurrence in common discourse, and its
occasional use by good writers and speakers. Furthermore it is said, that as
you is used in the singular number, the verb may also be singular to agree
with it. But the common rule for the agreement of a verb with its subject-
nominative, is thus violated in respect to both number and person; and
nothing but unquestionable authority can justify so palpable a solecism.

Imperfect tense.

Singular.
1. I loved.
2. Thou lovedst.
3. He loved.

Plural.
1. We loved.
2. You loved.
3. They loved.

Perfect tense.   Sign — *have.*

Singular.
1. I have loved.
2. Thou hast loved.
3. He has loved.

Plural.
1. We have loved.
2. You have loved.
3. They have loved.

Pluperfect tense.   Sign — *had.*

Singular.
1. I had loved.
2. Thou hadst loved.
3. He had loved.

Plural.
1. We had loved.
2. You had loved.
3. They had loved.

First Future.   Sign — *shall* or *will.*

Singular.
1. I shall or will love.
2. Thou shalt or wilt love.
3. He shall or will love.

Plural.
1. We shall or will love.
2. You shall or will love.
3. They shall or will love.

Second Future.   Sign — *shall* or *will have.*

Singular.
1. I shall have loved.
2. Thou shalt or wilt have loved.
3. He shall or will have loved.

Plural.
1. We shall have loved.
2. You shall or will have loved.
3. They shall or will have loved.

POTENTIAL MODE.

Present tense.   Sign — *may, can* or *must.*

Singular.
1. I may love.
2. Thou mayst love.
3. He may love.

Plural.
1. We may love.
2. You may love.
3. They may love.

Imperfect tense.   Sign — *might, could, would* or *should.*

Singular.
1. I might love.
2. Thou mightst love.
3. He might love.

Plural.
1. We might love.
2. You might love.
3. They might love.

Perfect tense. Sign — *may, can* or *must have.*

Singular.	*Plural.*
1. I may have loved.	1. We may have loved.
2. Thou mayst have loved.	2. You may have loved.
3. He may have loved.	3. They may have loved.

Pluperfect tense. Sign — *might, could, would,* or *should have.*

Singular.	*Plural.*
1. I might have loved.	1. We might have loved.
2. Thou mightst have loved.	2. You might have loved.
3. He might have loved.	3. They might have loved.

IMPERATIVE MODE.

Singular.	*Plural.*
Love or love thou.	Love or love you.

SUBJUNCTIVE MODE.

Present tense.

Singular.	*Plural.*
1. If I love or may love.	1. If we love or may love.
2. If thou lovest, &c.	2. If you love, &c.
3. If he loves, &c.	3. If they love, &c.

Or thus:

Singular.	*Plural.*
1. If I love.	1. If we love.
2. If thou love.	2. If you love.
3. If he love.	3. If they love, &c.

NOTE. — Conjugate the remaining forms like the corresponding tenses of the indicative, except as mentioned before.

SECTION XXXI.

PROGRESSIVE FORM.

331. A verb in this form is conjugated by annexing the present participle to the different forms of the verb *Be.*

EXAMPLE.

INDICATIVE MODE.

Present tense.

Singular.	*Plural.*
1. I am,	1. We are,
2. Thou art, } loving.	2. You are, } loving.
3. He is,	3. They are,

Imperfect tense.

	Singular.			Plural.	
1.	I was,		1.	We were,	
2.	Thou wast,	} loving.	2.	You were,	} loving.
3.	He was,		3.	They were,	

So with the other modes and tenses, which the learner may be required to repeat.

PASSIVE VOICE.

332. A verb in the passive voice is conjugated by annexing the perfect participle to the different forms of the verb *Be*.

EXAMPLE.

INDICATIVE MODE.

Present tense.

	Singular.			Plural.	
1.	I am,		1.	We are,	
2.	Thou art,	} loved.	2.	You are,	} loved.
3.	He is,		3.	They are,	

Imperfect tense.

	Singular.			Plural.	
1.	I was,		1.	We were,	
2.	Thou wast,	} loved.	2.	You were,	} loved.
3.	He was,		3.	They were,	

The other forms may be recited in a similar manner.

INTERROGATIVE FORM.

333. A verb is conjugated interrogatively by placing the subject nominative after the verb, or the first auxiliary to it, (when there is more than one,) in the different tenses of the *indicative* and *potential* modes.

EXAMPLES.

INDICATIVE MODE.

Present tense.

	Singular.		Plural.
1.	Am I ?	1.	Are we ?
2.	Art thou ?	2.	Are you ?
3.	Is he ?	3.	Are they ?

9*

Singular.	*Plural.*
1. Do I love ?	1. Do we love ?
2. Do you love ?	2. Do you love ?
3. Does he love ?	3. Do they love ?

Imperfect tense.

Singular.	*Plural.*
1. Was I ?	1. Were we ?
2. Wast thou ?	2. Were you ?
3. Was he ?	3. Were they ?

Singular.	*Plural.*
1. Did I love ?	1. Did we love ?
2. Didst thou love ?	2. Did you love ?
3. Did he love ?	3. Did they love ?

POTENTIAL MODE.

Singular.	
1. Can I be ?	1.
2. Canst thou be ?	2.
3. Can he be ?	3

Singular.	
1. Can I love ?	1.
2. Canst thou love ?	2.
3. Can he love ?	3.

EMPHATIC FORM.

384 In addition to the ordinary forms of the present and imperfect tenses of the indicative and subjunctive modes, there is another, called the *Emphatic form,* made by placing *do* or *did* before the principal verb.

EXAMPLE.

INDICATIVE MODE.
Present tense.

Singular.	*Plural.*
1. I do love.	1. We do love.
2. Thou dost love.	2. You do love.
3. He does love.	3. They do love.

Imperfect tense.

Singular. | *Plural.*

1. I did love.
2. Thou didst love.
3. He did love.

1. We did love.
2. You did love.
3. They did love.

EXERCISE.

The verbs used in this exercise are conjugated like the verb *love.* The learner is desired to tell the *mode, tense, number,* and *person* of each, and also its *form* and *agreement.*

I have labored. He has proved. He created. They commanded. We have commanded. It will rain. It has rained. The children mocked. The soldiers were marching, (*Progressive form.*) It was raining. We were hoping. The time is approaching. I have been listening. Were you listening? (*Interrogative form.*) Was he learning? Did he learn? Do you believe? Can you walk? We will walk. We shall be walking. Shall we walk? The world was created, (*Passive form.*) The world has been created. The soldiers were commanded. They will be commanded. The work will be accomplished. The work might be accomplished. They might accomplish the work. I do believe, (*Emphatic form.*) We do affirm. They did maintain.

To be written on the Board or Slate.

Write the common forms of the verb *love,* in the indicative mode. — The progressive forms. — The passive forms. — The interrogative forms. Write the common forms of the verb *love,* in the potential mode. — Progressive forms. — Passive forms.— Interrogative forms. Write all the forms of the Imperative mode — of the Infinitive mode — of the Participles — of the Subjunctive mode.

SECTION XXXII.

IRREGULAR VERBS.

335. Irregular verbs are those which do not form their imperfect tense and perfect participle by the addition of *ed* or *d* to the present; as, *go, went, gone.*

A LIST OF IRREGULAR VERBS.

Those verbs in the list that have their imperfect tense and perfect partici
ple designated by *R*, have both a regular and an irregular form.

Present.	Imperfect.	Perf. Part.
Abide	abode	abode
Am	was	been
Arise	arose	arisen
Awake	awoke, R.	awaked
Bear, *to bring forth,*	bare	born
Bear, *to carry,*		borne
Beat		beat, beaten
Begin		begun
Bend		bent
Bereave		bereft, R.
Beseech	besought	besought
Bid		bid, bidden
Bind		bound
Bite		bitten, bit
Bleed		bled
Blow		blown
Break		broken, broke
Breed		bred
Bring		brought
Build		built
Burst	burst	burst
Buy	bought	bought
Cast	cast	cast
Catch	caught, R.	caught, R.
Chide	chid	chidden, chid
Choose	chose	chosen
Cleave*		
Cleave, *to split*	clove *or* cleft	cloven, cleft
Cling	clung	clung
Clothe	clothed	clad, R.
Come	came	come
Cost	cost	cost
Creep	crept	crept
Crow	crew, R.	crowed

* Cleave, *to adhere,* is regular.

Present.	Imperfect.	Perf. Part.
Cut	cut	cut
Dare,* *to venture*	durst	dared
Deal	dealt, R.	dealt, R.
Dig	dug, R.	
Do	did	
Draw	drew	
Drink	drank	
Drive	drove	driven
Dwell	dwelt, R.	
Eat	ate	eaten, eat
Fall	fell	fallen
Feed	fed	fed
Feel	felt	felt
Fight	fought	fought
Find	found	
Flee	fled	
Fling	flung	
Fly, *as a bird*	flew	
Forget	forgot	forgot
Forsake	forsook	forsaken
Freeze	froze	
Get	got	
Gild	gilt, R.	gilt, R.
Gird	girt, R.	
Give	gave	
Go	went	
Grave	graved	
Grind	ground	
Grow	grew	
Hang	hung, R.	
Have	had	had
Hear	heard	
Hew	hewed	
Hide	hid	hidden, hid
Hit	hit	hit
Hold	held	held
Hurt	hurt	hurt

* Dare, *to challenge*, is regular.   † *Drunk* is used chiefly as an adjective.

Present.	Imperfect.	Perf. Part.
Keep	kept	kept
Knit	knit, R.	knit, R.
Know	knew	
Lade	laded	
Lay	laid	
Lead	led	
Leave	left	
Lend	lent	
Let	let	
Lie, *to lie down*	lay	
Load	loaded	laden, R.
Lose	lost	
Make	made	
Meet	met	
Mow	mowed	
Pay	paid	
Put	put	
Read	read	read
Rend	rent	
Rid	rid	
Ride	rode	
Ring	rung, rang	
Rise	rose	
Rive	rived	
Run	ran	run
Saw	sawed	sawn, R.
Say	said ·	said
See	saw	seen
Seek	sought	sought
Sell	sold	
Send	sent	
Set	set	
Shake	shook	
Shape	shaped	
Shave	shaved	
Shear	sheared	
Shed	shed	
Shine	shone, R.	

Present.	Imperfect.	Perf. Part.
Shoot	shot	shot
Sweat	sweat, R.	sweat, R.
Show*	showed	shown
Shred	shred	shred
Shrink	shrunk	shrunk
Shut.	shut	shut
Sing	sung, sang	sung
Sink	sunk, sank	sunk
Sit		sat
Slay		slain
Sleep		slept
Slide		slidden
Sling		slung
Slink		slunk
Slit	slit, R.	slit, R.
Smite	smote	smitten
Sow	sowed	sown, R.
Speak	spoke	spoken, spoke
Speed	sped	sped
Spend	spent	spent
Spill	spilt, R.	spilt, R.
Spin	spun	spun
Spit	spit, spat	spit
Split	split	split
Spread	spread	spread
Spring	sprung, sprang	sprung
Stand	stood	stood
Steal	stole	stolen
Stick	stuck	stuck
Sting	stung	stung
Stink	stunk	stunk
Stride	strode *or* strid	stridden
Strike	struck	struck *or* stricken
String	strung	strung
Strive	strove	striven
Strow *or* strew	strowed *or* strewed	{ strown, strowed, strewed

---

* This verb is sometimes written *show, showed, shown.*

Present.	Imperfect.	Perf. Part.
Shoe	shod	shod
Swear	swore	sworn
Swell	swelled	swollen, R.
Swim	swam, swum	swum
Swing	swung	swung
Take	took	taken
Teach	taught	taught
Tear	tore	torn
Tell	told	told
Think	thought	thought
Thrive	throve, R.	thriven, R.
Throw	threw	thrown
Thrust	thrust	thrust
Tread	trod	trod, trodden
Wax	waxed	waxen, R.
Wear	wore	worn
Weave	wove	woven, wove
Weep	wept	wept
Win	won	won
Wind	wound	wound
Work	wrought, R.	wrought, R.
Wring	wrung	wrung
Write	wrote	written

NOTE. 1. — The forms *sang, swang, spake, sprang, forgat, spat, gat, brake, &c.*, are now obsolete, or nearly so.

NOTE 2. — Many words which were used in the days of Shakspeare and Bacon, are now laid aside; others are used only in books, while others are obsolescent, being occasionally used; and a few of the old participles having lost their verbal character are used only as attributes, as; *fraught, drunken, molten, beholden, shorn, bounden, cloven. Holden, swollen, gotten,* are nearly obsolete in common parlance.— *Webster.*

NOTE 3. — Such verbs as are irregular only in familiar discourse, and which are improperly terminated by *t* instead of *ed*, as, *spelt*, &c., are not inserted in the table. Some contractions of *ed* into *t*, however, are unexceptionable; and others, the only established forms of expression, as *crept, dwelt, gilt,* &c. —*Murray.*

EXERCISE.

Sentences to be corrected in which the irregular verb is improperly used.

The horses drawed the carriage. The timber was drawed a great distance. The horses were drove too fast. Does a glutton know when he has ate enough? The birds have flew away. The stream has froze over. A stone laid in the street. It has laid there a month. The old man has laid down his burden. He lay down his book and walked to the door.

They have wrote to-day. The bell has just rang. The meeting has began. I begun my work yesterday. She sang* a song. They have set there until they are weary. I sat the instrument down at your door. The sun sat in a cloud last evening. I saw him setting by the wayside. A tree was laying across the street. They done their work faithfully. He has mistook the way. His garments are nearly wore out. The coach was drawed by four elegant horses. My watch was stole last night. The tempest blowed the ship ashore.

The wind blowed violently last evening. The chaff has blowed away. The building was blowed up. The rioters throwed stones. The ball was throwed dexterously. The sailor throwed away his money. The leaves were shook from the tree. The blossoms have fell to the ground. The leaves are tore out. Have you tore your book? The letter was so badly wrote that I read it with difficulty. Have you wrote to-day?

SECTION XXXIII.

FORMATION OF TENSES.

INDICATIVE MODE.

NOTE.—The directions below have reference to the first person singular of each tense.

1. The first person singular of the *Present* tense, is the root of the verb; as, "I command."

2. The *Imperfect* tense is formed from the present in regular verbs, by adding *ed* to the present. Silent *e* is dropped when the verb ends with that letter, before adding the *ed.* In irregular verbs the imperfect can be learned from the list of irregular verbs.

3. The *Perfect* tense is formed by placing the auxiliary *have*, before the perfect participle: as, "I *have* loved. I *have* gone."

4. The *Pluperfect* tense is formed by placing *had* before the perfect participle.

---

* *Sang*, according to Webster, is obsolete.

5. The *First Future* tense is formed by placing *shall* or *will* before the *present* or root ; as, " I *shall* or *will* command. "

6. The *Second Future* tense is formed by placing *shall have* before the per·fect participle ; as, "I *shall have* gone."

NOTE.—*Shall have* or *will have* may be placed before the participle in second and third persons of this tense.

THE POTENTIAL, INFINITIVE AND PARTICIPLES.

1. The *Present* tense is formed by placing *may, can* or *must*, before the present ; as, " I *may* or *can* go."

2. The *Imperfect* tense is formed by placing *might, could, would* or *should* before the present ; as, "I *might* go."

3. The *Perfect* tense is formed by placing *may have, can have,* or *must have* before the perfect participle ; as, "I *may, can,* or *must have* read."

4. The *Pluperfect* tense is formed by placing *might, could, would* or *should have*, before the perfect participle ; as, " I *might, &c.,* have loved."

5. The *Present* tense of the *Infinitive* mode has *to* before the root ; as, " *To love.*"

6. The *Perfect* tense of the *Infinitive* mode has *to have* before the perfect participle ; as, " *To have* read."

7. The *Present participle* ends in *ing.*

8. The *Perfect participle* of regular verbs ends in *ed.*

9. The *Perfect participle* of irregular verbs may be found in the list of irregular verbs.

10. The *Compound participle* is formed of the present participle *having*, and a perfect participle.

11. The tenses of the *Subjunctive mode* are formed like the tenses of the Indicative and Potential, with the signs *if, unless, admit, grant, &c.,* prefixed.

12. The *Imperative* mode is the simple form of the verb, and its subject nominative is generally omitted ; as, *Go, do, see ; thou* or *you* is omitted.

DEFECTIVE VERBS.

336. A Defective Verb is one which wants some of the modes or tenses. The following are verbs that belong to this class :

1. The auxiliary verbs *can, shall, may,* have two forms only, *present* and *past ;* as, *can, could, &c.*

2. *Ought* is defective, and is used in one form only. " Had ought or could ought " is improper.

3. *Quoth* is defective, and usually stands before its nominative ; as, " *Quoth* he." *Beware* is defective, and is used chiefly in the imperative and infinitive modes ; but occasionally in the *future* indicative and the *imperative* potential.

4. *To wit,* " To know," is now used only in the infinitive, in the sense of ' namely," or " that is to say."

IMPERSONAL VERBS.

337. An Impersonal Verb is one which is used only in the form of the third person singular, with the pronoun *it ;* as, "It *rains.*" "It *thunders.*" "It *hails.*"

SECTION XXXIV.

ANALYSIS AND PARSING.

In the exercises that follow, the learner should give particular attention to the parsing of the verbs, after carefully analyzing each sentence.

EXERCISE I.

INDICATIVE MODE.

Victory perches upon our banner — our arms triumphed, and the enemy suffered severely.

We have compared the vast relics of decayed and mouldering literature to animal and vegetable remains.

He has been diligent.   He will probably succeed.

Did you see the beautiful rainbow after the shower to-day ?

They have resolved, examined their hearts, and made new plans.

His words of this day are planted in my memory, and will there remain till the last pulsation of my heart.

I shall see his face and hear his voice no more.

EXERCISE II.

POTENTIAL MODE.

It may be expected that I should accompany the resolution with some suitable remarks.

His intercourse with the living world is now ended ; and those who* would hereafter find him, must seek him in his grave.

Thou canst do every thing.   No thought can be withholden from thee.

---

* "Who" is a relative pronoun, and the subject of *would find.*   "Those" is the subject of *must seek.*

To meet death as becomes a man, is a privilege bestowed on few. I would endeavor to make it mine.

We might have succeeded in our undertaking.

EXERCISE III.

IMPERATIVE MODE.

Incline my heart unto thy testimonies.

Keep my commandments and live. Bind them upon thy fingers, write them upon the table of thine heart.

Hear instruction, and be wise and refuse it not.

And Reuben said unto them, Shed no blood, but cast him into this pit and lay no hand on him.

EXERCISE IV.

INFINITIVE MODE.

RULE XII.

838. The Infinitive mode is generally used to limit a *verb, noun,* or *adjective.*

Model.

SENTENCE. — *The scholar loves to study.*

Analyzed. — "Scholar" is the subject. "Loves" is the predicate, modified or limited by the verb *to study* in the Infinitive.

The Infinitive parsed. — "To study" is a verb, in the infinitive mode, and limits the verb loves. RULE.

SENTENCES.

Birds love to sing. The youth tries to learn. The man has a desire to hear. Learn to obey. He may hope to succeed. It is kind to forbear. It is pleasant to hear the sweet music of birds.

Ask the hero, ask the statesman, whose * wisdom you have been accustomed to revere, and he will tell you.

The rain began to patter down in broad and scattered drops.

Influenced by a desire to stamp on these expressions their merited disgrace, and to preserve dignity and decorum in our deliberations, I felt it my duty to call the gentleman to order.

---

* "Whose" is a relative pronoun in the possessive case and limits *wisdom.*

SECTION XXXV.

ADJECTIVES.

339. Adjectives are divided into two general classes, *descriptive* and *definitive*.   (108, 109, 110.)

DESCRIPTIVE ADJECTIVES.

340. A Descriptive Adjective is one that expresses a quality of an object; as, "A *white* rose." "Glass is *brittle*."

Those derived from proper nouns are called Proper Adjectives; as, *American, English*.

341. Those derived from verbs, having the form of participles, are called Verbal Adjectives; as, "*Enduring* friendship." "A *bereaved* parent."

342. An adjective used in the predicate with the verb to complete an affirmation, is called a Predicate Adjective; as, "The sea is *rough*."   "He is esteemed *wise*."

343. An adjective used to modify the meaning of a verb and its subject, is called an Adverbial Adjective; as, "The moon looks *pale*." The adjective "pale" describes "moon" and at the same time modifies "looks;" that is, it does the office of both an adverb and an adjective, and may properly be termed an *Adverbial Adjective*.

344. An adjective preceded by the article "the" is often used as a plural noun; as, "The *wise*; the *good*; the *great*."

ANALYSIS AND PARSING.

Particular attention should be given to the different classes of adjectives.

The office of a great general does not differ widely from the office of a great mechanician.

The Christian benevolence of a private American association casts its eye upon them.

The closing hour has passed; a monarch lies in his lonely state.

In the deadly strife of European ambition, the arms of civilization acquired irresistible preponderance.

Gentle eyes grew sorrowful and dim.

The bells sounded soft and pensive.

Magnesia feels smooth; calcareous earths feel dry.

10*

DEFINITIVE ADJECTIVES.

345. Definitive Adjectives are such as *define* or *limit* the meaning of nouns and pronouns. (112.)

This class includes Articles, Numerals, and the Pronominal adjectives.

346. *An* or *a*, and *the*, are called articles. They are placed before nouns which they define, and may be properly termed definitive adjectives.

NOTE 1. — *An* stands before words beginning with a *vowel sound*. *A* stands before words beginning with a *consonant sound;* "*A* bird," "*a* use," "*a* yew tree."

NOTE 2. — *A* is used before words beginning with vowels which can be sounded only with the assistance of the consonants *y* or *w;* as, *A* [y] *union*, *a eulogy*.

NOTE 3. — *An* is used before words beginning with *h* and accented on the second syllable; as, "*An* historical poem" "*An* heroic act" and before words beginning with a silent *h;* as, "*An* honor."

347. *An* from the Saxon *an, ane*, and our word *one*, are the same. By custom "one" is used in numbering, while "an" is employed as a definitive adjective to denote an individual, either definitely or indefinitely.

348. When used definitely, "an" or "a" designates an individual object as known, certain or specified; as, "I hear *a* sound;" "I see *an* elephant;" "it weighs *an* ounce;" that is, *one* ounce.

349. When used indefinitely, "an" or "a" denotes some individual of a class or species, but does not specify any particular one; as, "*A* kingdom for *a* horse;" "a" specifies no particular kingdom or horse, although it denotes but one of each kind.

350. The definitive "the" is used before specific individuals or classes of objects, as distinguished from others of the same kind; as, "*The* laws of morality;" "*the* hope of the Christian;" "*the* sun;" "*the* earth."

It is also used in the singular number to denote the whole species or an indefinite number; as, "*The* almond tree shall flourish."

"The" is also used indefinitely; as, "Give sorrow to *the* winds."

EXERCISE.

Let the following expressions be corrected; and let the reason be given in each instance for the correction made.

The clock is a hour and an half too fast. A honest man sold me a ox. A Indian is a hard master. Such an one can be a upright judge. A early pear will keep but an short time. A old coat is an useless garment. A idle man stole an horse from a honest one. A ounce of prevention is worth an hundred pounds of cure.

351. *Numeral Adjectives* are such as denote number; as, *one, two, first, second.*

PRONOMINAL ADJECTIVES.

352. Those definitives which are sometimes used as adjectives and sometimes as pronouns, are called Pronominal Adjectives.

853. They are *this, that, these, those,* (demonstratives;) *each, either, neither,* (distributives); *some, any, one, all, such,* (indefinites;) *other, another, none, much, many, few, both, same, several, former, latter.* *One* and *other* are thus declined.

		Singular.	*Plural*
Nom.	One,	Other,	Others.
Poss.	One's,	Other's,	Others'.
Obj.	One.	Other.	Others.

NOTE.—In parsing, *an* or *a* and *the* may be called articles, and the definitives, *this, that, &c.,* may be called *adjectives* when they stand before nouns; and *pronouns* when they stand alone.

ANALYSIS AND PARSING.

Model.

SENTENCE. — *This is true charity.*

Analyzed. " This " is the subject; " is true charity " is the modified predicate.

The pronominal adjective parsed. "This" is a pronominal adjective used without a noun. It is in the nominative case and the subject of " is."

This day will be remembered. That event has been recorded. One * is apt to love one's self. Some were wise, others were foolish. He pleases some; he disgusts others. Much labor has been bestowed. Many hours have been wasted. A few days will determine his destiny. Others may boast; I will be silent. All must die; none can escape. A thousand soldiers were encamped.

---

* The noun, after most of the Pronominal adjectives used alone, can be easily supplied; as, *Some,* that is, some persons. *Others* however, in the plural, is strictly a pronoun, as it cannot be used before a noun either expressed or understood.

COMPOSITION.

1. Connect two descriptive adjectives with each of the following nouns.

Model.

— — days.   — — glass.   — — sea.

Bleak cold days.   *Clear smooth* glass.   *Dark blue* sea.

NOUNS.

Sky, cloud, sun, tempest, mountain, lake, wood, river, valley, island, shore, cliff, beach, sand, waves, forests, fields, cloud, eye, gardens, roses.

2. Connect three descriptive adjectives with each of the following nouns.

Model.

A — — — pebble.   A — — — Frenchman.

A *white, smooth, round* pebble.   A *tall, handsome, active* Frenchman.

NOUNS.

1. Cat, dog, wolf, fox, horse, butterfly.
2. American, Indian, Englishman.
3. Rose, tree, poppy, lily, flower.
4. Serpent, viper, snake, frog, lizard.

SECTION XXXVI.

COMPARISON OF ADJECTIVES.

354. The quality in one object is often spoken of in comparison with the same quality in itself, or in some other object.

EXAMPLES.

The same quality in three different objects may be compared as follows :
Iron is *hard ;* hardness is a quality in iron.

Steel is *harder* than iron ; hardness is a quality in steel, but this quality exists in a higher degree in steel than in iron.

Diamond is the *hardest* of the three ; hardness is a quality in diamond, but this quality exists in a higher degree than it does either in iron or steel.

The same quality in three different persons may be compared as follows.

A *wise* man ; a *wiser* man than he ; the *wisest* man of the three, or of all.

A *good* man ; a *better* man than he ; the *best* man of the three, or of all.

A *great* man; a *greater* man than he; the *greatest* man of the three, or of all.

The boy was *mischievous* at home, *more mischievous* at school, but the *most mischievous* at church.

355. Comparison is the variation of an adjective to denote the same quality in different degrees.

356. There are three principal degrees of comparison, called the *positive*, the *comparative*, and the *superlative*.

357. The *positive* denotes the simple quality, without specifying the degree of it ; as, Mild, great.

358. The *comparative* denotes a higher state of the same quality than the positive ; as, Milder, greater.

359. The *superlative* denotes a higher or lower state of the same quality than that expressed by the *comparative ;* as, Mildest, greatest.

REGULAR COMPARISON.

360. Adjectives of one syllable are commonly compared by annexing to the positive, *er* for the *comparative*, and *est* for the *superlative*.

361. When the *positive* ends in silent *e*, it drops the *e* on receiving the endings *er* and *est*.

362. The final consonant of certain adjectives is doubled before receiving the *er* or *est ;* as, Fit, fitter, fittest ; hot, hotter, hottest.

363. Some adjectives of two syllables are compared with *er* and *est* when they can be easily pronounced ; as, Lofty, loftier, loftiest ; handsome, handsomer, handsomest.

364. When an adjective ends in *y* after a consonant, this letter is dropped, and *i* is added before *er* and *est ;* as, Happy, happier, happiest.

365. Adjectives of more than one syllable are generally compared by means of the adverbs *more* and *most*, or *less* and *least ;*

as, Skilful, *more* skilful, *most* skilful; learned, *more* or *less* learned; *most* or *least* learned.

366. An *imperfect degree* is expressed by the ending *ish;* as, Blue-*ish*, dark-*ish.*

IRREGULAR COMPARISON.

367. The following adjectives are irregular in their comparison.

Pos.	Com.	Sup.	Pos.	Com.	Sup.
Good,	better,	best.	Fore,	former,	foremost, or first.
Bad, or ill,	worse,	worst.	Old,*	elder,	eldest.
Little,	less,	least.	Late,	later,	latest, or last.
Much,	more,	most.	Far,	farther,	farthest.
Many,	more,	most.	Near,	nearer,	nearest, or next.

368. Some words add *most* to form the superlative; as, Hind, hinder-*most ;* in, inner, inner-*most ;* up, upper, upper-*most,* &c.

369. Adjectives which express qualities that cannot be increased or diminished, do not admit of comparison; as, *Square, spherical, triangular,* &c.

370. Various degrees of comparison are expressed by means of *adverbs, adjuncts,* and by *emphasis ;* as, *Very* sick, *exceedingly* great, *in the highest degree* censurable.

EXERCISE.

Give the comparative and superlative.

High.   Grateful.   Good.   Ill.
Low.   Unmindful.   Little.   Generous.
Small.   Cheerful.   Happy.   Penurious.
Great.   Attractive.   Lofty.   Extravagant.

NOTE.—The word *more* should never be prefixed to the comparative degree of an adjective ; nor the word *most* to the superlative degree. Double comparatives and double superlatives should be carefully avoided.

EXAMPLES TO BE CORRECTED.

Who was a more wiser man than Solomon ? It was the beautifulest sight I ever saw. A more honester man you can-

---

* Thus compared only when applied to persons. The regular form *old, older, oldest,* is applied either to persons or things.

not find. My master is more kinder than my mistress. Summer is the delightfulest season of the year. The pine is more tall than the cedar. The good are more happy than the bad. Socrates was much more wiser than Alcibiades. Have you seen a rounder ball than this? The book is more square than the block.

REVIEW.

1. Into what two general classes may adjectives be divided?
2. What are descriptive adjectives? Proper adjectives? Participial adjectives? Give examples of each.
3. What are definitive adjectives? What does this class include?
4. Name the articles. What is the difference between *an* and *a*?
5. What are pronominal adjectives? Name them.
6. Define comparison. How many states?
7. What does the positive denote? The comparative? The superlative?

Section XXXVII.

RELATIVE PRONOUNS.

371. A Relative Pronoun is one that refers to a preceding noun or pronoun, which is called the *antecedent.**

EXAMPLES.

The man *who* is happy; "who" is the relative; it refers to man; *man* is the antecedent.

The sight *which* I saw; "which" is the relative; "sight" is the antecedent.

The people *who* are assembled; point out the *relative* and the *antecedent.*

372. The relative pronouns are *who, which* and *that; who* refers to persons or to things personified. *Which*† refers to irrational animals or things. *That* refers to persons, animals or things.

DECLENSION OF THE RELATIVES.

Singular and Plural.

Nom.	Who	Which	That
Poss.	Whose	Whose	——
Obj.	Whom	Which	That

Antecedent signifies "going before," or "preceding."

Sometimes, especially in poetry, the natural order of the words is changed, and the relative refers to a noun or pronoun following it.

† sometimes refers to ersons.

373. The relatives *who* and *which*, when used in asking questions, are called *interrogatives*.

374. The noun to which the interrogative refers is found in the answer to the question ; as, Who did this ? Ans. James ; that is, it was James who, &c.

EXERCISE.

Fill the blanks with relatives.

Note. — The objective case of the relative generally stands *before* the transitive verb which governs it, and *after* the preposition.

The people — we saw.

The king — commanded, was obeyed.

The birds — fly in the air.

The man — has no music in himself.

The events — are passing.

EXAMPLES TO BE CORRECTED.

The bird whom I caught has escaped. The friend which I loved is gone. There were some cities who aspired for liberty.

The rose whom we saw has faded. The son in which my hopes were placed was lost at sea.

PARSING.*

RULE XIII.

375. The relative pronoun agrees with its antecedent in *gender*, *number*, and *person*.

Note 1. — The relative in the different cases is parsed like other pronouns.

Parse the relatives.

The master *who* taught us will be gratefully remembered.

The trees *which* were planted grow thriftily.

---

* As the relative is a connective, the sentences in which it occurs cannot be properly analyzed until compound sentences have been explained.

He, *who* preserves me, to *whom** I owe my being, *whose* I am, and *whom†* I serve, is eternal.

The city *which* Romulus built is called Rome.

The boy *who* reads good books will become intelligent.

The letter *which* I have received, contains good news.

The rose *which* we saw is fading.

The tree *that* we passed has withered.

Whose book is this, *which* you gave me?

COMPOUND PRONOUNS.

376. The word *self* is often added to the personal pronouns *him, her, my, thy, it,* to express emphasis; as, Himself, itself, &c.

Singular.

	First person.	Second person.	Third person.
Nom. and Obj.	My*self.*	Thy*self.*	It*self.*

Plural.

Nom. and Obj.	Our*selves.*	Your*selves.*	Them*selves.*

Self (plural selves) is used alone as a noun. When prefixed to other words it makes a part of a compound adjective; as, *Self-complacent, self-taught.*

377. *What* is a compound relative including both the antecedent and the relative.

In the singular it represents *that which,* and in the plural *those which,* or the *things which.*

EXAMPLES.

I heard *what* you said; that is, *that which* you said.

I know *what* will please you; that is, *the things which,* &c.

378. " What " is sometimes used to represent an entire clause; as, " I tell thee *what,* corporal, I could tear her." " What " represents the whole clause, " I could tear her," which is in apposition with it.

---

* *Whom* is governed by the preposition *to.*

† *Whom* is in the objective case and governed by *serve.*

379. " What " is often used as a definitive adjective ; as, "It is unknown in *what* character he appeared." *What* is an adjective limiting the meaning of character.

380. " What," is much used in asking questions ; as, " *What* art thou ? " " *What* will you do ? " In the first sentence, *what* is the predicate nominative. In the second, *what* is in the *objective case*, and limits *do*. " You will do *what ?* "

381. " What " is sometimes used in poetry, before a noun in the sense of *the* ; as, " *What time* the morn mysterious visions bring ; " that is, *the* time.

382. " What " is likewise sometimes used elliptically, with *though*, or *if*, and also in exclamations ; as, " *What* though, in solemn silence ; " that is, *what imports it, though ?* " *What !* could ye not watch with me one hour ? " that is, *what is this ?* or *what means this ?*

383. *Whoever, whosoever, whatever*, and *whatsoever*, are compound words, used instead of two pronouns ; as, " *Whoever* dreads punishment, deserves it ; " that is, *he who* dreads, &c.

384. *Whatever, whatsoever, whichever*, and *whichsoever*, are often used as adjectives ; as, " *Whatever* measure."

EXERCISE IN PARSING.

Model of Parsing WHAT.

SENTENCE. — *I have heard what has been alleged.*

" What " is a compound relative, and is used in the sense of *that which.*
" That " is in the objective case, and is the object of heard.   " Which " is in the nominative case, and is the subject of " has been alleged."

Parse *what* in the following sentences.

I have done *what* you commanded.
You will know *what* I have said.
What you have said is true.
They are informed of *what* you did on the last night.
They know *what* is right.
It is not material *what* names are assigned them.
What consequence will follow the adoption of this measure ?
What news have you heard to-day ?

SECTION XXXVIII.

ADVERBS.

Mention the office of different kinds of adverbs.　(See 136 — 45.)

385. Most adverbs are used to express the same meaning as might be expressed by a combination of other words; as, "He acted *wisely*," i. e., he acted *with wisdom*; "he stopped here," i. e., in this place; "*when* shall I see you?" i. e., *at what time* shall I see you? "he visits me *often*," i. e., *many times.* "*Whence* art thou?" i. e., from what place; "*Where* are you?" i. e., in what place.

386. An *adverbial phrase* is often formed by a union of some other parts of speech; as, " *By and by; in truth; by far.*"

387. Adverbs may be divided into various classes; as, Adverbs of manner; of time; of place; of assent, denial, or doubt; of comparison and quality; of interrogation; of quantity, &c.

COMPARISON.

388. Adverbs ending in *ly* are commonly compared by more and most, or less and least: as *Justly*, (pos.) *more justly*, (comp.) *most justly*, (sup.); *wisely*, (pos.) *less wisely*, (comp.) *least wisely*, (sup.)

389. A few adverbs add *er* for the comparative, and *est* for the superlative; as, soon, soon*er*, soon*est*; oft*en*, often*er*, often*est*.

390. A few are compared irregularly; as,

> Little, less, least.
> Much, more, most.
> Badly or ill, worse, worst.
> Far, farther, farthest.
> Forth, further, furthest.
> Well, better, best.

NOTE. — The adverbs in the list, except *forth* and *badly*, are adjectives when they qualify nouns; as, A *far* country; *most* men; it is *well*; *much* money.

ANALYSIS AND PARSING.

His features are not a little changed.
All left the world much as they found it.
Wisdom alone is truly fair.
Things most truly are most fitly spoken.
He pushed his researches very far into antiquities.

COMPOSITION.

NOTE. — Abverbs should be placed near the verbs which they modify. *N* and *never* should stand after the auxiliary verbs, *may, can, shall, will, might, would, should, could, did;* as, " I will *never* distrust ;" not, " I *never* will," &c.

Compose sentences which shall contain the following Adverbs.

Anxiously.	Much.	Often.
Occasionally.	Too.	Sometimes.
Frequently.	Very.	When.
Immediately.	Chiefly.	Until.

EXAMPLES TO BE CORRECTED.

Adjectives are sometimes improperly used as adverbs ; as, " Henry wri careless ;" it should be *carelessly.*

He did not conduct proper. He acts foolish. She behaved ruder (it should be *more rudely,*) than she ought. He acted bolder than was expected. I shall never think mean of you. James reads distinct, writes neat, and recites correct. Do not walk so slow.

SECTION XXXIX.

EXERCISES IN ANALYSIS AND PARSING.

NOTE. These exercises are designed to call the attention of the learner to principles already explained.

EXERCISE I.

The noun and the verb. The subject and predicate. Simple sentences.

The king rules. Boys play. Time flies. Cæsar commanded. The bird was singing. Trees will grow. The king will conquer. The day had arrived. The sun had set. The hands should labor. Scholars should learn. The Americans might have submitted. The king should yield.

EXERCISE II.

Noun. Verb. Adverb. Modified predicate.

The storm rages violently. The sluggard sleeps soundly. The birds were singing sweetly. The time was passing pleasantly. The hour will soon arrive. The ship sailed yesterday. The news came to-day. Themistocles could not rest. Friends will certainly part. The man will never listen. Perhaps the child will recover. Roots grow downward.

EXERCISE III.

Adjective. Noun. Verb. Adjunct. Modified Subject. Modified Predicate. Object.

Cruel war desolates flourishing cities. A kind friend rescued me from danger. The hunter killed a ferocious panther in the forest.

Grapes hang in clusters on the vine. Prosperous gales waft the light ship over the sea. Some birds hang their nests on a slender twig of the highest branch of a tree.

EXERCISE IV.

A simple sentence gradually extended by the use of adjuncts or modifying words.

The storm drove.

A furious *storm drove* the ship.

A furious *storm from the north drove* the ship violently against the rocks.

The wind blew.

The gentle wind blew softly.

The gentle *south wind* blew softly over the sea.

Knowledge enlarges.

A knowledge of the works of nature enlarges the understanding.

An extensive knowledge of the works of nature enlarges the understanding of men, in a variety of ways.

11*

EXERCISE V.

Passive form.　Interrogative form.

The debt will undoubtedly be cancelled.

The village was shaken violently by the earthquake.

The store was plundered by a gang of robbers.

No season of life should be spent in idleness.

Will he be persuaded to go ?　Art thou he ?

May I be permitted to go ?　Is the rumor confirmed ?　Can
he succeed in his undertaking ?　Whither shall I flee ?　How,
could he do the cruel deed ?

EXERCISE VI.

The contented mind spreads ease and cheerfulness around it.

The school of experience teaches many useful lessons.

The eyes of fishes, compared with those of terrestrial animals,
exhibit a certain distinctness of structure, adapted to their state
and element.

Birds in general, procure their food by means of their beak.

A nature infinitely wise can hardly be supposed to employ
itself in vain.

The spirit of liberty had planted itself deeply among the Vir-
ginians.

A foraging party of the colonists, headed by Argall, having
stolen the daughter of Powhattan, demanded of her father a
ransom.

SECTION XL.

COMPOSITION.

EXERCISE I.

Compose sentences which shall contain in each one the following expressions.

　　　　duty of the inexperienced to

The traffic in ardent spirits

Perseverance and industry will

The advantages of a good education consist
　　　　to your letter which I have lately received
It would afford me great satisfaction
　　　　in reply to your
　　　　acquainted with
　　　　a delightful morning
The follies of youth
　　　　in the highest degree valuable.

EXERCISE II.

1. Let the parts of the following objects be enumerated.

A ship.	A plough.	A clock.
A book.	A chair.	A carriage.
A house.	A tree.	An ear of corn.
A table.	A fence.	A sleigh.

2. Mention the uses of the same objects. A composition of several lines may be written on each, in describing the various uses, &c.

EXERCISE III.

QUALITIES OF OBJECTS.

Every object admits of an adjective or adjunct, to express its quality or condition, its form, size, or comparative excellence : as, A *book* ; a *large* book, or, the book is *large* ; a *good* book, or, the book is *useful* ; a book abounding in excellent sentiments.

Express some of the qualities or conditions of the following objects by adjectives or modifying adjuncts.

An apple.	A man.	The ocean.
A tree.	A horse.	A ship.
A house.	The sun.	Gold.

EXERCISE IV.

The learner in this exercise may state such ideas and facts, as he can gain by reflection or reading on the following subjects.

EXAMPLE.

Subject. —IRON. Iron is the most valuable of all metals. Its use to some extent was known at a very early period, and has followed the progress of civilization in the world. In its natural state it is found in beds of ore, from which, by an ingenious process, it is extracted and prepared for use. The value of this metal, which abounds in almost every region of the earth, can be estimated only by reflecting upon the uses to which it is applied.

The plough.
A ship.   The co
Silver.

In this Exercise let some
ing objects and provisions, be specified in writing.

The ocean.	Roads.	Rain.
Rivers.	Railroads.	Wind.
Mountains.	Steam Engine.	Sun.

EXERCISE VI.

Expand the following expressions according to the model.

Model.

I write.
I write this letter.
I write this letter to inform you that your son is well.
I write this letter to inform you that your son is well and in excellent spirits.
I write this letter to inform you that your son is well and in excellent spirits, and is perfectly contented in his new situation.

NOTE. — Each expression may be expanded to a much greater length than in the model.

I am contented.	He went.
I believe.	They stopped.
Alonzo was not to blame.	The choir sung.
I love to read.	Have you heard?

The learner can now write short compositions on subjects which are easy and familiar, like the following:

SUBJECTS.*

A visit.	The advantages of an education.
The sagacity of a dog.	A dialogue on the stars.
A sleigh ride.	A story of an elephant.

A dialogue on the study of grammar.
An anecdote about Washington.

---

* The word *subject* in this connection signifies *theme*, or that about which we may write or converse.

LETTER WRITING.

The following is a proper example for imitation, in respect to the dating, beginning and closing of a letter.

Olney, June 16, 1769.

My Dear Friend :

I am obliged to you for your invitation, but being long accustomed to retirement, which I was always fond of, I am now more than ever unwilling to visit those noisy scenes which I never loved, and which I now abhor. I remember you with all the friendship I ever professed, which is as much as I ever entertained for any man.

I love you and yours; I thank you for your continued remembrance of me, and shall not cease to be their and your

Affectionate Friend,

William Cowper.

Joseph Hill, Esq.

REMARKS.

Letters should be written in an easy and natural style, but with a strict regard to neatness in the penmanship, and to propriety in the complimentary address and close, and also to pointing, folding and superscribing.

The learner should occasionally write letters to be examined and corrected by the teacher.

PART IV.

—

SYNTAX.

SECTION XLI.

391. Part III. was principally devoted to the structure of simple propositions. It now remains to combine these so far as is necessary for continued discourse, and to present some practical rules and principles to aid the learner in the art of composing.

COMPOUND SENTENCES.

392. A compound sentence is one which is made up of two or more simple propositions, connected together.

393. The propositions that make up a compound sentence are termed clauses.

EXAMPLES.

"The wind subsides and the clouds disperse."

"The wind subsides" is one proposition. "The clouds disperse" is another proposition. When united by "and" they form a compound sentence.

"He was travelling towards Rome when they met him at Milan."

This compound sentence consists of two clauses connected by "when."

"You will freely communicate to our young monarch that knowledge which will fit him to govern himself."

This is a compound sentence, consisting of two clauses. The last clause "which will fit him," &c., is connected with the word "knowledge" for the purpose of limiting its meaning.

CLASSIFICATION OF CLAUSES.

394. The clauses of a compound sentence may be divided into three general classes, namely; *Independent, Principal,* and *Subordinate.*

395. An *Independent Clause* is one which makes complete sense by itself.

" God spake, and it was done."

This compound sentence consists of two independent clauses, connected by " and."

" Socrates was wise ; Plato was also wise."

This sentence likewise consists of two independent clauses, connected by " also."

" I have been young, but now I am old."

How many independent clauses does this sentence consist of ?   How are they connected ?

396. A *Principal Clause* is one on which another clause depends.

NOTE. — The modifying or depending clause is sometimes connected with a single word in the principal clause; as, " Here is the man *who befriended me.*"

397. A *Subordinate Clause* is one connected with the principal clause, or with some word in it, to extend or modify its meaning.

" I hope that you are well."

" I hope " is the principal clause. " You are well " is the subordinate clause, connected with the principal clause by the conjunction " that."

"When I am old, forsake me not."

The principal clause is " forsake me not." The subordinate clause denotes time and is connected by the adverb " when."

" God, who made all things, is acquainted with our most secret thoughts."

The principal clause is, " God is acquainted," &c. The subordinate clause " who made all things," is connected with the word " God " to extend its meaning.

Model of analyzing a compound sentence.

SENTENCE. — " In the beginning of this address I said, and I have endeavored to keep my word so far, that I would plead only for intellectual interests."

First principal clause.—"I said." "I" is the subject. "Said" is the predicate.

Second principal clause.—"I have endeavored to keep my word so far." The conjunction "and" is the connective. "I" is the subject—"have endeavored to keep," &c., is the modified predicate.

Subordinate clause.—"That I would plead only for intellectual interests." The conjunction "that" connects the subordinate clause with the first principal clause. The subordinate clause is used as a noun in the objective case after "said," and therefore may be termed a *substantive clause.*

SENTENCES.

I come to you in the spirit of peace, yet you will not receive me.

My wrong was dreadful, and I cried aloud.

Cicero in his youth was covered with glory, but his old age was disturbed by the misfortunes of the republic.

Conjunctions do not merely in a vague manner denote a relation; they also determine the nature of the relation.

The drum and fife can sometimes drown the battle's noise, when there is no way to escape it.

If study were valuable for nothing else, yet it would be highly so for this—that it makes man his own companion.

898. Subordinate Clauses may be divided into *Substantive, Adjective, Adverbial and Conditional Clauses.*

Section XLII.

SUBSTANTIVE CLAUSES.

899. A Substantive Clause is one used in the office of a noun in the nominative or objective case.

A substantive clause may be used,

1. In apposition with a noun.
2. As the subject nominative of a verb.
3. As the predicate nominative.
4. As the object of a transitive verb or preposition.

EXAMPLES.

"The question 'what shall I do?' was asked by the trembling jailer."

The substantive clause " what shall I do ?" is in apposition with " question." The clause explains the meaning of " question," in this connection.

" Know thyself," was written over the gate of the Delphian temple.

The substantive clause " know thyself," is the subject nominative of the verb " was written."

" My wish is that you may be happy."

The clause " that you may be," &c., is the predicate nominative.

" We believe true religion was never propagated by the sword."

The clause " true religion," &c., is the object of " believe."

400. A substantive clause is sometimes used in the place of a noun.

EXAMPLES.

" The victory of Cyrus over the enemy was announced."

A substantive clause may be used in the place of " victory over the enemy ; " as, " It was announced that Cyrus had conquered the enemy."

" He showed who had plotted the conspiracy ; " that is, " the author of the conspiracy."

401. Direct and indirect quotations belong to this class of clauses.

402. A quotation is *direct* when the words of a person are given unaltered in the form in which they were stated ; as, " He would turn about and say, ' Hang such a one for disobedience.' "

403. A quotation is *indirect* when the words of a person are quoted in the form of a narration ; as, " He said that ' the French infantry would soon become tired of their virtue.' "

ANALYSIS AND PARSING.

The substantive clauses in the following sentences may be parsed, in the first place, as nouns in the nominative or objective case. Then the words can be parsed separately, as in other clauses.

He seized my hand, pressed it, and replied with strong emotion — " You have guessed the truth ; you have judged me rightly." [Direct quotation.]

" O ! " replied he, " there is fortunately one tract of literature which forms a kind of neutral ground." [Direct quotation.]

12

I am always at a less to know how much to believe of my own stories.

"Where am I?" murmured she faintly. "All is safe!" exclaimed I.

His constant request was that I would permit him to sit by me in my saloon.

It is in vain that their names are posted on the doors of country churches.

SECTION XLIII.

ADJECTIVE CLAUSES.

404. An Adjective Clause is one which is used like an adjective or an adjunct, to express a quality or attribute ; as, "The man *who is prudent* is often saved from disappointment."

405. An adjective clause is commonly connected with some noun or pronoun of the principal clause by the relative *who, which,* or *that ;* but sometimes by the adverbs *while, when, where, why,* &c. ; and it frequently serves to define the state, quality, or condition of an object, more exactly than a single adjective, adjunct or participle could do ; as, "I am he, *who teaches the truth.*"

COMPOSITION.

The learner may expand the *italicised words* into clauses, so as not to alter the meaning of the expression.

Model.

There are *idiomatic* expressions in English *suited* to the grave style.

EXPANDED. — There are expressions in English *which are idiomatic,* [and] *which are suited to the grave style.*

In conversing on *grave* subjects we should not use *lively* and *familiar* forms of expression.

We often use *incorrect* and *obscure* expressions in conversation.

Some, *presuming* on the good nature of their friends, write their letters in a *hasty* and *disconnected* manner.

Often there is nothing in the object *compared, fitted* to excite emotions *of the ludicrous.*

ADVERBIAL CLAUSES.

406. An Adverbial Clause is one used in the office of an adverb or an adjunct to denote *time, place, manner, consequence, effect, cause,* &c.

"We all know that it adds much to the point of a witty remark, when its author has founded it on an expression just dropped by another."

This compound sentence consists of three clauses, — one principal and two subordinate clauses. "That it adds much," &c., is a substantive clause, and is the object of the verb "know." The *adverbial clause* is, "when its author has," &c. It denotes both *time* and *cause*.

"His predictions were only too true, as the event proved."

"As the event proved" is the adverbial clause, it is nearly equivalent to the adjunct "according to, or corresponding with, the event."

407. Adverbial clauses are very numerous. They are sometimes merely adverbs or adjuncts expanded into clauses, but more generally modify the verb or adjective in the principal clause by a more extended explanation than a single adverb or adjunct could give.

CONDITIONAL CLAUSES.

408. A Conditional Clause is one which expresses something contingent or doubtful.

409. Conditional clauses are united to the principal clause by some word or phrase that implies a condition or supposition.

EXAMPLES.

"If he is in health, I am content."
The conditional clause is, "if he is in health."

"On condition that he come, I will consent to stay."
"On condition that he come," is the conditional clause.

ANALYSIS AND PARSING.

The different kinds of clauses may be pointed out in this exercise.

He drew up a petition in which he too freely represented his own merits.

The measure is so exceptionable that we cannot by any means permit it.

They have all been treated by me with candor, which they have not been careful of observing to one another.

"I do not know," says Germain, "whether he was mandarin and apostle at the same time."

Do you believe his story, that there are forty millions of in-
habitants in Pekin?

Rich gifts wax poor when givers prove unkind.

Let the doors be shut upon him, that he may play the fool
nowhere but in his own house.

If one man prefers a life of industry, it is because he has an
idea of comfort and wealth.

It is certain that I am indebted to him for some flagrant civil-
ities.

Section XLIV.

CONNECTIVES. *

410. A number of words is employed to denote certain relations or connection in discourse. These words have been termed by different writers, *particles, abbreviations, ligaments, connectives,* &c.

411. These words differ from each other in their import, but
have one property in common, which is indicated by the general term, *connective.* But they receive particular names according to their peculiar offices.

412. Some of these connect words only; as *prepositions.*

413. Some connect words with clauses; as *relatives.*

414. Some connect clauses, or parts of clauses with one another; as *conjunctions, adverbs.*

415. Some of this last class have a still more general office
in connecting paragraphs, sections, or chapters; as the words
wherefore, therefore, then, now, &c.

---

* The connective parts of sentences are of all others the most important,
and require the most care and attention; for it is by these chiefly that the
train of thought, the course of reasoning, and the whole progress of the mind
in continued discourse of all kinds are laid open; and on the right use of these,
perspicuity, that is, the first and greatest beauty of style principally depends.
— *Lowth's Introd.* p. 136.

CONNECTION OF CLAUSES.

416. The clauses which make up a compound sentence are connected as follows:

       1. By conjunctions.
       2. By adverbs.
       3. By relative words, or phrases.
       4. By incorporation.

CLAUSES CONNECTED BY CONJUNCTIONS.

Here review §153. Repeat the list of conjunctions, § 154.
Do conjunctions connect words? Give an example. Give other examples.

EXERCISE I.

In this exercise and the three following, the learner may explain how the clauses are connected.

You have departed from the example of other nations, and you have become an example to them.

Is this sentence simple or compound? Of how many clauses is it composed? What word connects these clauses?

You not only excel modern Europe, but you excel what she can boast of old.

The desert shall rejoice and the wilderness shall blossom.

Disappointment sinks the heart; but the renewal of hope gives consolation.

I complained and my spirit was overwhelmed.

Ask now the beasts and they shall teach thee.

If you would please to employ your thoughts on that subject, you would easily conceive our miserable condition.

This compound sentence consists of two clauses or simple sentences. 1. From *if* to *subjects.* 2. From *you* to *condition.*
The conjunction *if* connects them.

If he approve my endeavors, it will be an ample reward.

If I had known the distress of my friend, it would have been my duty to relieve him.

I thought that Titius was your friend.

That is the conjunction, and connects the two clauses.

I see that you are sad.

I respect him because he is sincere.

12*

CLAUSES CONNECTED BY ADVERBS.

EXERCISE II.

Adverbs which connect clauses are called *conjunctive adverbs*; they gener ally denote time, place, or quantity.

When he is in town, he lives in Soho square.

This sentence consists of two clauses. 1. "He is in town." 2. "He lives in Soho square." They are connected by the conjunctive adverb *when*.

Whilst I was lamenting this sudden desolation, the whole scene vanished.

Whilst connects the two clauses.

Where I am there shall ye be.

The rest will I set in order when I come.

CLAUSES CONNECTED BY RELATIVE WORDS OR PHRASES.

EXERCISE III.

417. Relative words are, *who, whose, which, that, whom, what,* and their compounds; also, expressions that denote comparison; as, *the more, the better,* and the like.

He came to the Alps, which separate Italy from Gaul.

This compound sentence is composed of two clauses. 1. "He came to the Alps." 2. "Separate Italy from Gaul." The relative *which* connects them, and stands in the place of *Alps*, to which it refers as its antecedent.

I read the letter which he received.

It is God whom we worship.

I am Miltiades, who conquered the Persians.

The city which Romulus built is called Rome.

418. Conjunctive Phrases are, *in order that, in as much as, to the intent that, on condition that, &c.*

CLAUSES CONNECTED BY INCORPORATION.

EXERCISE IV.

419. A clause is connected by incorporation when it is used as an essential part of a proposition, or as explanatory of some word in it. As such it is employed either in the nominative or objective case.

NOTE. — This kind of connection exists in fact with every form of substantive and adjective clauses. But in practice it may be better to restrict it to direct quotations, and to those cases in which the connective is not used as a word of relation, and in which no connective is expressed.

" You will depart with but a small retinue," said the Baronet.

There is no connective between these two clauses. And one cannot be supplied without changing the form. Still there are two distinct clauses, each having its subject expressed, but the former is an essential part of the latter; namely, the *object* of " said."

" Much depends upon who the commander is."

The clause " who the commander is," is the object of the preposition " upon," and together with the preposition, is an adjunct of the verb in the principal clause.

" Stop ! " said the German in a tone of anger.

" I do not mean," said the Antiquary, " to intrude upon your lordship."

" That your worship is right, is perfectly manifest."

" You are a tyrant," he answered with a sort of sigh.

SECTION XLV.

ABRIDGED OR SUBSTITUTED CLAUSES.

420. Subordinate Clauses frequently admit of being changed to shorter or different forms of expression without alteration in the sense.

421. An Adjective Clause is sometimes represented by an adjective ; as, " Every work *that is fictitious*," that is, " every *fictitious* work, should be favorable to good morals."

422. A subordinate clause is sometimes represented by a verb in the infinitive mode ; as, " I have come to Paris *that I may learn* the French language," that is, *to learn*, or in order *to learn*. " I hope *that I may see* you here ; " that is, I hope *to see* you, &c.

423. Subordinate clauses are often changed so as to become adjuncts of the principal clauses.

EXAMPLES.

I heard yesterday *that he is appointed judge.*
Changed. I heard yesterday *of his being appointed judge.*

In such examples the whole subordinate clause becomes the object of the preposition in the substituted form, and the noun that was the predicate nominative remains unchanged.

424. A subordinate clause is sometimes abridged by using a participle in place of the verb, omitting the connective, and making the subject independent.

EXAMPLES.

" Since our work is finished, let us depart."
Abridged. " Our *work being finished,* let us depart."
" While *Tarquinius was reigning,* Pythagoras came into Italy."
Abridged. " *Tarquinius reigning,* Pythagoras came into Italy."

In these examples the change has been made by substituting for the verb "is finished" and "was reigning," the participles "being finished" and "reigning," and omitting the connectives "since" and "while." The subject is now independent, that is, it is no longer used as the subject of the proposition.

425. Almost every form of expression admits of some change without alteration in the sense. That form should be chosen, which expresses thought in the most natural and forcible manner. For this end the taste and intelligence of the writer or speaker avails more than rules.

EXERCISE.

In this exercise the learner may abridge the subordinate clauses in the following sentences according to the examples given above.

Since life is short, it becomes us to be diligent. As the way was steep and difficult, we proceeded slowly. When shame is lost, all virtue is lost. When hope fails, the mind sinks in discouragement. Since you are our leader, we have nothing to fear. (See Rule XII, *Syntax.*) I am sorry that I have offended you. I am glad to hear that he is elected senator The being who created all things must be omnipotent.

SECTION XLVI.

PHRASES.

426. Phrases may be divided into three classes, *Substantive*, *Adjective*, and *Adverbial*.

427. A Substantive Phrase is a combination of words not forming a clause, used in the office of a noun in the nominative or objective case.

1. A substantive phrase may be the subject or predicate nominative ; as, " *To live soberly* is required of all."

2. It may be the object of a transitive verb or preposition ; as, " Most men love *to be called great.*" "Averse to *the nation's involving itself in another war.*" " The crime of *being a young man.*"

3. A substantive phrase may also be in apposition with a noun or the pronoun *it*. Is " it " an easy *thing to become a poet ?*

428. An Adjective Phrase is an adjunct of a noun, and consists of a preposition and its object. This kind of phrase is explained in Part II. See 121, 126.

429. An Adverbial Phrase is an adjunct of a verb or adjective, and consists also of a preposition and its object. This is likewise explained in Part II. See 147.

430. The Adjective and Adverbial Phrases serve a most important purpose in speech.

431. The adjective phrase modifies a noun by expressing :

1. Quality ; as, " An act *of justice.*" 2. Property ; as, " The writings *of Johnson.*" 3. Origin or source ; as, " The products *of the soil.*" 4. Condition or circumstance ; as, " A prisoner *in chains.*" 5. Place ; as, " A ship *in the harbor.*" 6. Identity ; as, " The city *of Athens.*" 7. Time ; as, "A period *of twenty years.*"

432. The adverbial phrase modifies the meaning of a verb, by expressing :

1. Cause ; as, " The ground is warmed *by the sun.*" 2. Manner ; as, " He writes *with care.*" 3. Place ; as, " He has resided *in Paris.*" 4. Object or end ; as, "He seeks *for office.*" 5. "Accompaniment; as, " He travelled *with*

his family." 6. Likeness; as, *"He seemed like his brother."* 7. Time; as, *" He will be absent during the summer."* 8. Distance; as, *" He travelled thirty miles in a day."*

NOTE.—The preposition is commonly omitted before nouns that denote time, distance, &c.

433. Connected with an adjective the adverbial phrase denotes, 1. The end to which the quality is directed; as, *" Fit for use."* 2. The object or cause of some affection or emotion of the mind; as, *" Fond of fruit." " Harassed with debt."* 3. The whole, when preceded by a partitive word; as, *" The best of all." " Fifty of the soldiers."* It likewise expresses the difference in degree; as, *" Greater by far." " Higher by fifty feet."*

434. Other combinations frequently occur, which have no modifying power, but serve as connectives, and might be termed conjunctive phrases, or prepositional phrases, according to their office in a sentence.

NOTE.—In the general analysis of sentences, phrases may be treated in the same manner as the parts of speech for which they respectively stand.

ANALYSIS AND PARSING.

Particular attention to be given to clauses and phrases and abridged propositions.

I recollect hearing a traveller, of poetical temperament, expressing the kind of horror which he felt in beholding, on the banks of the Missouri, an oak of prodigious size which had been in a manner overpowered by an enormous wild grape vine.

The vine had clasped its huge folds round the trunk, and from thence had wound about every branch and twig, until the mighty tree had withered in its embrace.

It seemed like Laocoon struggling ineffectually in the hideous coils of the monster Python.   It was the lion of trees perishing in the embrace of a vegetable boa.

Happiness is found in the arm-chair of dozing age, as well as in the sprightliness of the dance, or the animation of the chase.

RULES OF SYNTAX.

Section XLVII.

The following rules or statements of grammatical principles have been gradually developed in the progress of the work. The learner is now to verify them by analyzing the sentences arranged in exercises under the Rules respectively. A number of these was given in Parts II. and III. which are further extended and illustrated in this part.

THE NOUN AND PRONOUN.*

RULE I.

435. A noun or a pronoun limiting another noun, and denoting the same person or thing, is put, by apposition, in the same case ; as, " Cicero, the *orator*." See 115.

REMARKS.

1. A noun is sometimes in apposition with a *clause ;* as, " The eldest son was always brought up to that employment, a *custom* which he and my father followed."

2. A clause or a phrase is sometimes in apposition with a noun preceding it ; as, " I would only mention at present one article, *that of maintenance of the clergy.*"

3. A noun in apposition is frequently connected with the one that is limited by the conjunction *as ;* as, " My father intended to devote me *as the tythe* of his sons.

Note. — The word *as* appears to be used frequently in the sense of the Latin preposition *pro, instead of, in place of, for,* or *in the capacity of.*

4. When two nouns in apposition come together in the possessive case, the sign is omitted after the first ; as, " John the Baptist's head."

5. A noun in apposition with two or more nouns, is put in the plural.

6. A noun in apposition is sometimes used without the possessive sign, to limit a pronoun in the possessive case ; as, " His office as *judge* must be responsible." In this sentence judge refers to *his,* although it appears to be in the same case with office. This construction is anomalous, but something analogous to it is found in other languages.

7. The limiting noun is sometimes used with a preposition ; as, " The city *of* Boston ; " " The title *of* king."

---

* For Exercises in composition, the learner is referred to the section following General Exercise III. after Syntax.

ANALYSIS AND PARSING.

Herschel, the *astronomer*, discovered the planet *Uranus.*

Washington, the *commander-in-chief* of the American army, was born near the banks of the Potomac.

Webster, a dramatic *poet* of the seventeenth century, was clerk of the parish of St. Andrew.

The Tippecanoe, a *river* of Indiana, is rendered famous for a battle between the Americans and Indians.

I dined with him at our friend *Davies's.*

I received this reply, " He is *better.*"

You are too humane and considerate ; things which few people can be charged with.

I am pleased with your appointment as chaplain.

REVIEW.

Define the word *apposition.* Repeat the rules for nouns in apposition. Can words of different meaning be in apposition? Give some examples of nouns in apposition. Explain the rule of apposition, by the expressions, *George, the king ; Alexander, the conquerer.* Can a noun be in apposition with a clause or a sentence? *This was a saying of Franklin ; "Time is money."* What words are in apposition in this sentence? *Samuel Johnson.* Are these words in apposition? See 172. Sect. XV.

RULE II.

436. A noun in the predicate after an intransitive verb, is in the same case as the subject when both words refer to the same person or thing ; as, " *It* is *he ; he* has become a *poet.*" See 105.

NOTE. — This rule is chiefly applicable to the verbs *to be, to become,* and some other intransitive verbs, and also to some transitive verbs in the *passive form ;* such as denote *to name, to render, to make,* and the like.

REMARKS.

1. This rule applies also to the infinitive and participles of verbs of the same class ; as, " I desire to be a *poet.*" " I believe *him* to be a *knave.*"

2. In expressions like the following there is found, perhaps, an exception to the remark above ; " He is angry with me on account *of my being a friend* to his enemy." The phrase " of my being a friend " is an abridged expression equivalent to " *because I am a friend,*" in which " friend " is in the nominative case ; so in the following, " I am suspicious of *his being a rogue ;* " that is, *that he is a rogue.*

In the abridged form the entire phrase *my being a friend,* or *his being a rogue,* is the object of the proposition, but the words "friend" and "rogue" may be considered in the same case as they would be in the unabridged form.

3. The construction of a noun after the verbs *to be, to become, &c.*, when they form together a substantive phrase, may be explained in a similar way. In the sentence "to be a learned *man* is no easy attainment," the whole phrase "to be a learned man" is the subject of *is*, and the noun "man" may be considered in the nominative case after "to be."*

4. A phrase or a proposition is sometimes used as the predicate nominative as, "To steal is to break the law."

5. Both words sometimes stand before, and sometimes after the verb; as, "Art *thou he?*" "Am *I* a *traitor?*" "*Monster* as *thou* art, I will yet obey thee."

ANALYSIS AND PARSING.

Intransitive Verbs.

Clement was the name of many popes.

A coronation is a solemn inauguration of a monarch.

The diamond is the most valuable gem.

The youth will become a poet.

Stephen died a martyr to his faith.

Passive form.

Washington *is called* the *father* of his country.

Napoleon Bonaparte, an inhabitant of Corsica, *was styled* the *Emperor* of France.

In England, a kind of trident is used for catching eels, *called* an *eel-spear.*

Cicero and *Antonius* were called *consuls.*

I *am tired* of being an *idler.*

I cannot *bear* the thought of being an *exile* from my country.

TO BE CORRECTED.

Show by Rule II. wherein these examples are incorrect.

I that speak unto thee am *him.*   *It* was not *him* that said it. *It* cannot be *him. Whom* are *you? Whom* do men say that *I* am? *Who* do they represent *me* to be?   I do not think *it* is *him.* Did you believe *it* to be *he?*   I did not think of its being *him.* If I were *him* I would not tolerate it.

---

* This explanation accords with the views of N. Butler and S. S. Green. Bullions considers the noun or pronoun in such relations to be in the objective case.

REVIEW.

Repeat Rule II. How does Rule II. differ from Rule I? *Ans.* Cases of Rule II. occur where a verb separates the two nouns ; as, "Time *is* money ;" *is* separates *time* and *money ;* in cases of Rule I. no verb intervenes ; as, "*Cicero, the orator.*" Give some examples of nouns in apposition. "Cicero, the orator." Which Rule is applicable to this expression ? "Cicero *was* an orator." Which rule applies ? Give some examples of the same case *after* as *before* the verb. What sometimes supplies the place of one of the nouns ? Give an example. Why is the expression *it is me,* incorrect ?

Section XLVIII.

Rule III.

437. The subject of a finite verb must be in the nominative case.

Rule IV.

438. A verb must agree with its subject nominative in number and person.

Note. — The verbs *need* and *dare,* when intransitive, are sometimes used in the plural form with a singular nominative.

REMARKS.

1. A substantive clause or phrase is often the subject of a verb.

2. In *declarative* sentences or *conditional* clauses, the *subject nominative* usually precedes the verb ; but in *interrogative* and *imperative* sentences it commonly follows the verb, or its auxiliary.

Examples. — "*He* reads." "The *rain* falls." "If *I* go." "Believest *thou* this ?" "Who art *thou* ?"

3. The subject nominative also follows the verb when a supposition is expressed without the conjunction *if ;* as, "Were *it* not for this." "Had *I* been there." Also, when the verb is preceded by *there, here, then, thence ;* or by *neither* or *nor ;* as, "Ye shall not eat of it, *neither* shall ye touch it."

4. An intransitive verb between two nominatives of different numbers or persons, should agree with that which is more naturally the subject of the affirmation ; as, "His *meat* was locusts and wild honey." "The *wages* of sin is *death.*"

In such cases the verb more commonly agrees with the noun that precedes it.

5. *Methinks* (imperfect *methought,*) is called an impersonal verb, compounded of the pronoun *me,* in the objective case, and the verb *think,* which follows the analogy of some Latin and Greek verbs, and by custom is used with the

objective instead of the *nominative* case, and takes the form of the *third* person instead of the first.

6. *As regards, as concerns, as respects, as appears.* These are phrases without a nominative case expressed. The pronoun *it* is often used before these verbs, and is easily supplied when wanting.

7. *As follows.* The nominative case can be supplied before this verb as the connection requires. "He addressed the assembly *as follows.*" This can be analyzed thus, "He addressed the assembly in a manner *as this which follows.*"

By several authors, *as* is considered a relative pronoun when used before the verb follows; as, "The circumstances were *as* follow," [those *which* follow.]

8. A verb in the Imperative mode, and the transitive verbs *need, want* and *require,* sometimes appear to be used indefinitely without a nominative; as, "There *required* haste in the business;" "there *needs* no argument for proving;" "there *wanted* not men who would," &c. The last expressions have an active form with a passive sense, and should, perhaps, be considered elliptical rather than wanting a nominative; as, "Haste is required," "no argument is needed," &c.

9. The verb which agrees with the nominative case is sometimes omitted; as, "To whom the *monarch;*" *replied* is omitted. "What a bloom in that person!" The verb *is* is omitted.

ANALYSIS AND PARSING.

Varro was esteemed a learned man, but Aristides was called just.

Titus has been called the love and delight of the human race.

Shall a barbarian have these cultivated fields?

At Burlington, I made an acquaintance with many principal people of the province.

The first impression made by the proceedings of the American Congress on our people in general, was greatly in our favor.

To be natural is to be antiquated.

To use correct and elegant English is to plod.

To be ever active in laudable pursuits, is the distinguishing characteristic of a man of merit.

To see the sun is pleasant.

To excel in knowledge is honorable; but to be ignorant is base.

That you may enjoy every felicity, is my fervent prayer.

Promising and not performing, is evidence of insincerity.

Methinks this single consideration will be sufficient to extinguish all envy.

Methought I was admitted into a long spacious gallery.

I am indifferent as regards my personal security.

As appears from the evidence, he is guilty of an atrocious crime.

Let there be no strife betwixt me and thee.

"Marry," says* I, "if it be so, I am very well rewarded for all the pains I have been at."— *Addison.*

TO BE CORRECTED.

Show by the rule why these examples are incorrect.

The clouds has dispersed. The rivers has overflowed their banks. There was three Indians in the company. A variety of blessings has been conferred upon us. In piety and virtue consist the happiness of man. What names has the planets? There goes the ships freighted with treasure. There follows from thence these plain consequences. There is men who never reason. The smiles that encourage severity of judgment, hides malice and insincerity. Some foggy days, and about ten or twelve days in January, was cold and icy. How do your pulse beat? How does your plans succeed? What signifies good opinions when our practice is bad? There was more impostors than one. The virtue of these men and women are indeed exemplary.

REVIEW.

Repeat rules III. and IV. and explain them by examples. "To err is human."— Show how the rule applies in this sentence. *What* is human? what then is the nominative? which remark under rule IV, is applicable? "Whence art thou?"— Which word is the nominative? does the nominative generally stand *before* or *after* the verb? How is *methinks* explained? What is said of *as regards, as concerns,* &c.? Are any verbs used without a nominative case?

---

* There are *irregular* expressions occasionally to be met with, which usage or custom sanction, rather than analogy. Such as, "*says I,*" "*thinks I,*" &c. These however, are ungrammatical, and should not be imitated.

RULE V.

439. Two or more nominatives singular, connected by *and*, expressed or understood, generally require a plural verb; as, Charles, Thomas, and George *are* brothers.*

REMARKS.

1. When the nouns are taken *separately*, or are emphatically distinguished, they may be regarded as belonging to separate propositions; as, "*Every* officer and every soldier claims a superiority." "Ambition and not the safety of the state *was* concerned."

The nouns, in a compound subject, are taken separately when preceded by *every, each, no,* or *not;* or some other disuniting word; as, "*Every* adjective and every adjective pronoun *belongs,*" [not belong,] &c.†

2. If in such cases the nouns are of different numbers, the verb should agree with the first; as, "Diligent *industry,* and not mean savings, produces honorable competence."

3. When the nouns connected by *and* refer to the *same person or thing,* the verb is singular; as, "Why is *dust and ashes* proud?"

4. When the nominatives connected by *and* are of different *persons,* the verb agrees with the first person rather than with the second, and with the second, rather than with the third; as, "My brother and I are interested in the work." The verb *are* is in the *first person,* because *I* is of the first person; and it is in the *plural number,* because "brother" and "I" are connected by *and,* and make a compound subject.

ANALYSIS AND PARSING.

Model.

SENTENCE. — *Tranquillity and love dwell here.*

Analyzed. The sentence is simple, having a compound subject.

"Tranquility and love," is the compound subject; "and" is the connective.

---

* The best English authors sometimes imitate the Greek and Roman writers in using a singular verb after nouns connected by and; as, "Their safety and welfare *is* most concerned." — *Spectator.* The majority of Grammarians, however, do not approve this license.

† A nominative singular sometimes has an adjunct connected with it, by *with, in company with,* or by some other *connective phrase,* which gives, in reference to the whole subject, the idea of plurality, and occasionally such a subject is used with a plural verb; as, "The angle A. with the angles B. and C., *compose* [composes] the triangle;" "The king, with the lords and commons, *constitute* [constitutes] an excellent form of government." In all such examples, a *singular verb* is more strictly in accordance with the principles of construction, and with the usage of the best writers.

"Dwell" is the predicate modified by here. Or the sentence may be considered compound, and be resolved into two simple sentences; as, "Tranquillity dwells here, and love dwells here:" in this case "and" connects the verbs. The former method is preferable.

Reason and truth constitute intellectual gold.

Riches, honors, and pleasures, steal away the heart from religion.

The planetary system, boundless space, and the immense ocean, affect the mind with sensations of astonishment.

Prosperity with humility, renders its possessor truly amiable.

The useful arts improved by science, and science itself improved by philosophy, confer power on civilized and instructed man, and enable him to triumph over his fellows and over nature.

TO BE CORRECTED.

The reasons for the correction should be given in every instance.

Idleness and ignorance is the parent of many vices. Time and tide waits for no man. Patience and diligence, like faith, removes mountains. The forehead, the eyes, and the countenance, often deceives. Castor and Pollux was seen to fight on horseback. The following treatise, with those which accompany it, were written many years ago. His wisdom, not his money, produce esteem. The sides A. B. and C. forms the triangle. My uncle with his son were in town yesterday. That able scholar and grammarian have been refuted. The discomfiture and slaughter was very great. And so was also James and John. By whose power all good and evil is distributed.

RULE VI.

440. Two or more nominatives singular, connected by *or* or *nor*, require a singular verb; as, Ambition *or* pride controls him.

REMARKS.

1. If either of the nominatives thus connected is plural, the verb usually agrees with it; as, "Neither poverty nor riches were injurious to him." But se the plural nominative should be placed next to the verb.

2. If the nominatives connected by *or* or *nor*, are of different persons, the verb agrees with the person placed next to it ; as, " Either *thou* or *I* am mistaken."

8. Of two or three pronouns of different persons, the second is usually placed before the third, and the first should always be placed nearest to the verb ; as, " George or I am the person." Such expressions as, " Either *you* or *I* am in fault," " *George* or *I* am the person," are inelegant, and may be easily avoided. It would be better to say, either *I* am to blame, or *you* are ; either *George* is in fault, or I *am*.

ANALYSIS AND PARSING.

The method of analyzing examples under this rule is similar to that presented in the model under Rule V.

Ignorance or negligence has caused the mistake.

John, James, or Andrew, intends to accompany you.

Death or some worse misfortune soon divides them.

History or geography is a proper study for youth.

Extreme heat or extreme cold is painful.

Man's happiness or misery is in a great measure put into his own hands.

One or both of the witnesses were present.

RULE VII.

441. The nominative of a collective noun requires a verb in the *singular* or *plural*, according as the noun denotes unity or plurality ; as, " The *class was large ;* my *people do* not consider."

REMARKS.

1. The *plural* form of the verb is more commonly used.
2. When the definitive *this*, or *that*, precedes the noun, the verb must be singular.

ANALYSIS AND PARSING.

A part mount the horses and guide the reins.

A great multitude hurl stones and darts.

The court has just ended.

In France the peasantry go barefoot, and the middle class make use of wooden shoes.

Why do the heathen rage and the people imagine a vain thing.

The people rejoice in that which should cause them sorrow.

The fleet was seen sailing up the channel.

The nobility are the pillars to support the throne.

A company of troops was detached.

TO BE CORRECTED BY RULES VI. AND VII.

James or Charles were in fault. Neither authority nor analogy support such an opinion. Either ability or inclination were wanting. Neither the father nor the son were saved. Neither the general nor the soldiers was charged with cowardice. The British parliament are composed of king, lords and commons. A council were called. The crowd were very great. This sort of goods are not fashionable. That party were in an error. This company are handsomely uniformed. The court of Rome were not without solicitude.

GENERAL REVIEW OF THE NOMINATIVE CASE.

Repeat Rules III. IV. V. VI. and VII. When must the verb be singular ? Give examples. When must a verb be plural ? Give examples. What besides a noun can be the subject of a verb ? When a nominative is a verb in the infinitive, or a sentence, what must be the person and number of the verb ? *Ans.* Third person, singular. If two infinitives are connected by *and*, in what number must the verb be ? *Ans.* Plural. When pronouns of different persons are connected by *and*, in which person must the verb be ? If connected by *or*, in which person.

SECTION XLIX.

THE POSSESSIVE CASE.

RULE VIII.

442. A noun or pronoun in the possessive case, limits the noun which denotes the object possessed. See 120.

REMARKS.

1. The noun denoting the thing *owned* or *possessed* is often omitted, when it can be easily supplied ; as, " We dined at Peter *Garrick's* ; " *house* is omitted. Vital air was a discovery of Priestley's ; that is, of Priestley's *discoveries; the* same as to say, " Vital air was one of Priestley's discoveries,

2. When two or more nouns imply joint possession, the sign ('s) is gen·erally omitted after the first, but annexed to the last; as, "*Sanborn* and *Carter's* bookstore." Sanborn and Carter, joint. owners, are both in the possessive case, and are governed by "bookstore;" but the *sign* is annexed to *Carter* only.

3. When two or more nouns denote *separate* ownership, each noun has the sign annexed; as, "*Cowper's, Thomson's* and *Coleridge's* works. "*Works*" is understood after each possessive.

4. When the possessive is denoted by two or more words so closely related as not to admit a pause between them, the last generally has the sign; as, " John *the Baptist's* head." "The king of *Great Britain's* prerogative." "At our friend Sir Robert Hinckley's." " The captain of *the guard's* house."

5. In case of possessives in apposition, if the limited word is omitted, the sign is generally annexed to the first, especially if it is limited by more than one word; as, "I dined at Walton's, an amiable and worthy man." "I left the parcel at Smith's, the bookseller and stationer."

6. The preposition *of* with its *objective case*, is often equivalent to the possessive case; as, " The advice of my father." Or, " My father's advice."

7. The possessive is often used to limit a participial noun, or a phrase beginning with a present participle; as, "Much will depend on the *pupil's* composing frequently." *Pupil's* is governed by the participial noun *composing.**

8. The use of the possessive case, in composing, is attended sometimes with harshness and obscurity, which may be avoided by employing the preposition *of*, or the expressions, *the property of*, or, *belonging to*; as, " This was my father and brother's farm;" — better thus, this farm *belonged to*, or, *was the property of*, my father and brother. "They condemned the prodigal's, as he was called, extravagant conduct;" — it should be, " they condemned the extravagant conduct of the prodigal," as he was called. " She began to extol the farmer's, as she called him, excellent understanding;"—it should be, "the excellent understanding of the farmer," as she called him.

ANALYSIS AND PARSING.

He spoke slightingly of Dyer's fleece.

I asked for Barkerville's edition of Barclay's Apology.

My ways are not thy ways.

He accompanied me to St. Mary's Church.

His lady was the daughter of Johnson's first schoolmaster.

I have received your letter.

Their insolence is intolerable.

---

* The participle used as a noun, still retains its verbal properties, and may govern the objective case, or be modified by an adverb or adjunct, like the verb from which it is derived.

My country has claims, my children have claims, and my own character has claims upon me.

You will see his sister at Mr. Hector's.

I found Dr. Johnson at Mr. Seward's.

Sometimes I smoke a pipe at Child's (coffee house.)

This was a discovery of Newton's.

There was also a book of De Foe's, and another of Dr. Mather's.

This took place at our friend Sir Joshua Reynold's.

The manner of a young lady's employing herself usefully in reading, will be the subject of another paper.

Very little time was necessary for Johnson's concluding a treaty with the bookseller.

He added an anecdote of Quin's relieving Thomson from prison.

He pathetically described the parent's and the son's misfortune.

He reminded Dr. Johnson of Mr. Murphy's having paid him the highest compliment that ever was paid to a layman.

I dined with him at our friend Davies's.

I gave him an account of my having examined the chest of books which he had sent to me.

TO BE CORRECTED BY THE REMARKS UNDER RULE VIII.

Webster or Johnson's Dictionary. Washington and Taylor's courage. Bancroft or Prescott's History. Ferdinand's and Isabella's reign. Hyde's, Lord's, and Duren's bookstore. Mr. Murphy mentioned Dr. Johnson having a design to publish an edition of Cowley. I dined with him at Mr. Thrale. Fanciful people may talk of a mythology being amongst them. There is no danger of that complaint being made at present. The bishop's of Landaff excellent works. I will not, for David's thy father's sake. Much depends on this rule being observed.

EXERCISE.

Change the following sentences into other forms which shall convey the same meaning.

Model.

This was the *king of England's* eldest son.
Changed. This was the eldest *son of the king of* England.
The declaration was published in the *army's* name.
Changed. The declaration was published in the *name of the* army.

Sentences to be changed.

A mother's tenderness and a father's care, are nature's gifts for man's advantage. This was John, Robert and Charles's estate. Very little time was necessary for Johnson's concluding a treaty with the bookseller. This property was my father's, my brother's, and my uncle's. This was John Johnson's eldest son's estate. This was a discovery of Sir Isaac Newton's. He is ignorant of the country's condition.

REVIEW.

What is the rule for the government of nouns or pronouns in the possessive case? What is the sign of the possessive case? When two or more nouns denote the joint owners of the same thing, to which is the sign annexed? When can the noun be omitted which governs the possessive case? Give some examples. When the possessive is governed by a participial clause, can the sign be properly omitted? Repeat the rule and remarks for the government and use of the possessive case.

SECTION L.

OBJECTIVE CASE.

RULE IX.

443. The object of a transitive verb, or a preposition, must be in the objective case; as, "The sun imparts *warmth* to the *ground.*"

NOTE. — Participles of transitive verbs in the active form, likewise govern the objective case.

REMARKS.

1. Some intransitive verbs are followed by an objective of a kindred signification to their own; as, "He dreamed *a dream*;" let him die *the death*"; "to run *the race*;" "to sleep *the sleep* of death;" "to live a *life* of ease;" "he went his *way.*"

2. Similar to this idiom are expressions like the following; "groves whose trees *wept* odorous gums." "The crispid brook *ran* nectar." "Her lips blushed deeper sweets." *

8. The objective *whom*, *which* or *that* should stand before the verb that governs it, and except in interrogative sentences before the subject of the verb ; as, " *Whom* ye seek." " The story *which* he told."

ANALYSIS AND PARSING.

Disappointment sinks the heart of man.

Foolish pursuits delight some persons.

A variety of pleasing objects charms the eye.

I have read your letter.   I commend your diligence.

The President's speech is so important to the public, that I know you will be anxious to see it as early as possible.

I will resign my office and remain with you.

That is the friend whom you must receive cordially, and whom you cannot esteem too highly.

They whom opulence has made proud, and whom luxury has corrupted, cannot relish the simple pleasures of nature.

TO BE CORRECTED.

Who did they send ?   He that is idle reprove.   He and they we know.   He invited my brother and I to examine his library. Ye hath he quickened.   Who shall I call you ?   He who committed the offence, you should correct, not I who am innocent. He who is in fault I will chastise.   Who shall I direct this letter to ?   Who will you vote for ?   He and they we know, but who are you.

RULE X.

444. Nouns which denote *time, quantity, measure, distance, value,* or *direction,* are often put in the objective case

---

* Some verbs were formerly used as transitive, which are no longer considered as such; as, "He repented *him*;" "flee *thee* away." *Cease,* however, is used as a transitive verb by our best writers; as, "Cease thy impious rage." *Webster.*

without a preposition ; as, " He is ten *years* old" ; "the rule is a *foot* in length."

NOTE. — In analyzing, such nouns with the adjectives joined to them are to be treated as adjuncts, modifying or limiting some other words in the sentence. Some grammarians prefer to have a preposition supplied in explaining the construction of such words. In some instances this is easily done, in others it is not admissible.*

REMARKS.

1. The word HOME after the verbs *come, go*, and the like, is generally in the objective case without a preposition ; as, " My intention is to *come* home, unless I receive a commission to St. James's."

NOTE. — When an adjective or an article is joined to the words *home, north,* &c. the preposition is used ; as, " He has gone to his home."

2. The words *like, near* and *nigh* are commonly followed by the objective case without a preposition ; as, " He is like his father;" " He lives *near* the river."

3. Nouns that denote particular points of time are generally used with a preposition, but not always ; as, "*At* that *hour* ;" " *In* the *morning*."

ANALYSIS AND PARSING.

Congress has been in session three months.

NOTE. — Three months answers to the question *how long?* and modifies the predicate of the sentence ; *months* is in the objective case without a preposition.

He was absent from his native country six years.

They excavated a pit twenty feet in depth.

One morning we walked out together.

Wednesday, Nov. 1st., we left Paris.

The storm burst upon us three leagues from the land.

They travelled north, south, east and west.

The people looked this way and that way, but discovered no means of escape.

RULE XI.

TWO OBJECTIVES

445. Verbs signifying *to ask, to teach, to call, to pay, to allow, to give, to make, to constitute,* and some others, fre-

---

* Lowth, followed by the whole tribe of writers on this subject, alleges some prepositions to be understood before these expressions of time. But this is a palpable error arising from preconceived notions of the necessity of such words. The fact is otherwise ; all these peculiar phrases are idiomatic, and are remains of the early state of our language. — *Webster.*

quently govern two objective cases; as, "He asked *me a question;*" "and God called the *firmament Heaven;*" "God seems to have made *him what* he was." "They chose or elected *him clerk.*" "*Simon*, he surnamed *Peter.*"

REMARKS.

1. A preposition is often used before one of the objectives following the verbs *ask, teach, pay, allow* and *promise*, and can easily be supplied when omitted.

2. An infinitive or an entire clause is often used as one of the objectives; as, "He asked me *to give* him money.

3. The verb *cost* is sometimes followed by two objectives; as, "It cost *me* much *labor.*"

4. Verbs which have two objectives in the *active form*, retain one of them in the passive, and the other becomes the subject; as "He asked *me* a *question.*" [active form.] "A *question* was asked me," or "*I* was asked a question" [passive form.] The last expression, namely, "I was asked a question," is anomalous, but authorized by good usage.

ANALYSIS AND PARSING.

Model.

SENTENCE.— *A wise man will teach his sons justice.*

ANALYZED.— "A wise man," is the modified subject. "Will teach his sons justice," is the modified predicate. The predicate *will teach*, is modified, 1st, by its direct object, *sons*; 2d, by *justice*, which may be called the indirect object of teach; if the preposition *of*, or *about*, were supplied before justice, the expression *of justice* would be the adjunct of *will teach.*

PARSED. — "Sons," is a common noun, third person, plural, masculine gender, objective case, and the object of teach.

"Justice" is a common noun, third person, singular, neuter gender, objective case, and the indirect object of teach. *Teach* is followed by two objectives

ANALYSIS AND PARSING.

In long journeys, ask your master leave to give ale to your horses. — *Swift.*

God called the light day, and the darkness he called night.

While they promise themselves liberty, they themselves are the servants of corruption.

He fashioned it with a graving tool, after he had made it a molten calf.

He allowed his son the third part of his inheritance.

His son was allowed the third part of his inheritance.

SECTION LI.

CASE INDEPENDENT.

The form of the independent case is usually that of the *nominative*, but its relations and office are quite different.

RULE XII.

446. A noun joined with a participle, standing unconnected with the subject or predicate of a sentence, is in the case absolute or independent; as, "The *oration having been spoken*, the assembly was dismissed." *

REMARKS.

1. The noun independent may have adjectives and modifying adjuncts.

2. In *analyzing*, the case absolute or independent, with the participle and other modifying words, is an abridged expression, which may be formed into a complete sentence, by substituting a verb for the participle, and supplying other necessary words; as, "Tarquinius reigning," "Pythagoras came into Italy." *Tarquinius reigning*, is an abridged expression, and is equivalent to *while Tarquinius was reigning.*

ANALYSIS AND PARSING.

Model.

SENTENCE. — *Mr. Welch's health being impaired, he was advised to try the effect of a warm climate.*

ANALYZED.— "He," is the subject; "was advised," &c., is the modified predicate. "Mr. Welch's health being impaired," is an abridged expression, equivalent to, "since Mr. Welch's health was impaired."

---

* A noun having no grammatical connection with the subject or predicate of a sentence, when joined with a participle is usually said to be in the case *absolute*, but when it is the name of an object *addressed*, it is said to be in the case *independent*. As either term indicates the fact that the noun is not grammatically connected with the leading parts of the sentence, it is deemed immaterial which term is employed.

" It " is frequently redundant, or is used indefinitely ; and when so used, it may be parsed in apposition with the infinitive or clause following ; as, " It is the mark of a generous spirit to forgive injuries ;" the proper subject of the verb is, " *to forgive injuries*," and " it " is redundant, or unnecessary to the sense ; but such a usage is authorized by the best writers.

5. The pronoun *whatever* or *whatsoever* is sometimes used for the sake of emphasis ; as, " No ground *whatever* ;" when used in this manner, it may be treated as an adjective belonging to a noun understood ; as, " No prudence whatever," that is, " no prudence, *whatever* prudence may exist, can deviate from this scheme."

6. The pronouns *himself, itself, themselves*, &c., are used in the nominative or objective case, and are frequently a mere repetition for the sake of emphasis, and in many instances are to be parsed in apposition with some noun or pronoun expressed or understood ; as, " He *himself* said it."

7. " What " is sometimes used adverbially in the sense of *partly* ; as, " *What* with the war ;" " *what* with the sweat," &c.

8. " What " is often improperly used for " that ;" as, " They will not believe but *what* I have been entirely to blame.

9. Every relative must have an antecedent to which it refers, either expressed or implied ; as, " Who is partial to others, is so to himself." In this sentence, " who " is used indefinitely, referring to some word not expressed ; as, " The *man* who," or " any *person* who," &c.

10. The relative *that*, may refer either to persons or things ; but it is generally used in preference to *who* or *which*, in the following instances :

I. After an adjective in the superlative degree ; as, " Humility is one of the most amiable virtues *that* we can possess. " Which," in this sentence, would sound harsh and disagreeable.

II. After the word *same* belonging to the noun which immediately precedes the relative ; as, " They are the *same persons that* we saw yesterday."

III. After " who," used interrogatively or after an antecedent introduced by *it* ; as, " Who *that* is prudent, would conduct in such a manner ;" " It is you *that* must bear the responsibility ; not I."

IV. When the antecedent consists of two or more words taken conjointly, one referring to a person, and the other to a thing ; as, " My memory fondly clings to the dear friends and country *that* I have left."

11. The relative frequently refers to a whole clause ; as, " You have overcome envy with glory, *which* is very difficult."

12. Two relatives occurring in different clauses of a compound sentence should be the same ; as, " It is remarkable, that Holland, against *which* the war was undertaken, and *that* in the very beginning was reduced to the brink of ruin, lost nothing." " Which " should be used instead of " that."

13. The relative *which* is appropriately used to refer to the words " child " and " children." " Which " refers to persons, when used to designate one of two individuals ; as, " *Which* of the two?"

REMARK.

Names, titles, captions, and *signatures,* standing unconnected, are abridged expressions, to which, in analyzing and parsing, such words can be added as are necessary to complete a sentence.

EXAMPLES.

The Spectator; that is, this book is entitled the Spectator. Rule V.; Chapter IV.; that is, this is Rule V., &c. Henry Martyn; that is, the memoir of Henry Martyn. *Spectator, Rule V., Chapter IV.,* are strictly parts of sentences, and can be parsed as nouns in the nominative after the verbs.

REVIEW.

What are the rules for nouns in the independent case? Give some examples under each. In what case are the nouns in the following expressions? " O liberty!" " O my country " " Our *work* being finished, we will play." Repeat the rule for the objective case; for two objectives. Give examples under each. Repeat the rules for the nominative case; for the possessive case; for the objective case; for the independent case. What rule is applicable to the nouns, in such expressions as the following; " I am busy *every day;* " " he has been absent *six weeks;* " " *six rods* wide;" " *ten feet* deep;" " much every *way;* " "the book is worth a *dollar;* " " it cost *me money;* " " he is like his *father.*"

SECTION LII.

PRONOUNS.

RULE XIV.

448. Pronouns must agree with their antecedents and words for which they stand, in *gender, number,* and *person;* as, "*Thou who* speakest." "*They* went *their* way."

REMARKS.

1. Pronouns which refer to *two* or *more nouns,* when the objects are taken together, must be in the plural number; as, " George and Thomas excel in *their* studies."

2. Pronouns which refer to two or more *singular* nouns, connected by *or* or *nor* must be in the singular number; as, " Neither James nor John is diligent in *his* studies;" not *their* studies.

3. When the nouns connected are of different persons, the *first person* is preferred to the *second,* and the *second* to the third.

4. The pronoun " it " often refers to nouns without regard to *number, gender* or *person;* to infinitives, to clauses, and even to whole paragraphs.

14*

Can any one, on their entrance into the world, be fully secure that they shall not be deceived ?

They which seek wisdom will certainly find her.

The child whom we have just seen is wholesomely fed.

REVIEW.

What is the general rule for the agreement of pronouns ? Explain the meaning of this rule. When two or more nouns are connected by *and*, in what number must the pronoun be which refers to them ? If nouns are connected by *or* or *nor*, what must be the *number* of the pronoun referring to them ? Repeat the rules for the construction of the *relative*. What kind of a pronoun is *what ?* How is it treated in parsing ? *Ans.* Generally, as a compound pronoun, equivalent to *that which* or *those which.*

Section LIII.

ADJECTIVES.

Rule XV.

449. An adjective belongs to the noun or pronoun which it qualifies or defines. (113.)

REMARKS.

1. Adjectives are frequently separated by intervening words from the nouns to which they belong; as, "The day is *pleasant.*" "*Great* is the Lord." "A river twenty rods *wide.*"

2. Adjectives are used to modify infinitives, parts of clauses, and whole propositions; as, "To see the sun is *pleasant;*" "to advance was *difficult;*" "to retreat *hazardous.*"

3. Adjectives are used to modify both the *action of the verb*, and its *subject;* as, "The wind was blowing *fresh;*" "he grew *old* in the service of his country."

The difference between an adverb and an adjective in such a connection, may be illustrated by the following examples :

He feels *warm* — adjective.

He feels *warmly* the insult offered him — adverb.

She looks *cold* — adjective.

She looks *coldly* on him — adverb.

Adjectives of this kind frequently follow those verbs for which the verb "be" might be substituted; as, The rose *smells* sweet; that is, *is* sweet. "Sweet" in this connection is an adjective. How *sweet* the hay smells, [is.] The apple tastes sour, [is.]

4. Adjectives are sometimes used to modify other adjectives; as, "*Deep*

14. When there are antecedents of different persons to which a relative in the nominative case refers, it is the general rule that the relative may agree with either ; as, "I am the Lord that *make* or *maketh* all things." It is better in most cases to place the relative as near as possible to the word to which it refers ; thus, instead of the expression, "I am the Lord who command you," it is better to say, "I who command you am the Lord."

15. Sometimes the relative precedes the *clause* to which it refers, without ambiguity in the sense "There was, therefore, *which* is all we assert, a course of life pursued by them different from that which they before led."

ANALYSIS AND PARSING.

In *parsing the pronoun*, inquire, what does it stand in place of? how declined? how governed? what is the rule for its agreement? what for its government?

The little bill must be paid, but I confess it alarms me. The expense of my son here, is greater than I ever imagined. Although his company is almost all the pleasure I have in life, yet I should not have brought him, if I had known the expense.

The cookery, and the manner of living here, *which* you know Americans were taught by their masters to dislike, are more agreeable to me than you can imagine.

It is the care of a very great part of mankind to conceal their indigence from the rest; they support themselves by temporary expedients, and every day is lost in contriving for the morrow.

TO BE CORRECTED.

Rebecca took goodly raiment, and put them upon Jacob.

One should not think too favorably of themselves.

The multitude eagerly pursue pleasure, as its chief good.

The council were divided in its sentiments.

The moon appears, but the light is not his own.

The men which seek wisdom will find him.

One cannot be too careful of their reputation.

My brother and I are employed in their proper business.

George and Charles are diligent in his studies.

Neither James nor John has gained to themselves much credit.

Each of the sexes should be kept within their particular bounds.

weakest of the two ;" it should be, " the weaker of the two." " The elder of the three ; " it should be, " the eldest of the three."

13. The superlative, however, is admissible where two things are compared, if there is no ambiguity from such a use ; as, " The weakest of the two, or the weaker of the two."

14. Double comparatives and superlatives should be avoided ; as, " A more serener temper;" " the most straitest sect."

15. In expressing a comparison, if both nouns relate to the same thing, the article should not be prefixed to the latter; if to different things it should not be omitted; as, " He is a much better general than statesman."

16. The word such is often improperly used for so; as, " He was such an extravagant person;" it should be so extravagant.

Position of Adjectives.

17. Adjectives are usually placed before the nouns to which they belong ; as, " A generous man."

18. The following are exceptions to this general rule :

I. When the adjective is limited by some word or adjunct following it, it stands after its noun; as, "Food convenient for me." "A rule, a foot long."

II. When the adjective expresses a title; as, " Alexander, the Great," it follows its noun.

III. Sometimes several adjectives belonging to one noun are placed after it; as, " A prince learned, wise, and brave."

IV. An adjective used emphatically to introduce a sentence is often separated from its noun by intervening words; as, "Great is the Lord."

V. When an adjective is preceded by an adverb, it generally follows its noun; as, " A man truly wise."

VI. The definitive all, is often separated from its noun by the; as, "All the people." " All," sometimes stands after several nouns, to impart energy to the sentence; as, " Ambition, interest, honor, all concurred."

VII. All adjectives are separated from their nouns by " a," when they are preceded by " so," or " as ; " as, " So wise a man." " As good a man."

ANALYSIS AND PARSING.

The young blood of modern literature ⋅ has put new life into the literature of the dead languages.

All the features of a great heroic age, — from which European civilization dates, and political and domestic order takes its rise, stand forth in living reality.

> The encumbered oar scarce leaves the hostile coast,
> Through purple billows and a floating host.

None were banished except the thirty tyrants.

I have not seen him these ten years.

That sort of books was a valuable present.

These studies were the delight of his declining years.

To die for one's country is sweet and becoming. To restrain anger is excellent. To excel in knowledge is honorable. The flame burns bright and clear. Keen blows the wind, and piercing is the cold. A great many stars are visible in a clear night. A light shineth in the path of the upright.

SENTENCES TO BE CORRECTED.

A new barrel of flour. A clear spring of water. A green load of wood. A new pair of boots. I have received them books which you sent me. I can never think so mean of him. They wandered about solitarily and distressed. She reads proper, writes neat, and composes accurate. They lived conformable to the rules of prudence. He was such an extravagant man, that he soon wasted his property. I never saw such large trees. Such a bad temper is seldom found. A tree fifty foot high. Twenty ton of hay. Two shilling a pound.

'T is more easier to build two chimneys than to maintain one. The tongue is like a race horse, which runs the faster the lesser weight it carries. The nightingale sings; hers is the most sweetest voice in the grove. The Most Highest hath created us for his glory and our own happiness. The Supreme Being is the most wisest, the most powerfulest, and the most best of beings. Virtue confers the supremest dignity on man, and should be his chief desire. His assertion was more true than that of his opponent; nay, the words of the latter were most untrue. His work is perfect; his brother's more perfect; and his father's the most perfect of all. Eve was the fairest of all her daughters. Profane swearing is, of all other vices, the most inexcusable. A talent of this kind would, perhaps, prove the likeliest of any other to succeed. He spoke with so much propriety, that I understood him the best of all the others who spoke on the subject. Such distinguished virtues seldom occur.

SECTION LIV.

PRONOMINAL ADJECTIVES.*

RULE XVI.

450. Pronominal adjectives limit the nouns to which they belong, or are used alone as pronouns ; as, *This* day, *few* men, *both* men, *many* people, the *latter* day, *some* think, *few* come, &c.

REMARKS.

Each other. One another.

1. These are elliptical expressions and may be explained as follows :

" Righteousness and peace have kissed *each other ;* " that is, *each* has kissed the *other.*

" We ought to love *one another ;* " that is, *one* ought to love, &c.

" When ye come together to eat, tarry *one* for *another ;* " it might be, for one another.

" Exhort *one another* daily ; " let each exhort the other, &c.†

2. The adjectives *this* and *these* refer to what is near or present ; but the adjectives *that* and *those* refer to what is more remote or absent ; as, " *This* man," that is, the man who is present or near ; " *That* man," that is, the man who is at a distance or absent.

3. The adjectives *each, every, either*, require, in construction, the noun, pronoun or verb, to be in the singular number ; as, " *Every* tree is known by its fruit." This rule is often violated, as in the following examples : " Let each fulfil *their* part ; " it should be *his.*

" Every " is sometimes joined to a noun, preceded by a numeral adjective ; as, " Every *six months.*" " Every *hundred years.*" As the noun and the numeral are together merely a complex term expressing a definite period, such examples do not in reality make an exception to the rule.

4. Even when several nouns are connected as the common subjects of a verb, if each one is limited by *each* or *every*, expressed or understood, the verb must be singular ; as, " Every leaf, every twig, and every drop of water, teems with life."

5. The words *means, news, amends*, &c., formerly plural nouns, are now used in the singular number, and take adjectives agreeing with them in the

---

* This class of words, in nearly every instance where they are used alone, admit of having a noun supplied ; but as it would be obviously improper to supply a noun in some cases, it is better to treat them as pronouns when they are used alone.

† The expressions, *each other, one another*, are sometimes termed reciprocal pronouns.

plural; as, "*This* means," not *these* means. "*One* means or *a* means," not one *mean.*

6 The pronominal *both*, is often used in the place of two nouns, connected together, or of a plural noun comprising only two individuals, the subject or object in a sentence; as, "Abraham took sheep and oxen, and gave them to Abimelech, and *both* of them made a covenant."

"Both" is sometimes used in apposition with a pronoun to give emphasis to the expression; as, "He forgave them *both*." "I will teach you *both*."

7. The pronominals *former* and *latter*; also *the one* — and *the other*, may properly represent nouns or clauses in contrast, when they are near in construction and occasion no obscurity.*

8. *One* is sometimes used in the plural; as, "The great *ones* of the world;" "the little *ones*." "One" used without a noun is often used indefinitely, signifying persons in general; as, "*One* ought to pity the distresses of mankind."

9. *None* is used in both numbers; as, "*None* is," or "*None* are." "*None* that go unto her return again."

10. *Either* is sometimes used for "each;" as, "Two thieves were crucified — on *either* side one."

11. "Them" used for "these" or "those" is a vulgarism; as, "*Them* books." "*Them* people." It should be, "*these* books," "*those* people."

ANALYSIS AND PARSING.

Pronominal Adjectives.

One day Alonzo made a discovery which startled him.

A great many people think that the Sabbath ends at sunset.

The boy hoped he had made some impression.

You know very well that such an expedition, with such companions, will not be keeping holy the Sabbath day.

Every feeling of gratitude is obliterated by one single interference with your wicked desires.

He soon learned, that it was one thing to see that his feelings were wrong, and another thing to feel right.

These omissions were more frequent than he imagined.

And the eyes of them both were opened.

Pronominal Adjectives used as Pronouns.

And he went after the man of Israel into the tent, and thrust both of them through.

---

* The injudicious use of *former* and *latter* and other substitutes are a great blemish in Campbell's Philosophy of Rhetoric. — *Webster.*

15

The same is equally true of the past.

In the evening he was occupied with some one of these enjoyments, and the next day he was planning another.

This he could not but strongly shrink from.

Let others serve whom they will ; as for me and my house, we will serve the Lord.

The dialogue between conscience and his heart was going on all the time ; the latter finally prevailed.

Many shall come in my name, saying, I am Christ, and shall deceive many.

Jubal was the father of such as dwell in tents.

I cannot go beyond the word of the Lord my God, to do less or more.

Let each fulfil his part.

TO BE CORRECTED.

These kind of indulgences. Those sort of favors. I have been waiting this two hours. Do you see those books lying on this table ? These men that stand yonder are soldiers. That breeze is refreshing. Where are these books which you took from the desk ? Both the sun, moon, and planets, turn on their axis. Do you see them people walking in the park ?

Rule XVII.

451. The article *an* or *a*, is used before nouns in the singular number only, individually or collectively. *The* is used before nouns in both numbers; as, " A man ; " " a thousand ; " " the houses ; " " the sea."

REMARKS.

1. Articles, when used, should be applied according to their signification, and as the sense requires. They are often properly omitted.

2. When the sense of words is sufficiently certain by the construction, the article may be omitted.

3. When the signification of the noun is general, and requires no limitation, the article is omitted; as, " Honor to whom honor is due." " Man is
 ʒl."

4. When two or more nouns occur in the same construction, the article may be used with the first and omitted with the rest; as, " There were many hours both of the night and day," or *the* day It is often used, however, in such instances for the sake of emphasis.

5. When two or more adjectives are used to express different qualities of the same object, the article may be used with the first, and omitted with the rest; as, " A large and convenient dwelling," referring to a single dwelling. But if it is intended to express qualities of different objects, the article may be used before each; as, "*A* large and *a* convenient dwelling," referring to two dwellings.

6. When the two nouns after a comparative refer to the same person or thing, the article should be omitted before the second; as, " He is a better soldier than scholar." The use of the article before " scholar," would change the meaning entirely; it then would mean, " He is a better soldier than a scholar is."

7. A nice distinction in the sense is sometimes made by the use or omission of the article before the words *little* and *few; as,* " He has a little reverence." This means that he has reverence in a slight degree. " He has little reverence." This implies a doubt whether he has any.

8. *An* or *a* is sometimes used in the sense of *each* or *every; as,* " Twice *a* day."

9. The article is often used to modify the meaning of an adjective; as, " A *hundred* men ;" " a *large* number of men ;" " a *few* things."

10. " The " is used before *comparatives* and *superlatives; as,* " *The* more — *the* better ;" " An estate, *the largest* in the city."

11. " The " is used before the antecedent of restrictive clauses; as, " *The* sight *which we saw.*"

12. " An or a " sometimes occurs between the adjective " many," and a singular noun; as, " Full many *a* gem ;" " many *a* youth."

TO BE CORRECTED.

Show how the articles are misapplied in the following sentences.

Reason was given to a man to control his passions. A man is the noblest work of creation. He is a much better writer than a reader. The king has conferred on him a title of a duke. Wisest and best men sometimes commit errors. At best his gift was but a poor offering. He has been censured for giving a little attention to his business.

REVIEW.

What is the rule for the agreement of adjectives ? What is an adjective ? Does the term adjective include the article ? Are adjectives ever separated from their nouns ? Give some examples. Can adjectives qualify *Infinitives,*

clauses or sentences? Give examples. In the expression, *that you are mistaken is certain,* which is the adjective? To what does it belong? In the expression, *she looks pale,* which is the adjective? What does it appear to modify? Give other examples of the same kind. Do adjectives modify other adjectives? Give some examples. Show wherein the following expressions are incorrect. *He was extreme prodigal; he writes neat; the stream flows rapid; the wind blows violent.* Repeat the rule and notes for the *agreement* and *use* of the article. Is there any difference in the following expressions? *Few people, a few people.* What is the rule for pronominal adjectives? Explain the phrases *each other,* and *one another.* What is the difference in use between the pronominals *this* and *that?* What is said of *each, every, either?* What should be the number of an adjective to agree with *means* or *news?* What is the rule for the agreement of the article *an* or *a?* of *the?* Mention some of the rules for the omission or the use of the articles.

SECTION LV.

VERBS.

THE INFINITIVE MODE.

RULE XVIII.

452. A verb in the Infinitive mode is generally used to limit the meaning of a *verb, noun,* or *adjective;* as, " I hope *to succeed;*" "a desire *to improve;*" "anxious *to hear.*"

REMARKS.

A verb in the Infinitive may also limit the meaning of

1. *As* or *than;* as "He is so conceited as to *disdain* to have any thing to do with books;" "he desired nothing more *than to know* his imperfections."*

2. *Adverbs;* as "The rope is strong *enough to suspend* a ton;" "I know not how to address you."

3. *Prepositions;* as, "What went ye out *for to see;*"† "my friend is about to take his departure."

4. The *Infinitive* is also used independently; as, " *To say the least* he has erred in judgment;" "but *to proceed* with our argument."

---

* The Infinite after *as* or *than,* more properly limits a verb understood; as, "He desired nothing more than *he desired* to know," &c.

† This form of expression is now obsolete; it occurs in the Scriptures and in ancient writings.

5. When the Infinitive denotes *purpose* or *design*, it is frequently preceded by the phrase *in order*, but this phrase is often omitted.

6. The phrase *to be sure* is often used adverbially, in the sense of *surely*, or *certainly.*

SPECIAL RULE.

453. The Infinitive mode has sometimes a subject in the objective case; as, "I believe *the sun* to be the centre of the solar system;" "I know *him* to be a man of veracity."

REMARKS.

1. This form of expression, far less common in our language than in the Latin and Greek, is equivalent to a subordinate clause introduced by *that;* "I believe *him* to be dishonest," that is, I believe *that* he is dishonest.

2. The Infinitive with its subject is sometimes introduced by *for;* as, "*For* him to die was gain." In such expressions the infinitive and the words connected with it, form the subject of the verb in the sentence, "For him to die" is the subject of *was.*

NOTE. — The use of the Infinitive as the *subject, object,* and *predicate nominative* has been explained under the Rules relating to these subjects. For the nature and properties of the Infinitive, see Sec. xxi, 255, 256.

ANALYSIS AND PARSING.

He was willing to risk all, for the excitement of a new revolution.

He delivered his brother Alfonzo into their hands, to be recognized as the lawful heir of the crown.

Not far from the city of Avila, they caused a scaffold to be erected, of sufficient elevation to be easily seen from the surrounding country.

A manifesto was then read, exhibiting in glowing colors the tyrannical conduct of the king, and the consequent determination to depose him.

It would be an unprofitable task to attempt to unravel all the fine-spun intrigues, by which the Marquis Villena contrived to defeat every attempt at an ultimate accommodation.

The abject mind of Henry was content to purchase repose, even by the most humiliating sacrifice.

Be not so greedy of popular applause, as to forget that the same breath which blows up a fire may blow it out again.

I understand him better, than to suppose he will relinquish his design.

RULE XIX:

454. The verbs which follow *bid*, *dare*, *durst*, *hear*, *feel*, *let*, *make*, *need*, *see*, and their participles, are used in the Infinitive without the sign *to ;*[*] as " He bid me go."

NOTE. — The verbs *watch, behold, know, observe, have, command, find*, and some others, are occasionally followed by the infinitive without the sign *to*.

ANALYSIS AND PARSING.

The name of Henry makes them leave me desolate.

My followers' base and ignominious treasons make me betake to my heels.

Dare any man be so bold to sound retreat or parley, when I command them kill? — *Shakspeare.*

Hark! I hear the herald angels say.

And the multitude wondered when they saw the lame walk and the blind see.

He had dared to think for himself. — *Coleridge.*

The haughty priests of learning banished from the schools all who had dared draw water from the living fountain. — *Coleridge.*

I found my friend express much satisfaction for the bargains he had made. — *Steele.*

TO BE CORRECTED.

You ought not walk too hastily. I need not to solicit him to do a kind action. I have seen some very young persons to conduct themselves very indiscreetly. And the multitude wondered when they saw the lame to walk, and the blind to see.

---

* The sign *to* is retained after these verbs when used in the passive form. The sign is also sometimes retained after *make* and *dare*.

PARTICIPLES.

RULE XX.

455. Participles belong to nouns or pronouns, which they limit or explain.

Present and compound participles govern the same case as the verbs from which they are derived.

REMARKS.

1. The participle is often used as a noun, either with or without an article; but when so used the present or compound participle of a transitive verb performs the office of a verb and a noun at the same time; as, "In return for your *inviting me.*"

2. When preceded by the article, the present participle, in most cases, must be followed by "of;" as, "The gaining *of* wisdom;" "The supplying *of* our wants." Expressions like the following are incorrect: "*The preaching* repentance;" "*The writing* an essay." "Of" should be used after "preaching," &c.*

3. The reverse of this rule should also be observed, namely; that the "of" should not be employed after the participle, when it is not preceded by the article; as, "By preaching of repentance." It should be, "by the preaching of repentance," or, "by preaching repentance." In general, both the article and the preposition should be used, or both should be omitted, except where the ellipsis of the preposition is obvious, or where another construction is required by the sense; as, "The *advising* or *attempting* to procure an insurrection." In this sentence the infinitive is used after the participial noun.

4. Present and compound participles often perform the office of a verb and noun at the same time; as, "He was displeased with the king's *having bestowed* the office upon a worthless man." In this sentence, the compound participle is used as a noun and governs "king's." It also, in the office of a verb, governs the noun "office," in the objective case.

5. Participles often belong to a clause or a part of a sentence; as, "*Owing* to the bad state of the roads, he was detained a day beyond the time of his appointment." In this sentence, "owing" agrees with the whole sentence, "he was," &c. The words *concerning, according, respecting, touching,* &c., are generally considered prepositions. They are, however, derived from verbs, and in most instances refer to some statement in the sentence.

6. Participles are sometimes used indefinitely, without reference to any

---

* This rule is often violated by our best writers, and to make it universal is to assume an authority much too dictatorial. The expression, "The making a will," is perfectly good English. — *Webster.*

noun or pronoun expressed; as, "It is not possible to act otherwise, *considering* the weakness of our nature." "*Generally speaking*, his conduct was very honorable."

For other uses of the participle, see Sec. XXIV.

7. Adjectives derived from verbs, and having the form of participles, are called *verbal* or *participial* adjectives.

ANALYSIS AND PARSING.

And they, continuing daily with one accord in the temple, and breaking bread from house to house, did eat their meat with gladness and singleness of heart, praising God, and having favor with all the people.

He has left town for Ireland without taking leave of either of us.

Having a little time upon my hands, I could not think of bestowing it better than in writing an epistle to the Spectator.

I cannot forbear troubling you with a letter upon that subject.

We considered man as belonging to societies; societies as formed of different ranks; and different ranks distinguished by habits.

Having been very well entertained by your specimen of clubs, I shall take the liberty to furnish you with a brief account of such a one as you have not seen.

TO BE CORRECTED.

By observing of truth. By the observing truth. By the sending proper information. Without the taking pains. Without taking of pains. The changing times and seasons, the removing and setting up kings, belong to Providence alone. Poverty turns one's thoughts too much upon the supplying one's wants. In tracing of his history, we discover little that is worthy of imitation.

SECTION LVI.

MODES. TENSES.

456. In the use of   regard
should be paid to their

1. The indicative mode must be used after conjunctions which are positive and unconditional in their nature; as, " He is esteemed, *because* he is generous."

2. The subjunctive mode is used after conjunctions which imply doubt, contingency or condition; as, " If he is expert in business, he will find employment." " Suppose we admit this fact."

3. In general, the form of the verb in the subjunctive, is the same as that of the indicative; but an elliptical form in the second and third person singular, should be used in the following instances:

4. *Future contingency* is expressed by the omission of the indicative termination; as, " If he go," for " if he *shall* go." " Though he slay me," i. e. " though he *should* slay me." " If thou injure another, thou wilt hurt thyself."

5. *Lest* and *that* annexed to a command, are followed by the elliptical form of the subjunctive; as, " Love not sleep lest thou come to poverty."

6. *If*, with *but* following it, when futurity is denoted, requires the elliptical form; as, " If he *do* but *touch* the hills they shall smoke."

7. But when future contingency is not denoted by the subjunctive clause, the indicative form is used; as, " If she *is* but sincere I am happy."

TO BE CORRECTED.

If he acquires riches, they will corrupt his mind, and be useless to others. Though he urges me yet more earnestly, I shall not comply, unless he advances more forcible reasons. I shall walk in the fields to-day, unless it rains. As the governess were present, the children behaved properly. Despise not any condition, lest it happens to be your own. Let him that is sanguine take heed lest he miscarries. Take care that thou breakest not any of the established rules. If he does but intimate his desire, it will be sufficient to produce obedience. At the time of his return, if he is but expert in the business, he will find employment. If he do but speak to display his abilities, he is unworthy of attention. If he be but in health, I am content. If thou have promised, be faithful to thy engagement. Though he have proved his right to submission, he is too generous to exact it. Unless he have improved, he is unfit for the office. If thou had succeeded, perhaps thou would not be the happier for it. Though thou did injure him, he harbors no resentment. Was he ever so great and opulent. this conduct would debase him. Was I to enumerate all her virtues, it would look like flattery. Though I was perfect, yet I would not presume. Unless thou can fairly support the cause, give it up honorably. Though thou might have foreseen the danger, thou could not have avoided it.

TENSES.

No very definite rules can be given for the proper use of the tenses in all cases, except such as are found in the definitions already given in Part III. The best rule, which is a very general one, is, to observe strictly what forms of the verb the sense requires.

It may be useful, however, to give a few examples of the manner in which the tenses are improperly employed.

Errors in Forms.

I *come* is very improperly used for I *came.*
I *done* is very improperly used for I *did.*
I *begun* is very improperly used for I *began.*

Done and *begun* are perfect participles, which are improperly used for the imperfect tense.

The river *has froze* over; it should be *has frozen.*
The school *has began;* it should be *has begun.*
The horse was *drove hard;* it should be *was driven.*
The thief *has stole* my watch; it should be *has stolen.*

Froze, began, drove, stole, are forms of the imperfect tense, which are improperly used for the perfect participles, *frozen, begun, driven,* &c.

The expressions "had rather," and "had better," though anomalous, are well authorized. But "had ought," or "had not ought," commonly contracted into "had n't ought," is a gross vulgarism. *Ought* is a defective verb used only in the present and imperfect tenses.

Sit, set, lie, lay.

The verbs *sit* and *lie* are often confounded with *set* and *lay*.

The verb *to sit*, signifies " to repose on a seat." Its principal parts are, PRES. sit; IMPER sat; PERF. PART. sat.

The verb *to set*, when transitive, signifies " to place." The principal parts are, PRES. set; IMP. set; PERF. PART. set. This verb is also used intransitively; as, " The sun sets." " The moon has set."

The verb *to lie* signifies " to repose," " to lie down." Its principal parts are, PRES. lie; IMP. lay; PERF. PART. lain. There is also a regular verb *lie*, which signifies to utter a falsehood.

The verb *to lay*, signifies " to place." Its principal parts are, PRES. lay; IMP. laid; PERF. PART. laid.

Errors in Connection.

INCORRECT.	CORRECTED.
I should be glad if he *will* write.	*Would* write.
I *have* completed the task two days ago.	I *completed.*
They *have* resided in Italy till two months ago.	They *resided.*
His style *has formerly been* admired.	*Was formerly admired.*
Next new year's day, I *shall be* at school six months.	I *shall have been.*
After we *visited* London we returned, content and thankful, to our retired habitation.	After *we had visited* London, &c.

TENSES OF THE INFINITIVE MODE.

457 As a verb in the infinitive mode is strictly nothing more than a verbal noun, that is, the name of some action, it will be easy to determine which tense of the infinitive should be employed, by inquiring whether the action expressed by the infinitive refers to past, present, or future time; for example:

" I intended to write;" i. e. I intended writing; not, I intended *to have written*, or, having written, for this expression would refer the act to a time before there was an *intention* to act.

" I hoped to see you;" not *to have seen* you.

" I commanded him *to do* it;" not, *to have done* it, i. e. *the doing* would not be before the command. Hence, in regard to verbs of this class the following rule may be observed for the use of the infinitive.

SPECIAL RULE.

458. After verbs signifying *to hope, to intend, to desire, to*

The same is equally true of the past.

In the evening he was occupied with some one of these enjoyments, and the next day he was planning another.

This he could not but strongly shrink from.

Let others serve whom they will ; as for me and my house, we will serve the Lord.

The dialogue between conscience and his heart was going on all the time ; the latter finally prevailed.

Many shall come in my name, saying, I am Christ, and shall deceive many.

Jubal was the father of such as dwell in tents.

I cannot go beyond the word of the Lord my God, to do less or more.

Let each fulfil his part.

TO BE CORRECTED.

These kind of indulgences. Those sort of favors. I have been waiting this two hours. Do you see those books lying on this table ? These men that stand yonder are soldiers. That breeze is refreshing. Where are these books which you took from the desk ? Both the sun, moon, and planets, turn on their axis. Do you see them people walking in the park ?

RULE XVII.

451. The article *an* or *a*, is used before nouns in the singular number only, individually or collectively. *The* is used before nouns in both numbers; as, " A man ; " " a thousand ; " " the houses ; " " the sea."

REMARKS.

1. Articles, when used, should be applied according to their signification, and as the sense requires. They are often properly omitted.

2. When the sense of words is sufficiently certain by the construction, the article may be omitted.

3. When the signification of the noun is general, and requires no limita- tion, the article is omitted; as, "Honor to whom honor is due." " Man is al."

4. When two or more nouns occur in the same construction, the article may be used with the first and omitted with the rest ; as, " There were many hours both of the night and day," or *the* day   It is often used, however, in such instances for the sake of emphasis.

5. When two or more adjectives are used to express different qualities of the same object, the article may be used with the first, and omitted with the rest ; as, " A large and convenient dwelling," referring to a single dwelling. But if it is intended to express qualities of different objects, the article may be used before each ; as, " *A* large and *a* convenient dwelling," referring to two dwellings.

6. When the two nouns after a comparative refer to the same person or thing, the article should be omitted before the second ; as, " He is a better soldier than scholar." The use of the article before " scholar," would change the meaning entirely ; it then would mean, " He is a better soldier than a scholar is."

7. A nice distinction in the sense is sometimes made by the use or omission of the article before the words *little* and *few ;* as, " He has a little reverence." This means that he has reverence in a slight degree. " He has little reverence." This implies a doubt whether he has any.

8. *An* or *a* is sometimes used in the sense of *each* or *every ;* as, " Twice *a* day."

9. The article is often used to modify the meaning of an adjective ; as, " A *hundred* men ;" " a *large* number of men ;" " a *few* things."

10. " The " is used before *comparatives* and *superlatives ;* as, " *The* more — *the* better ;" " An estate, *the largest* in the city."

11. " The " is used before the antecedent of restrictive clauses ; as, " *The* sight *which we saw.*"

12. " An or a " sometimes occurs between the adjective " many," and a singular noun ; as, " Full many *a* gem ;" " many *a* youth."

TO BE CORRECTED.

Show how the articles are misapplied in the following sentences.

Reason was given to a man to control his passions. A man is the noblest work of creation. He is a much better writer than a reader. The king has conferred on him a title of a duke. Wisest and best men sometimes commit errors. At best his gift was but a poor offering. He has been censured for giving a little attention to his business.

REVIEW.

What is the rule for the agreement of adjectives ? What is an adjective ? Does the term adjective include the article ? Are adjectives ever separated from their nouns ? Give some examples. Can adjectives qualify *Infinitives,*

clauses or sentences? Give examples.   In the expression, *that you are mistaken is certain*, which is the adjective?   To what does it belong?   In the expression, *she looks pale*, which is the adjective?   What does it appear to modify?   Give other examples of the same kind.   Do adjectives modify other adjectives?   Give some examples.   Show wherein the following expressions are incorrect. *He was extreme prodigal; he writes neat; the stream flows rapid; the wind blows violent.*   Repeat the rule and notes for the *agreement* and *use* of the article.   Is there any difference in the following expressions?   *Few people, a few people.*   What is the rule for pronominal adjectives?   Explain the phrases *each other*, and *one another*.   What is the difference in use between the pronominals *this* and *that?*   What is said of *each, every, either?*   What should be the number of an adjective to agree with *means* or *news?*   What is the rule for the agreement of the article *an* or *a?* of *the?*   Mention some of the rules for the omission or the use of the articles.

SECTION LV.

VERBS.

THE INFINITIVE MODE.

RULE XVIII.

452. A verb in the Infinitive mode is generally used to limit the meaning of a *verb, noun,* or *adjective*; as, "I hope *to succeed*;" "a desire *to improve*;" "anxious *to hear.*"

REMARKS.

A verb in the Infinitive may also limit the meaning of

1. *As* or *than;* as "He is so conceited as to *disdain* to have any thing to do with books;" "he desired nothing more *than to know* his imperfections."*

2. *Adverbs;* as "The rope is strong *enough to suspend* a ton;" "I know not how to address you."

3. *Prepositions;* as, "What went ye out *for to see;*"† "my friend is about to take his departure."

4. The *Infinitive* is also used independently; as, "*To say the least* he has erred in judgment;" "but *to proceed* with our argument."

---

* The Infinite after *as* or *than*, more properly limits a verb understood; as, "He desired nothing more than *he desired* to know," &c.

† This form of expression is now obsolete; it occurs in the Scriptures and in ancient writings.

5. When the Infinitive denotes *purpose* or *design*, it is frequently preceded by the phrase *in order*, but this phrase is often omitted.

6. The phrase *to be sure* is often used adverbially, in the sense of *surely*, or *certainly*.

SPECIAL RULE.

453. The Infinitive mode has sometimes a subject in the objective case; as, " I believe *the sun* to be the centre of the solar system;" " I know *him* to be a man of veracity."

REMARKS.

1. This form of expression, far less common in our language than in the Latin and Greek, is equivalent to a subordinate clause introduced by *that;* " I believe *him* to be dishonest," that is, I believe *that* he is dishonest.

2. The Infinitive with its subject is sometimes introduced by *for;* as, "*For* him to die was gain." In such expressions the infinitive and the words connected with it, form the subject of the verb in the sentence, "For him to die " is the subject of *was.*

NOTE. — The use of the Infinitive as the *subject, object,* and *predicate nominative* has been explained under the Rules relating to these subjects. For the nature and properties of the Infinitive, see Sec. xxi, 255, 256.

ANALYSIS AND PARSING.

He was willing to risk all, for the excitement of a new revolution.

He delivered his brother Alfonzo into their hands, to be recognized as the lawful heir of the crown.

Not far from the city of Avila, they caused a scaffold to be erected, of sufficient elevation to be easily seen from the surrounding country.

A manifesto was then read, exhibiting in glowing colors the tyrannical conduct of the king, and the consequent determination to depose him.

It would be an unprofitable task to attempt to unravel all the fine-spun intrigues, by which the Marquis Villena contrived to defeat every attempt at an ultimate accommodation.

The abject mind of Henry was content to purchase repose, even by the most humiliating sacrifice.

Can any one, on their entrance into the world, be fully secure that they shall not be deceived ?

They which seek wisdom will certainly find her.

The child whom we have just seen is wholesomely fed.

REVIEW.

What is the general rule for the agreement of pronouns ? Explain the meaning of this rule. When two or more nouns are connected by *and*, in what number must the pronoun be which refers to them ? If nouns are connected by *or* or *nor*, what must be the *number* of the pronoun referring to them ? Repeat the rules for the construction of the *relative*. What kind of a pronoun is *what ?* How is it treated in parsing ? *Ans.* Generally, as a compound pronoun, equivalent to *that which* or *those which.*

Section LIII.

ADJECTIVES.

Rule XV.

449. An adjective belongs to the noun or pronoun which it qualifies or defines. (113.)

REMARKS.

1. Adjectives are frequently separated by intervening words from the nouns to which they belong ; as, " The day is *pleasant.*" " *Great* is the Lord." " A river twenty rods *wide.*"

2. Adjectives are used to modify infinitives, parts of clauses, and whole propositions ; as, " To see the sun is *pleasant ;*" " to advance was *difficult ;*" " to retreat *hazardous.*"

3. Adjectives are used to modify both the *action of the verb*, and its *subject ;* as, " The wind was blowing *fresh ;*" " he grew *old* in the service of his country."

The difference between an adverb and an adjective in such a connection, may be illustrated by the following examples :

He feels *warm* — adjective.

He feels *warmly* the insult offered him — adverb.

She looks *cold* — adjective.

She looks *coldly* on him — adverb.

Adjectives of this kind frequently follow those verbs for which the verb " be " might be substituted ; as, The rose *smells* sweet; that is, *is* sweet. " Sweet " in this connection is an adjective. How *sweet* the hay smells, [is.] The apple tastes sour, [is.]

4. Adjectives are sometimes used to modify other adjectives ; as, " *Deep*

blue," " a *witch* hazel mineral rod," "*pale* red." Several adjectives are sometimes joined to a single noun; as, " *Liverpool deep blue earthen* pitchers."

5. The adjective is often used alone, the noun with which it agrees being
understood; as, " *The brave*," " *the righteous*," " *the beautiful*."

6 The adjective is sometimes used indefinitely, without direct reference
to any noun; as, " To be *wise* and *good*, is to be *great* and *noble*." A noun
however, can generally be supplied in such instances; as, " For one to be
wise, is for one to be *great*," &c.

7. The expressions *two first*, *first two*, are both authorized by good usage.✻

8. An adjective is sometimes used to modify a noun and another adjective; as, " A *poor* old man."

9. Adjectives are sometimes improperly used for adverbs; as, " *Miserable*
poor," for " *miserably* poor ;" " *excellent* well," for " *excellently* well ;" " he behaved himself conformable to that great example ;" it should be *conformably* to.

" He acted *agreeable* to my advice." It should be *agreeably* to, because
agreeably shows the manner of acting ; but, *Agreeable* to my promise *I now
write*, is correct, as will appear by analyzing : " *I now write, this* is agreeable to,"
&c.; *agreeable* does not show the manner of writing, but qualifies the clause,
" *I now write*." Much care is necessary to avoid errors of this kind. The
true meaning of the sentence should be sought by a careful and rigid analysis.

Comparison of Adjectives.

10. The comparative degree generally refers to two objects distinct from
each other ; as, " the sun is brighter than the moon."

11. The superlative refers to objects belonging to the same class, some
times to two only, but more commonly to more than two; as, " Sirius is the
brightest of the fixed stars."

It would be incorrect to say, " Sirius is brighter than a fixed star," because it would imply that Sirius is not a fixed star. It should be compared
with a single object of the kind distinct from itself, thus ; " Sirius is brighter
than Arcturus," is correct.

It would also be incorrect to say, " Sirius is the brightest of the planets,"
because it would imply that Sirius is a planet.

It is incorrect to say, " Solomon was the wisest of the Roman kings," because he did not belong to that class of kings. But it is correct to say, " Solomon was wiser than any Roman king," for the reason already mentioned.

12. Comparative and superlative degrees are also incorrectly used in instances like the following : " He is of *all others*, the most insensible ;" it should
be, " he is the most insensible *of all* ;" " the vice of covetousness enters deepest
into the soul of man of any other ;" it should be, "*deeper than any other*." " The

---

✻ The question whether the numerals *two, three, four*, should stand before
the words *first* or *last*, or whether *first* or *last* should stand before the numerals,
does not appear to be settled by usage. There are good authorities on both
sides. Grammarians generally favor the use of *first* and *last*, before the nu
meral. When objects are spoken of in *pairs, triplets*, &c., it is manifestly
proper to place the numeral *last*.

weakest of the two ;" it should be, " the *weaker* of the two." " The *elder* of the three ; " it should be, " the *eldest* of the three."

13. The superlative, however, is admissible where two things are compared, if there is no ambiguity from such a use; as, " The *weakest* of the two, or the *weaker* of the two."

14. Double comparatives and superlatives should be avoided ; as, " A *more serener* temper;" "the *most straitest* sect."

15. In expressing a comparison, if both nouns relate to the *same* thing, the article should not be prefixed to the latter; if to different things it should not be omitted; as, " He is a much better general than statesman."

16. The word *such* is often improperly used for *so;* as, " He was *such* an extravagant person ;" it should be *so* extravagant.

Position of Adjectives.

17. Adjectives are usually placed before the nouns to which they belong; as, " A *generous* man."

18. The following are exceptions to this general rule:

ɪ. When the adjective is limited by some word or adjunct following it, it stands after its noun; as, " Food *convenient* for me." " A rule, a foot *long*."

ɪɪ. When the adjective expresses a title; as, " Alexander, the Great," it follows its noun.

ɪɪɪ. Sometimes several adjectives belonging to one noun are placed after it; as, " A prince *learned, wise,* and *brave*."

ɪᴠ. An adjective used emphatically to introduce a sentence is often separated from its noun by intervening words; as, "*Great* is the Lord."

ᴠ. When an adjective is preceded by an adverb, it generally follows its noun; as, " A man *truly wise*."

ᴠɪ. The definitive *all,* is often separated from its noun by *the;* as, "All the people." " All," sometimes stands after several nouns, to impart energy to the sentence; as, " Ambition, interest, honor, *all* concurred."

ᴠɪɪ. All adjectives are separated from their nouns by " a," when they are preceded by " *so*," or " *as;* " as, " *So* wise a man." " *As* good a man."

ANALYSIS AND PARSING.

The young blood of modern literature · has put new life into the literature of the dead languages.

All the features of a great heroic age, — from which European civilization dates, and political and domestic order takes its rise, stand forth in living reality.

> The encumbered oar scarce leaves the hostile coast,
> Through purple billows and a floating host.

None were banished except the thirty tyrants.

I have not seen him these ten years.

That sort of books was a valuable present.

These studies were the delight of his declining years.

To die for one's country is sweet and becoming. To restrain anger is excellent. To excel in knowledge is honorable. The flame burns bright and clear. Keen blows the wind, and piercing is the cold. A great many stars are visible in a clear night. A light shineth in the path of the upright.

SENTENCES TO BE CORRECTED.

A new barrel of flour. A clear spring of water. A green load of wood. A new pair of boots. I have received them books which you sent me. I can never think so mean of him. They wandered about solitarily and distressed. She reads proper, writes neat, and composes accurate. They lived conformable to the rules of prudence. He was such an extravagant man, that he soon wasted his property. I never saw such large trees. Such a bad temper is seldom found. A tree fifty foot high. Twenty ton of hay. Two shilling a pound.

'T is more easier to build two chimneys than to maintain one. The tongue is like a race horse, which runs the faster the lesser weight it carries. The nightingale sings; hers is the most sweetest voice in the grove. The Most Highest hath created us for his glory and our own happiness. The Supreme Being is the most wisest, the most powerfulest, and the most best of beings. Virtue confers the supremest dignity on man, and should be his chief desire. His assertion was more true than that of his opponent; nay, the words of the latter were most untrue. His work is perfect; his brother's more perfect; and his father's the most perfect of all. Eve was the fairest of all her daughters. Profane swearing is, of all other vices, the most inexcusable. A talent of this kind would, perhaps, prove the likeliest of any other to succeed. He spoke with so much propriety, that I understood him the best of all the others who spoke on the subject. Such distinguished virtues seldom occur.

SECTION LIV.

PRONOMINAL ADJECTIVES.*

RULE XVI.

450. Pronominal adjectives limit the nouns to which they belong, or are used alone as pronouns ; as, *This* day, *few* men, *both* men, *many* people, the *latter* day, *some* think, *few* come, &c.

REMARKS.

Each other. One another.

1. These are elliptical expressions and may be explained as follows :

" Righteousness and peace have kissed *each other* ; " that is, *each* has kissed the *other*.

" We ought to love *one another* ; " that is, *one* ought to love, &c.

" When ye come together to eat, tarry *one* for *another* ; " it might be, for one another.

" Exhort *one another* daily ; " let each exhort the other, &c.†

2. The adjectives *this* and *these* refer to what is near or present ; but the adjectives *that* and *those* refer to what is more remote or absent ; as, " *This* man," that is, the man who is present or near ; " *That* man," that is, the man who is at a distance or absent.

3. The adjectives *each*, *every*, *either*, require, in construction, the noun, pronoun or verb, to be in the singular number ; as, " *Every* tree is known by its fruit." This rule is often violated, as in the following examples : " Let each fulfil *their* part ; " it should be *his*.

" Every " is sometimes joined to a noun, preceded by a numeral adjective ; as, " Every *six months*." " Every *hundred years*." As the noun and the numeral are together merely a complex term expressing a definite period, such examples do not in reality make an exception to the rule.

4. Even when several nouns are connected as the common subjects of a verb, if each one is limited by *each* or *every*, expressed or understood, the verb must be singular ; as, " Every leaf, every twig, and every drop of water, teems with life."

5. The words *means*, *news*, *amends*, &c., formerly plural nouns, are now used in the singular number, and take adjectives agreeing with them in the

---

* This class of words, in nearly every instance where they are used alone, admit of having a noun supplied ; but as it would be obviously improper to supply a noun in some cases, it is better to treat them as pronouns when they are used alone.

† The expressions, *each other*, *one another*, are sometimes termed reciprocal nouns.

plural ; as, " *This* means," not *these* means. " *One* means or *a* means," not one *mean.*

6 The pronominal *both*, is often used in the place of two nouns, connected together, or of a plural noun comprising only two individuals, the subject or object in a sentence; as, " Abraham took sheep and oxen, and gave them to Abimelech, and *both* of them made a covenant."

" Both " is sometimes used in apposition with a pronoun to give emphasis to the expression ; as, " He forgave them *both*." " I will teach you *both*."

7. The pronominals *former* and *latter ;* also *the one* — and *the other*, may properly represent nouns or clauses in contrast, when they are near in construction and occasion no obscurity.*

8. *One* is sometimes used in the plural ; as, " The great *ones* of the world ;" " the little *ones.*" " One " used without a noun is often used indefinitely, signifying persons in general ; as, " *One* ought to pity the distresses of mankind."

9. *None* is used in both numbers ; as, " *None* is," or " *None* are." " *None* that go unto her return again."

10. *Either* is sometimes used for " each ;" as, " Two thieves were crucified — on *either* side one."

11. " Them " used for " these " or " those " is a vulgarism ; as, " *Them* books." " *Them* people." It should be, " *these* books," " *those* people."

ANALYSIS AND PARSING.

Pronominal Adjectives.

One day Alonzo made a discovery which startled him.

A great many people think that the Sabbath ends at sunset.

The boy hoped he had made some impression.

You know very well that such an expedition, with such companions, will not be keeping holy the Sabbath day.

Every feeling of gratitude is obliterated by one single interference with your wicked desires.

He soon learned, that it was one thing to see that his feelings were wrong, and another thing to feel right.

These omissions were more frequent than he imagined.

And the eyes of them both were opened.

Pronominal Adjectives used as Pronouns.

And he went after the man of Israel into the tent, and thrust both of them through.

---

* The injudicious use of *former* and *latter* and other substitutes are a great blemish in Campbell's Philosophy of Rhetoric. — *Webster.*

The same is equally true of the past.

In the evening he was occupied with some one of these enjoyments, and the next day he was planning another.

This he could not but strongly shrink from.

Let others serve whom they will ; as for me and my house, we will serve the Lord.

The dialogue between conscience and his heart was going on all the time ; the latter finally prevailed.

Many shall come in my name, saying, I am Christ, and shall deceive many.

Jubal was the father of such as dwell in tents.

I cannot go beyond the word of the Lord my God, to do less or more.

Let each fulfil his part.

TO BE CORRECTED.

These kind of indulgences. Those sort of favors. I have been waiting this two hours. Do you see those books lying on this table? These men that stand yonder are soldiers. That breeze is refreshing. Where are these books which you took from the desk? Both the sun, moon, and planets, turn on their axis. Do you see them people walking in the park?

Rule XVII.

451. The article *an* or *a*, is used before nouns in the singular number only, individually or collectively. *The* is used before nouns in both numbers; as, " A man; " " a thousand; " " the houses; " " the sea."

REMARKS.

1. Articles, when used, should be applied according to their signification, and as the sense requires. They are often properly omitted.

2. When the sense of words is sufficiently certain by the construction, the article may be omitted.

3. When the signification of the noun is general, and requires no limitation, the article is omitted; as, "Honor to whom honor is due." "Man is mortal."

4. When two or more nouns occur in the same construction, the article may be used with the first and omitted with the rest ; as, " There were many hours both of the night and day," or *the* day It is often used, however, in such instances for the sake of emphasis.

5. When two or more adjectives are used to express different qualities of the same object, the article may be used with the first, and omitted with the rest ; as, " A large and convenient dwelling," referring to a single dwelling. But if it is intended to express qualities of different objects, the article may be used before each ; as, " *A* large and *a* convenient dwelling," referring to two dwellings.

6. When the two nouns after a comparative refer to the same person or thing, the article should be omitted before the second ; as, " He is a better soldier than scholar." The use of the article before " scholar," would change the meaning entirely ; it then would mean, " He is a better soldier than a scholar is."

7. A nice distinction in the sense is sometimes made by the use or omission of the article before the words *little* and *few ;* as, " He has a little reverence." This means that he has reverence in a slight degree. " He has little reverence." This implies a doubt whether he has any.

8. *An* or *a* is sometimes used in the sense of *each* or *every ;* as, " Twice *a* day."

9. The article is often used to modify the meaning of an adjective ; as, " A *hundred* men ;" " a *large* number of men ;" " a *few* things."

10. " The " is used before *comparatives* and *superlatives ;* as, " *The* more — *the* better ;" " An estate, *the largest* in the city."

11. " The " is used before the antecedent of restrictive clauses ; as, " *The* sight *which we saw.*"

12. " An or a " sometimes occurs between the adjective " many," and a singular noun ; as, " Full many *a* gem ;" " many *a* youth."

TO BE CORRECTED.

Show how the articles are misapplied in the following sentences.

Reason was given to a man to control his passions. A man is the noblest work of creation. He is a much better writer than a reader. The king has conferred on him a title of a duke. Wisest and best men sometimes commit errors. At best his gift was but a poor offering. He has been censured for giving a little attention to his business.

REVIEW.

What is the rule for the agreement of adjectives ? What is an adjective ? Does the term adjective include the article ? Are adjectives ever separated from their nouns ? Give some examples. Can adjectives qualify *Infinitives,*

clauses or *sentences?* Give examples. In the expression, *that you are mistaken
is certain*, which is the adjective? To what does it belong? In the expression, *she looks pale*, which is the adjective? What does it appear to modify?
Give other examples of the same kind. Do adjectives modify other adjectives?
Give some examples. Show wherein the following expressions are incorrect.
*He was extreme prodigal; he writes neat; the stream flows rapid; the wind blows
violent.* Repeat the rule and notes for the *agreement* and *use* of the article. Is
there any difference in the following expressions? *Few people, a few people.*
What is the rule for pronominal adjectives? Explain the phrases *each other*,
and *one another*. What is the difference in use between the pronominals *this*
and *that?* What is said of *each, every, either?* What should be the number
of an adjective to agree with *means* or *news?* What is the rule for the agreement of the article *an* or *a?* of *the?* Mention some of the rules for the omission or the use of the articles.

SECTION LV.

VERBS.

THE INFINITIVE MODE.

RULE XVIII.

452. A verb in the Infinitive mode is generally used to
limit the meaning of a *verb, noun*, or *adjective*; as, "I
hope *to succeed;*" "a desire *to improve;*" "anxious *to
hear.*"

REMARKS.

A verb in the Infinitive may also limit the meaning of

1. *As* or *than;* as "He is so conceited as to *disdain* to have any thing to do
with books;" "he desired nothing more *than to know* his imperfections."*

2. *Adverbs;* as "The rope is strong *enough to suspend* a ton;" "I know not
how to address you."

3. *Prepositions;* as, "What went ye out *for to see;*"† "my friend is about
to take his departure."

4. The *Infinitive* is also used independently; as, "*To say the least* he has
erred in judgment;" "but *to proceed* with our argument."

---

* The Infinite after *as* or *than*, more properly limits a verb understood; as,
"He desired nothing more than he *desired* to know," &c.

† This form of expression is now obsolete; it occurs in the Scriptures and
in ancient writings.

5. When the Infinitive denotes *purpose* or *design*, it is frequently preceded by the phrase *in order*, but this phrase is often omitted.

6. The phrase *to be sure* is often used adverbially, in the sense of *surely*, or *certainly.*

SPECIAL RULE.

453. The Infinitive mode has sometimes a subject in the objective case; as, " I believe *the sun* to be the centre of the solar system;" " I know *him* to be a man of veracity." ·

REMARKS.

1. This form of expression, far less common in our language than in the Latin and Greek, is equivalent to a subordinate clause introduced by *that;* " I believe *him* to be dishonest," that is, I believe *that* he is dishonest.

2. The Infinitive with its subject is sometimes introduced by *for;* as, "*For* him to die was gain." In such expressions the infinitive and the words connected with it, form the subject of the verb in the sentence, " For him to die " is the subject of *was.*

NOTE. — The use of the Infinitive as the *subject, object,* and *predicate nominative* has been explained under the Rules relating to these subjects. For the nature and properties of the Infinitive, see Sec. xxi, 255, 256.

ANALYSIS AND PARSING.

He was willing to risk all, for the excitement of a new revolution.

He delivered his brother Alfonzo into their hands, to be recognized as the lawful heir of the crown.

Not far from the city of Avila, they caused a scaffold to be erected, of sufficient elevation to be easily seen from the surrounding country.

A manifesto was then read, exhibiting in glowing colors the tyrannical conduct of the king, and the consequent determination to depose him.

It would be an unprofitable task to attempt to unravel all the fine-spun intrigues, by which the Marquis Villena contrived to defeat every attempt at an ultimate accommodation.

The abject mind of Henry was content to purchase repose, even by the most humiliating sacrifice.

Be not so greedy of popular applause, as to forget that the same breath which blows up a fire may blow it out again.

I understand him better, than to suppose he will relinquish his design.

RULE XIX:

454. The verbs which follow *bid, dare, durst, hear, feel, let, make, need, see,* and their participles, are used in the Infinitive without the sign *to ;* as " He bid me go."

NOTE. — The verbs *watch, behold, know, observe, have, command, find,* and some others, are occasionally followed by the infinitive without the sign *to.*

ANALYSIS AND PARSING.

The name of Henry makes them leave me desolate.

My followers' base and ignominious treasons make me betake to my heels.

Dare any man be so bold to sound retreat or parley, when I command them kill ? — *Shakspeare.*

Hark ! I hear the herald angels say.

And the multitude wondered when they saw the lame walk and the blind see.

He had dared to think for himself . — *Coleridge.*

The haughty priests of learning banished from the schools all who had dared draw water from the living fountain. — *Coleridge.*

I found my friend express much satisfaction for the bargains he had made. — *Steele.*

TO BE CORRECTED.

You ought not walk too hastily. I need not to solicit him to do a kind action. I have seen some very young persons to conduct themselves very indiscreetly. And the multitude wondered when they saw the lame to walk, and the blind to see.

---

* The sign *to* is retained after these verbs when used in the passive form. The sign is also sometimes retained after *make* and *dare.*

PARTICIPLES.

RULE XX.

455. Participles belong to nouns or pronouns, which they limit or explain.

Present and compound participles govern the same case as the verbs from which they are derived.

REMARKS.

1. The participle is often used as a noun, either with or without an article; but when so used the present or compound participle of a transitive verb performs the office of a verb and a noun at the same time; as, "In return for your *inviting me*."

2. When preceded by the article, the present participle, in most cases, must be followed by "of;" as, "The gaining *of* wisdom;" "The supplying *of* our wants." Expressions like the following are incorrect: "*The preaching* repentance;" "*The writing* an essay." "Of" should be used after "preaching," &c.*

3. The reverse of this rule should also be observed, namely; that the "of" should not be employed after the participle, when it is not preceded by the article; as, "By preaching of repentance." It should be, "by the preaching of repentance," or, "by preaching repentance." In general, both the article and the preposition should be used, or both should be omitted, except where the ellipsis of the preposition is obvious, or where another construction is required by the sense; as, "The *advising* or *attempting* to procure an insurrection." In this sentence the infinitive is used after the participial noun.

4. Present and compound participles often perform the office of a verb and noun at the same time; as, "He was displeased with the king's *having bestowed* the office upon a worthless man." In this sentence, the compound participle is used as a noun and governs "king's." It also, in the office of a verb, governs the noun "office," in the objective case.

5. Participles often belong to a clause or a part of a sentence; as, "*Owing* to the bad state of the roads, he was detained a day beyond the time of his appointment." In this sentence, "owing" agrees with the whole sentence, "he was," &c. The words *concerning, according, respecting, touching,* &c., are generally considered prepositions. They are, however, derived from verbs, and in most instances refer to some statement in the sentence.

6. Participles are sometimes used indefinitely, without reference to any

---

* This rule is often violated by our best writers, and to make it universal is to assume an authority much too dictatorial. The expression, "The making a will," is perfectly good English. — *Webster*.

noun or pronoun expressed; as, "It is not possible to act otherwise, *consider ing* the weakness of our nature." " *Generally speaking*, his conduct was very honorable."

For other uses of the participle, see Sec. XXIV.

7. Adjectives derived from verbs, and having the form of participles, are called *verbal* or *participial* adjectives.

ANALYSIS AND PARSING.

And they, continuing daily with one accord in the temple, and breaking bread from house to house, did eat their meat with gladness and singleness of heart, praising God, and having favor with all the people.

He has left town for Ireland without taking leave of either of us.

Having a little time upon my hands, I could not think of bestowing it better than in writing an epistle to the Spectator.

I cannot forbear troubling you with a letter upon that subject.

We considered man as belonging to societies; societies as formed of different ranks; and different ranks distinguished by habits.

Having been very well entertained by your specimen of clubs, I shall take the liberty to furnish you with a brief account of such a one as you have not seen.

TO BE CORRECTED.

By observing of truth. By the observing truth. By the sending proper information. Without the taking pains. Without taking of pains. The changing times and seasons, the removing and setting up kings, belong to Providence alone. Poverty turns one's thoughts too much upon the supplying one's wants. In tracing of his history, we discover little that is worthy of imitation.

SECTION LVI.

MODES. TENSES.

456. In the use of   regard
should be paid to their

1. The indicative mode must be used after conjunctions which are positive and unconditional in their nature; as, "He is esteemed, *because* he is generous."

2. The subjunctive mode is used after conjunctions which imply doubt, contingency or condition; as, "If he is expert in business, he will find employment." "Suppose we admit this fact."

3. In general, the form of the verb in the subjunctive, is the same as that of the indicative; but an elliptical form in the second and third person singular, should be used in the following instances:

4. *Future contingency* is expressed by the omission of the indicative termination; as, "If he go," for "if he *shall* go." "Though he slay me," i. e. "though he *should* slay me." "If thou injure another, thou wilt hurt thyself."

5. *Lest* and *that* annexed to a command, are followed by the elliptical form of the subjunctive; as, "Love not sleep lest thou come to poverty."

6. *If*, with *but* following it, when futurity is denoted, requires the elliptical form; as, "If he *do* but *touch* the hills they shall smoke."

7. But when future contingency is not denoted by the subjunctive clause, the indicative form is used; as, "If she *is* but sincere I am happy."

TO BE CORRECTED.

If he acquires riches, they will corrupt his mind, and be useless to others.   Though he urges me yet more earnestly, I shall not comply, unless he advances more forcible reasons.   I shall walk in the fields to-day, unless it rains.   As the governess were present, the children behaved properly.   Despise not any condition, lest it happens to be your own.   Let him that is sanguine take heed lest he miscarries.   Take care that thou breakest not any of the established rules.   If he does but intimate his desire, it will be sufficient to produce obedience. At the time of his return, if he is but expert in the business, he will find employment. If he do but speak to display his abilities, he is unworthy of attention. If he be but in health, I am content. If thou have promised, be faithful to thy engagement. Though he have proved his right to submission, he is too generous to exact it. Unless he have improved, he is unfit for the office. If thou had succeeded, perhaps thou would not be the happier for it. Though thou did injure him, he harbors no resentment. Was he ever so great and opulent. this conduct would debase him. Was I to enumerate all her virtues, it would look like flattery. Though I was perfect, yet I would not presume. Unless thou can fairly support the cause, give it up honorably. Though thou might have foreseen the danger, thou could not have avoided it.

TENSES.

No very definite rules can be given for the proper use of the tenses in all cases, except such as are found in the definitions already given in Part III. The best rule, which is a very general one, is, to observe strictly what forms of the verb the sense requires.

It may be useful, however, to give a few examples of the manner in which the tenses are improperly employed.

Errors in Forms.

I *come* is very improperly used for I *came*.
I *done* is very improperly used for I *did*.
I *begun* is very improperly used for I *began*.

Done and *begun* are perfect participles, which are improperly used for the imperfect tense.

The river *has froze* over; it should be *has frozen*.
The school *has began*; it should be *has begun*.
The horse was *drove hard*; it should be *was driven*.
The thief *has stole* my watch; it should be *has stolen*.

Froze, began, drove, stole, are forms of the imperfect tense, which are improperly used for the perfect participles, *frozen, begun, driven,* &c.

The expressions "had rather," and "had better," though anomalous, are well authorized. But "had ought," or "had not ought," commonly contracted into "had n't ought," is a gross vulgarism. *Ought* is a defective verb ~d only in the present and imperfect tenses.

Sit, set, lie, lay.

The verbs *sit* and *lie* are often confounded with *set* and *lay*.

The verb *to sit*, signifies "to repose on a seat." Its principal parts are, PRES. sit; IMPER sat; PERF. PART. sat.

The verb *to set*, when transitive, signifies "to place." The principal parts are, PRES. set; IMP. set; PERF. PART. set. This verb is also used intransitively; as, "The sun sets." "The moon has set."

The verb *to lie* signifies "to repose," "to lie down." Its principal parts are, PRES. lie; IMP. lay; PERF. PART. lain. There is also a regular verb *lie*, which signifies to utter a falsehood.

The verb *to lay*, signifies "to place." Its principal parts are, PRES. lay; IMP. laid; PERF. PART. laid.

Errors in Connection.

INCORRECT.	CORRECTED.
I should be glad if he *will* write.	*Would* write.
I *have* completed the task two days ago.	I *completed.*
They *have* resided in Italy till two months ago.	They *resided.*
His style *has formerly been* admired.	*Was formerly admired.*
Next new year's day, I *shall be* at school six months.	I *shall have been.*
After we *visited* London we returned, content and thankful, to our retired habitation.	After *we had visited* London, &c.

TENSES OF THE INFINITIVE MODE.

457 As a verb in the infinitive mode is strictly nothing more than a verbal noun, that is, the name of some action, it will be easy to determine which tense of the infinitive should be employed, by inquiring whether the action expressed by the infinitive refers to past. present, or future time ; for example :

"I intended to write ;" i. e. I intended writing; not, I intended *to have written*, or, having written, for this expression would refer the act to a time before there was an *intention* to act.

"I hoped to see you ; " not *to have seen* you.

"I commanded him *to do* it ; " not, *to have done* it, i. e. *the doing* would not be before the command. Hence, in regard to verbs of this class the following rule may be observed for the use of the infinitive.

SPECIAL RULE.

458. After verbs signifying *to hope, to intend, to desire, to*

command, and the like, the present tense of the infinitive should be used; as, " I hoped *to see* you." " I desired *to hear* from my friend."

After verbs of other significations, a strict regard should be paid to the time of the action denoted by the infinitive, compared with the tense or time of the verb on which it depends.

TO BE CORRECTED.

Let the reason be given for the correction made in each instance.

They laid down to rest. A beggar was setting by the wayside. A stone was laying in the street. The tree has laid there several days. Let us set down. It is injurious to health to set up late nights. He set up, and began to speak. Sin layeth at the door.

It will give our parents much pain *to have heard* of your misconduct. They desired *to have seen* you respected and esteemed, but alas! their hopes *have been* unexpectedly cut off. They intended *to have devoted* you to the service of your country and mankind; but when the sad intelligence *reaches* them, how *would* they sink under the burden of their disappointment, and how will they weep bitter tears, when they *have reflected* upon the happiness they *have anticipated,* from your advancement to an honorable condition in life. I expected *to have seen* them before the news *should have reached* them, but urgent duties *will have prevented.*

Section LVII.

ADVERBS.

Rule XXII.

459. Adverbs generally modify *verbs, participles, adjectives,* and *other adverbs.*

REMARKS.

1. Adverbs should generally be placed before adjectives, after verbs in the simple form, and frequently between the auxiliary and the verb; as, " He is very anxious;" " He spoke *kindly*;" " He is *busily* employed."

This rule is too genera. to be of much service, since the exceptions to it are very numerous. The good sensé and taste of the writer are generally the safest guide in the appropriate use of this class of words. In the following example, the position of the adverb depends upon the sense intended; " We *always* find them ready ; " " We find them *always* ready."

The position of the adverb is right in both instances; but the meaning conveyed is different. From the first it is not certain that they are *always* ready, as it is asserted in the second expression, but that we *always* find them so.

2. Adverbs are sometimes used for adjectives ; as, " The *then* ministry ; " " The *above* discourse ; " * " *To-morrow* morning ; " " The men *only*."

NOTE. — When " only " refers to a noun, it should be placed near it, to avoid ambiguity.

3. Adverbs are sometimes used as nouns ; as, " Until *now ;* " " Yet a little *while*."

4. *From* is sometimes *unnecessarily* used before *whence, thence, hence;* as " *From* whence art thou ? " for " *whence*," &c.

5. The adverb *there* often stands at the beginning of a sentence, without particular reference to any other word ; as, " *There* are many who believe," &c.

6. The word modified by the adverb is sometimes omitted; as, " I 'll *hence* to London."

7. Two negatives in the same clause are equivalent to an affirmative; as, " *Nor* did they *not* perceive," that is, *they did perceive*.

8. An adverb sometimes modifies the word *a*, used in the sense of *one ;* as, "Almost *a* year ; " " not *a* dollar."

9. The word *but* in the sense of *only* is used as an adverb ; as, "All are *but* parts of one stupendous whole ; " "I have *but* one request to make."

10. *As* in the sense of *so*, is an adverb ; " *As* well ; *as* much."

11. The adverb *now* frequently stands at the beginning of paragraphs, in argumentative and familiar discourse, as a *general connective*, without modifying any particular word ; as, " *Now*, it is evident," &c.

12. A preposition with its object is sometimes equivalent to an adverb ; as, ' *In truth*," for truly, &c.

13. Adverbs are not unfrequently absolute ; that is, they qualify no particular word, but usually refer to the whole preceding sentence; as, " *Yes, no, therefore, then, however*," &c., and not unfrequently they are expletives, that is, qualify nothing ; as, " *Why, well, there*," &c.

14. Adverbs sometimes modify *prepositions, adjuncts, phrases,* and *entire clauses ;* as, " *Just* below the surface ; *nearly* round the world ; I hear *almost* in vain ; *independently* of these considerations."

---

* Such expressions, though not destitute of authority, are exceedingly inelegant and irreconcilable with authority. — *Crombie.*

15. The adverbs *here*, *there*, and *where*, are frequently used in the sense of *hither*, *thither*, *whither*.

SENTENCES TO BE ANALYZED AND PARSED.

There,* there.* now we have had enough for one lecture.

Well,* sir, said I, how did you like little Miss? I hope she was fine enough.

Alas! madam, said he one day, how few books are there, of which one ever can possibly arrive at the last page. — *Johnson.*

Well, he brought him home, and reared him at the then Lord Valdez's cost. — *Coleridge.*

The wall tottered, and had well-nigh fallen right on their heads. — *Id.*

And not a † vanity is given in vain.

The women and children only were saved from the conflagration.

Little children, yet a little while I am with you.

Stoop down, my thoughts that used to rise,
Converse a while with death.

He then, having received the sop, went immediately out.

SECTON LVIII.

PREPOSITIONS.

RULE XXIII.

460. Prepositions connect words and show the relation between them. The object of a preposition must be in the objective case. See 123.

REMARKS.

1. *But*, in the sense of except, appears sometimes to be used as a preposition; as, "All but *one*."

---

* These adverbs are used independently.

† Not modifies *a*, which is used in the sense of *one*.

2. *Than* is sometimes followed by the objectives *whom* and *which;* as, " Al fred, *than whom*," &c. " Beelzebub, *than whom*," &c.

3. The article *a* is in a few instances employed in the sense of a preposition, as, " Simon Peter said, I go *a* [to] fishing." It is also used for *at.*

4. Two or more words combined, are sometimes treated as a compound preposition; as, *According to, in respect to, in regard to, from above, from below, as to, as for, over against, instead of, out of, &c.*

5. The words *allowing, considering, concerning, during, respecting, supposing, notwithstanding, excepting, past,* are sometimes termed *verbal prepositions,* * and also *save* and *except.*

6. In poetry the preposition is sometimes placed after its object; as, " The woods among." And in familiar style sometimes also it stands after its object, as " *What* is he aiming *at !* "

7. Two prepositions, each in a different clause, sometimes have reference to the same noun ; as, "I am interested in, and labor for, the promotion of human happiness." Expressions of this kind are very common, but cannot be considered elegant. A better form can be easily substituted; as, "I am interested in the promotion of human happiness, and labor to promote it."

8. The following are correct examples of the use of prepositions :

Abandoned to — abhorrence of — abound in — absent from — abstain from — beguile of —

Careful of — careless about — careless of — differ from — discourage from — encouragement to —

Familiar with — interfere with — influence on — impatient at — inspection into — partiality to

Prejudice against — provide for — suitable to — participate in — conscious of — correspond to — correspond with —

Derogate from — derogation to — contiguous to — bereave of — difficulty in — differ with —

Disappointed of — discouragement to — expert in — influence over — influence with — connect with —

Impatient for — inspection over — partiality for — provide with — provide against — suitable for — peculiar to —

REVIEW.

Repeat the general rule for adverbs. With what parts of speech can adverbs be connected? What is the use of adverbs? Do they govern cases? Do they connect clauses? Do adverbs ever modify prepositions? Nouns?

---

* Some grammarians prefer to treat this class of words as participles, under all circumstances, agreeing with the whole sentence, or some word understood ; and *save* and *except* as verbs in the imperative mode.

Articles? What adverbs are sometimes used independently? Rule for prepositions? Remarks. In what sense is *but* used as a preposition? As an adverb? Is *but* ever an adjective? A conjunction? What participles and verbs are sometimes considered as prepositions? Can they be parsed otherwise than as prepositions?

461. Prepositions are not unfrequently united with other words, forming a compound expression, equivalent in meaning to a single word; as, "I *looked on* Virgil as a majestic writer."

Looked on is a compound *transitive* verb, equivalent in meaning to "regarded," or "considered." It has, like other transitive verbs, a *passive* form; as, "Virgil *was looked on*," &c.

REMARKS.

1. Prepositions are sometimes connected with certain verbal adjectives, forming what may be termed *compound adjectives.* The event was *unlooked for:* the measure was *uncalled for:* he lived neglected and *uncared for.*

2. Prepositions are often inseparably united with nouns, adjectives, verbs adverbs, and with other prepositions; as, "Afternoon, imprudent, to-day, to-morrow."

EXERCISE.

Analyze the sentences and parse the compound verbs.

We must *look out for* words as beautiful as can be found. — *Felton.*

Words must *be looked out for* as beautiful as can be found.

Politeness of manners, and knowledge of the world, should principally be *looked after* in a tutor. — *Locke.*

NOTE. — Some intransitive verbs admit of a passive form, which includes the preposition that followed the verb in the active form; as,

He *referred to* the civil war in his remarks. [Active form.]

The civil war *was referred to* in his remarks. [Passive form.]

He sincerely *repented of* his sins. [Active form.]

His sins *were* sincerely *repented of.* [Passive form.]

He *disposed of* his property. [Active.]

His property *was disposed of.* [Passive.]

Section LIX.

CONJUNCTIONS.

462. Conjunctions connect words, phrases, adjuncts, or sentences; as, " He reads *or* writes." " To do wrong *and* to suffer wrong." " In the morning *and* in the evening." " I sought the Lord *and* he heard me."

Note.— The list of the principal conjunctions may be found in Part II. Their general use has been already illustrated in the analysis of compound sentences.

REMARKS.

1. Conjunctions unite the words, or phrases, which form the compound subjects of a preposition; also two or more objects of a transitive verb or a preposition. Words united in such relations must, therefore, be in the same case. It would be improper to say, " He and me are brothers;" because " me " cannot be a part of the compound subject. " You *as well as him* are accountable." "You" and "him" are in different cases, and still both are intended to be the subjects of the same verb. It should be, " You as well as he."

2. The rule given by Murray and copied by many others, "that conjunctions must connect similar modes and tenses of verbs," is erroneous, as may be seen from a few examples. " He neither receives nor can give delight."— *Johnson.* "There *may be* and usually *is* an ellipsis of the verb."— *Webster.* " For thou *wast* slain and *hast* redeemed us."— *Rev. V.* " So that neither angel, man, nor world, *could* stand, or *can* stand."

3. Writers have sometimes fallen into errors by observing this rule too strictly. " If I *should ask* any one whether ice and water *were* two distinct species of things." " Were " is in the *imperfect subjunctive*, to correspond with *should ask*, in the first clause. But the inquiry is not intended to be whether "ice and water were," but " whether they *are*," &c. The *present tense* is used in expressing facts " which exist at all times," or " general truths." " The alchemists supposed that bodies *wére* composed of salt, sulphur and mercury." It should be *are composed.* "They said that man was an animal." It should be, *is an animal.*

4. After *than*, there is usually an ellipsis of some word or adjunct necessary to a complete sentence; as, "He that cometh after me is mightier *than* I;" that is, than I *am.* " He loves his money more than his honor;" that is, more than *he loves* his honor. Sometimes this conjunction appears to assume the office of a preposition, and to govern an objective case. This use was mentioned under prepositions. See 460.

5. There is often an ellipsis of some word, phrase, or clause after the conjunctions, *yet, though, if,* and *as;* as, "False flew the shaft, *though* pointed well;" that is, though *it was* pointed, &c. " He was treated *as a son.*"

16*

6. The word *as*, has various offices and uses.

I. "As," is used as an adverb in the sense of *equally*; as, "*As* good." "*As* great." "*As* well." In such instances it usually corresponds with another *as*, in the same clause; as, "I have seen it as well *as* you."

II. "As," is used as a connective, — 1, to unite clauses or words expressing comparison, equality, or contrast; as, "I believe it is *as* you represent." — 2, to connect words in apposition; as, "The government sent him *as* commissioner."— 3, to join adjectives or participles to the words which they modify; as, "I regard him as ruined and lost beyond recovery." *As* appears to be used as a relative pronoun in the nominative or objective case; as, "Give me such information *as* you possess." "The books are such *as* will please him." In the first instance "as," is the *object* of "possess." In the second, it is the subject of "will please." In such instances, however, *that which*, or *those which*, can generally be supplied, and "as" may be treated as a conjunction. Some prefer this method of analyzing sentences of this kind. "As" is sometimes combined with prepositions; as, "As to." "As for." In this as in some other use it is difficult to explain the office of this word.

7. "As," is also sometimes combined with the conjunctions *if, though*, and likewise with *what*; as, "*As if*," "*as though*," "*what if*," "*what though*."

8. After expressions which denote *doubt, fear*, or *denial*, the conjunction *that* should be employed; as, "I do not doubt *that* he is honest." It is a very common fault to use *lest*, or *but that*, instead of *that* in such a connection, as, "I do not doubt *but that* he will succeed." "I fear *lest* he will not recover."

9. The connection of words, phrases or clauses, is sometimes rendered more emphatic by employing two or more connectives, which are usually separated by some intervening word or phrase; as, "*Both* you *and* I." "Socrates was wise, *and* Plato was *also* wise." He was *not only* forgiven, *but* he was *even* rewarded."

10. The word *both* is used as a *conjunction*, adjective, or pronoun, and should be always employed to refer to only two persons, things or statements. The sentence, "Both *men, women* and *children* ran out to meet him," is faulty, because "both" is used to refer to *three* different objects.

11. *That* is used in the office of a *conjunction, relative pronoun*, or *adjective*; as, "I learn *that* he is better." "It is the same man *that* I met yesterday." "*That* man is not worthy of regard."

CORRESPONDING CONJUNCTIONS.

463. Some conjunctions and adverbs must be followed by certain corresponding conjunctions. In composing they should follow each other in the order given in the list below.

1. *Conjunctions corresponding with Conjunctions.*

Either — or; as, "I will *either* send it *or* bring it."
Neither — nor; as, "He will *neither* listen *nor* obey."

Though, although — yet, still, nevertheless; as, " *Though* he slay me, *yet* wil. I trust in him."

Whether — or ; as, " *Whether* he will go, *or* not, is uncertain."

2. *Conjunctions corresponding with Adverbs.*

As — as; (expressing equality) as, " She is *as* amiable *as* her sister."

As — so; (expressing equality) as, " *As* the stars, *so* shall thy seed be."

So — as; as, " He is not *so* wise *as* he thinks himself to be." " Live *so as* to be happy." " Pompey was not *so* great a man *as* Cæsar."

So — that; (expressing a consequence) as, " He was *so* fatigued, *that* he could scarcely move."

Not only — but also; as, " He was *not only* rich, *but also* generous."

3. *Conjunctions corresponding with Adjectives.*

Such — as: as, " We have seldom had *such* a season *as* the present."

Such — that: as, " *Such* is the difficulty attending the enterprise, *that* I am compelled to relinquish it."

The conjunction *than* is used after the adverb *rather,* and after adjectives and adverbs in the comparative degree.

The expressions, *The more — the more, The better — the better, The less — the less,* &c., may be considered as *correlatives,* serving the purpose of uniting the clauses of a compound sentence in an emphatic manner.

There are some abridged expressions, which it is convenient to call *compound connectives:* such as, *As well as, inasmuch as, in order that, but that,* &c. ; these, however, can generally be analyzed intelligibly, and each may be parsed separately, by supplying such words as the sense will allow.

ANALYSIS AND PARSING.

All this is done, *and* all this expenditure is incurred.

In order to produce it now, we diminish the productiveness of all other labor. *And* the only effect is to postpone it to a still more distant period.

Here are two distinct sentences, the general train of thought being connected by *and,* standing at the beginning of the *second,* after the period.

Different men are constituted by the Creator with different aptitudes for different pursuits, *and* with different dispositions towards those pursuits.

A great public *as well as* private advantage, arises from every one's devoting himself to that occupation which he prefers, and for which he is specially fitted.

It is also evident *that,* by each nation's devoting itself to that branch of production for which it has the greatest facilities, either original or acquired, its own happiness will be better promoted, and a greater amount of production created, *than* in any other manner.

This compound sentence consists of four members or clauses. " That " connects the clause, " it is also evident," &c., with the clause, " its own hap piness will be promoted ;" of which the phrase, " by each," &c., is an adjunct; " and " connects the clause following it with the one before ; " than " connects " will be created," and " will be promoted," understood, to the same words ex pressed ; " for which," &c., is a *relative* clause, and refers to " production." " Either "   " or," are corresponding conjunctions, and connect " original " and " acquired."

TO BE CORRECTED.

There is no man so miserable, who does not enjoy something. *Neither* he or *I* am able to do it. I know not ·*if* it was James *or* his brother that performed the work. He asked me *if* I would call and see his brother; it should be *whether.* I asked him *if* he knew me. The judge asked the foreman if the prisoner was guilty or not guilty.

I have travelled both in Europe, in France, and in America.

SECTION LX.

INTERJECTIONS.

RULE XXV.

464. Interjections have no governing power, and have no dependence on other words.

REMARKS.

1. Interjections often stand before nouns independent, and before whole clauses ; as, " O virtue ! "   " O for a lodge in some vast wilderness ! "   Some words must be supplied before such clauses, to complete the sentence ; as, " O how I long for a lodge," &c.
2. " Ah me ! " " Ah sinful nation ! " " They have forsaken the Lord !" " Oh me !"   Such expressions may be considered elliptical, and words can be supplied to make a complete sentence ; as, " Ah *pity* me," " Ah *this* is a sinful

nation," " Oh *save* me ;" or they may be treated as the case independent, which is not necessarily confined to the nominative form.

3. Certain verbs are used in exclamations; as, " Behold ! how good and how pleasant it is for brethren to dwell together in unity ! " So in like man ner, " Hush ! " " Hark ! " " See ! "

4. The word *what* is sometimes used to denote *surprise* or *wonder :* as, " What ! could ye not watch with me one hour ?" The phrase, " *What ho !* " may be parsed also as an interjection.

NOTE. — It is not necessary to consider the verbs mentioned above and the pronoun *what* as interjections ; for in all such broken expressions, governing words can be supplied; as, What ! [say you ?] or what [does this mean ?] Hark ! [ye.] See ! [thou.]

SECTION LXI.

GENERAL EXERCISES ON THE RULES OF SYNTAX.

EXERCISE I.

Instances in which the same words are used in different offices, or as different parts of speech.

Calm was the day, and the scene delightful. We may expect a *calm* after a storm: To prevent passion is easier than *to calm* it.

Better is a *little*, with content, than a great deal, with anxiety. The gay and dissolute think *little* of the miseries which are stealing softly after them. A *little* attention will rectify some errors.

Though he is out of danger, he is *still* afraid. He labored to *still* the tumult. *Still* waters are commonly the deepest.

Damp air is unwholesome. Guilt often casts a *damp* over our sprightliest hours. Soft bodies *damp* the sound much more than hard ones.

Though she is rich and fair, *yet* she is not amiable. They are *yet* young, and must suspend their judgment *yet* a while.

Many persons are better than we suppose them to be. The *few* and the *many* have their prepossessions. *Few* days pass without some clouds.

The *hail* was very destructive. *Hail !* virtue ! thou source of every good. We *hail* you as friends.

Have you seen the book *that* I purchased yesterday? Give me *that* book. I study *that* I may improve.

A new broom *sweeps* better than an old one. The boatman labored at the *sweeps* all day.

We had been to the *fair*, and seen a *fair* lady. His lot is hard but *fair*.

Much money is corrupting. Think *much* and speak little. He has seen *much* of the world, and been *much* caressed.

His years are *more* than hers; but he has not *more* knowledge. The *more* we are blessed, the *more* grateful we should be. The desire of getting *more* is rarely satisfied.

He has *equal* knowledge, but *inferior* judgment. She is his *inferior* in sense, but his *equal* in prudence.

Every being loves its *like*. We must make a *like* space between the lines. Behave yourselves *like* men. We are too apt to *like* pernicious company. He may go or stay as he *likes*.

They strive *to* learn. He goes *to* and fro. *To* his wisdom we owe our privilege. The proportion is ten *to* one.

He has served them with his *utmost* ability. When we do our *utmost*, no more is required.

He is esteemed *both* on his own account, and on that of his parents. *Both* of them deserve praise.

Yesterday was a fine day. I rode out *yesterday*. I shall write *to-morrow*. *To-morrow* may be brighter than *to-day*. We shall arrive *to-day*.

You must *either* go or stay, and you may do *either*, as you please.

Behold! how pleasant it is to see the sun. I *behold* men as trees, walking.

EXERCISE II.

A collection of idiomatic or peculiar expressions, difficult to analyze and parse, taken from writers of standard authority.

As.	As if.	So as.

In singing *as* in piping you excel. — *Dryden.*

I live *as* I did, I think *as* I did, I love you *as* I did. — *Swift.*

Mad *as* I was, I could not bear his fate with silent grief. — *Dryden.*

Darest thou be *as* good *as* thy word now ? — *Shakspeare.*

As thou art a prince I fear thêe. — *Id.*

The objections that are caused against it *as* a tragedy, are as follow.

> The noise pursues me wheresoe'er I go,
> *As* fate sought only me. — *Dryden.*

At either end it whistled *as* it flew. — *Id.*

He answered their questions *as if* it were a matter that needed it. — *Locke.*

Each man's mind has some peculiarity *as well as* his face. — *Id.*

These should be gently treated, *as though* we expected to be in their condition. — *Sharp.*

Sempronius is *as* brave a man *as* Cato.

As for the rest of those who have written against me, they deserve not the least notice. — *Dryden.*

Is it not every man's interest, that there should be *such* a government of the world *as* designs our happiness ? — *Tillotson.*

A bottle swinging at each side, *as* hath been said or sung. — *Cowper.*

They pretend, in general, to great refinements, *as to* what regards christianity. — *Addison.*

What.   Whatever.   Whatsoever.

In these cases we examine the why, the *what*, and the how of things.

Let them say *what* they will, she will do *what* she lists. — *Drayton.*

Mark *what* it is, his mind aims at in this question, and not *what* words he expresses. — *Locke.*

What ! canst not thou bear with me half an hour ? — *Sharp.*

What if I advance an invention of my own to supply the defect of our new writers ? — *Dryden.*

What though none live my innocence to tell ?

Theu balmy sleep had charmed my eye to rest

What time the morn mysterious visions brings. — *Pope.*

The enemy having his country wasted, *what* by himself and *what* by the soldiers, findeth succor in no places. — *Spenser.*

Whatever is read, differs from what is repeated. — *Swift.*

Whatsoever is first in the invention, is last in the execution. — *Hammond.*

What ho! thou genius of the clime, *what ho!* — *Dryden.*

Himself.   Itself.   So, &c.

He *himself* returned again.   David hid *himself* in the field.

With shame he remembers while *himself* was one of the same herd, *himself* the same had done. — *Denham.*

I viewed in my mind, *so* far as I was able, the beginning and progress of a rising world.

We think our fathers fools, *so* wise we 're grown,

Our wiser sons no doubt will think us *so.*

Deliver us from the nauseous repetition of As and So, which some *so so* writers, I may call them *so,* are continually sounding in our ears. — *Felton.*

O, *so,* and had you a counsel of ladies too ?

When.   While.   Then.

Kings may take their advantage when and how they list.

I was adopted heir by his consent,

Since *when* his oath is broke. — *Shakspeare.*

Pausing *a while* thus to herself she mused. — *Milton.*

One *while* we thought him innocent. — *Ben Jonson.*

Use your memory ; you will sensibly experience a gradual improvement, *while* you take care not to overload it.

The *then* bishop of London, Dr. Laud, attended on his majesty throughout that whole journey. — *Clarendon.*

Thee *then* a boy within my arms I laid. — *Dryden.*

Till *then* who knew the force of those dire dreams?— *Milton.*

That.   Both.

He wins me by *that* means I told you. — *Shakspeare.*

What is *that* to us ? See thou to *that.* — *Matthew.*

I 'll know your business, *that* I will. — *Shakspeare.*

    Treat it kindly *that* it may

    Wish at least with us to stay. — *Cowley.*

O *that* those lips had language ! — *Cowper.*

And the next day, *both** morning and afternoon, he was kept by our party.

Each other.   One another.

Loveliest of women ! heaven is in thy soul, beauty and virtue shine forever about thee, bright'ning *each other.* Thou art all divine. — *Addison.*

The storm beats the trees against *one another.* — *Johnson.*

This is the message that ye heard from the beginning, that we should love *one another.* — *John.*

Beloved, let us love *one another.* — *Id.*

Save.   But.†

    All the conspirators *save* only he,

    Did that they did in envy of great Cæsar. — *Shakspeare.*

    Night shades the groves, and all in silence lie,

    All *save* the mournful Philomel and I. — *Young.*

He that is washed needeth not, *save* to wash his feet.

And all desisted, all *save* him alone. — *Wadsworth.*

Who can it be, ye perjured Gods, *but* Lycon ?

    For who *but* he who arched the skies,

    Could raise the daisy's purple bud ?

---

* *Both* in this sentence would be considered a corresponding conjunction by most grammarians ; but if the sentence is analyzed carefully, it will be seen that *both* refers to the periods of time, namely, he was kept by our party, in both parts of the day, *morning* and *afternoon.* *Both*, therefore, is strictly an adjective. It may not, however, be worth while to deviate from the usual method of disposing of it.

†The words *save* and *but*, when, in the sense of " except," or " not includ ing," they are followed by an objective case, are considered prepositions.

When used in the sense of *except*, they are more commonly followed by a nominative, or by an entire clause ; and in this case they do the office of a connective, and are termed *conjunctions.*

· The word *save* is by some considered a verb in the Imperative in all connections. But this word, and nearly all the conjunctions and prepositions, appear to have lost their original *verbal* power, and are now used as connectives to show the relations of words or sentences, rather than to express the action of a subject.

The boy stood on the burning deck,
Whence all *but* him had fled. — *Hemans.*

Section LXII.

EXERCISE III.

465. False Syntax, or examples to be corrected according to previous Rules of Syntax.

I admire the generous sympathy of Lafayette, he who befriended America.

The tomb we visited, was Washington's, the man who is the boast and pride of America.

They slew Varus, he that was mentioned before.

Him it is whom they persecuted.

Whom do you think it is ?

Who do you think it to be ?

It was him that said it, not I.

Was it him of whom you spake ?

Man, though he has a great variety of thoughts, yet they are all within his own breast.

Trouble, though it may be long delayed, yet it will surely come.

There is a great many different ways of accumulating wealth.

Nothing but vain and foolish pursuits delight some persons.

What avails the best sentiments, if persons do not live suitably to them?

Thou who art the Author of life can restore it.

There is many occasions in life in which silence and simplicity is true wisdom.

Great pains was taken to reconcile the parties. [This is right.]

Note. — According to the best usage, the word pains in the sense of labor, trouble, &c., though of a plural form, is joined with a singular verb ; as, The pains they had taken *was* very great. — *Clarendon.* No pains is taken.—*Pope.* See Worcester's Dictionary.

He need not proceed in such haste. [right.]

He dare not touch a hair of Catiline. [right.]

He dare him to the trial. [wrong.]

We need our sympathy. [wrong.]

NOTE. — The verbs *need* and *dare*, are used both in a transitive and intransitive sense. When they are intransitive, good usage authorizes the plural form with nouns in the singular.

To live soberly and piously are required of all.

What signifies the counsel and care of teachers ?

One, added to nineteen, make twenty.

Idleness and ignorance is the parent of many vices.

In unity consists the welfare and security of society.

One or both of the scholars was present at the transaction.

The deceitfulness of riches, or the cares of life, has choked the seeds of virtue in many a promising mind.

The people rejoices in that which should give them sorrow.

The British parliament are composed of king, lords and commons.

The time of William making the experiment.

Such will ever be the effect of youth associating with vicious companions.

Who have I reason to esteem so highly as you ?

Ye who are dead hath he quickened.

And he that was dead set up and began to speak.

We have done no more than it was our duty to have done.

I always intended to have rewarded my son.

He appeared to have been a man of letters.

It was a pleasure to have received this approbation.

They whom he had most injured, he had the greatest reason to love. Who shall I call you ?

I am not recommending these kind of sufferings.

By this mean, he had them more at vantage.

There is no mean of escaping the persecution.

And with this amend he was content.

Peace of mind is an honorable amend for the sacrifices of self-interest.

NOTE. — The word *means* in the sense of "cause," and the word *amends* and several others, as, *alms*, *news*, *riches*, &c., have only the plural, form and may be used either in the singular or plural number.

Some men think exceeding clearly, and reason exceeding forcibly.

He acted in this business bolder than was expected.

They were seen wandering about solitarily and distressed.

Every leaf, every twig, every drop of water, teem with life.

Every man and every woman were numbered.

Man's happiness or misery are in a great measure put into his hands.

What black despair, what horror fills his mind.

Virtue confers the supremest dignity on man.

His work is perfect ; but his brothers is more than perfect.

Which of them two persons was in fault ?

We have a great many of them flowers in the garden.

Each of them in their turn receive favors.

Every person, whatever be their station, are bound by the duties of morality and religion.

Humility and love constitutes the essence of religion.

If one man prefer a life of industry and economy, it is because he has an idea of comfort and wealth.

Though the design be laudable, it will involve much anxiety and labor.

A large number of vessels is being built, the present season.

The army is being concentrated to invade the capital.

I intended to have called on my way home.

I had hoped to have seen the affair amicably settled.

It was said by somebody, I know not who, that Charles was the person who they imputed the crime to.

Neither despise the poor or envy the rich.

I should be obliged to him if he will gratify me.

The relations are so uncertain, as that they require much examination.

NOTE.— Prepositions are often incorrectly applied.

They arrived *in* Boston *at* 9 o'clock A. M. [at.]

The old man was sitting *upon* the ground *on* the side of the road.

I differ entirely *with* you in this particular. [from.]

He was resolved *of* going to the Persian court.

He was eager *of* recommending it to his fellow-citizens.

He accused the ministers *for* betraying the Dutch.

The history of Peter is agreeable *with* the sacred text.

It is a use that perhaps I should have thought *on.*

He was made much *on* at Argus.

Neither of them shall make me swerve *out* of my path.

Ye blind guides which strain *at* a gnat and swallow a camel. [out.]

466. PUNCTUATION.*

NOTE.— The general principles which govern the use of the points or marks, will be easily learned by oral instruction, or by writing sentences without marks, on the black board, and punctuating them according to the general rules given below.

THE USE OF THE COMMA.

The comma [,] which is the mark most frequently used in punctuation, may be inserted according to the following rules.

RULE I.

The comma should be used to separate the clauses of a compound sentence.

EXAMPLES.

A wise son maketh a glad father, but a foolish man despiseth his mother.

This is a compound sentence, consisting of two clauses, which are separated by a comma.

EXERCISE.

Analyze the following sentences and explain the use of the comma.

A stone is heavy, and the sand [is] weighty.   As cold water to a thirsty soul, so is good news from a far country.

The sun had risen bright and high,
And cloudless shone along the sky.

---

* Writers differ much in regard to punctuation; some use fewer marks than others ; some dispense entirely with the colon [:] ; some use the comma where others would use the semicolon [;].   There is, indeed, a great want of uniformity in punctuation, the principal object of which is, to separate the parts of a sentence, that their relations may not be misunderstood.

Insert commas in the proper places in the following compound sentences. Let each sentence by analyzed before inserting the comma.

When the graces of novelty are worn off admiration is succeeded by indifference. The ox knoweth his owner the ass his master's crib Israel doth not know my people do not consider. He who preserves me to whom I owe my being whose I am and whom I serve is eternal.

Note.— When the compound sentence consists of two clauses only, which are closely connected, the comma may be omitted; as, "The sluggard is wiser in his own conceit than seven men that can render a reason."

Rule II.

The comma should be used to mark the omission of some word or words, necessary to a complete grammatical construction.

EXAMPLE.

Self conceit, presumption, and obstinacy blast the prospects of many a youth.

EXERCISE.

Analyze the following sentences, and supply some word or words whose omission is indicated by the comma.

We hear nothing of causing the blind to see, the lame to walk, the deaf to hear, the lepers to be cleansed. The miseries of poverty, of sickness, of captivity, would without hope be insupportable. To err is human; to forgive, divine. His wisdom, not his talents, attracted attention.

Insert the comma to mark the ellipsis in the following sentences.

The earth the sea the rain the snow the night the day summer and winter seed time and harvest show forth the wisdom and goodness of the Creator. He was gigantic in knowledge in virtue in health.

Rule III.

The case independent, with its modifying words, all detached assertions and phrases, direct quotations, and adverbs used independently, or referring to the whole sentence, should be separated by commas ; as,

"Why, Mr. Pearson," said she, "you are just like Dr. Johnson, I think." *Mr. Pearson* is in the case independent; the adverb, *why*, is used independently, or it refers to the whole sentence; *said she*, is a *detached* assertion. *Why, Mr. Pearson*, and *said she*, are separated by commas, according to the rule.

NOTE.—The words, *yes, no, now, however, indeed, perhaps, again, finally*, and the phrases, *in short, at length, at least, in return*, and the like, are generally to be separated by commas from the words contiguous to them.

RULE IV.

A comma is sometimes used to separate words and clauses, expressing contrast or opposition ; as,

Liberal, not lavish, is kind nature's hand.
Though deep, yet clear ; though gentle, yet not dull.

RULE V.

When three or more nouns, adjectives, verbs, or adverbs occur in succession, they should be separated by commas ; as

A woman, gentle, sensible, well informed and religious. The husband, wife, and children, suffered extremely. In a letter, we may advise, exhort, comfort, request, and discuss.

RULE VI.

Clauses and phrases, which occur between words connected in construction, and words in apposition, when accompanied with adjuncts, are generally separated by commas ; as,

Johnson had repeated a psalm which he had translated, *during his affliction*, into Latin verses. Cowper, *the gifted poet*, died in the year 1800. Miltiades, *the son of Cimon*, the Athenian.

NOTE.— If the word in apposition is not limited by an adjunct, or qualified by an adjective, the comma should not be inserted; as, "Milton the poet."

RULE VII.

The parts of a simple sentence are not generally separated,

**except when they are long or interrupted by phrases or ex·
planatory words ; as,**

The eyes of the mind are like the eyes of the body.

To be very active in laudable pursuits, is the distinguishing characteristic
of a man of merit.

REMARK.

The insertion of a comma between contiguous words, closely connected in
construction, should be avoided, unless such words are particularly emphatic
or important.

SEMICOLON, COLON, AND PERIOD.

The semicolon [;] is placed between the clauses of a period,*
**which are less closely connected than such as are separated by
commas.**

NOTE.— It is impossible to give very definite rules for the use of the semicolon. Its use, like that of other pauses, must be learned in a great measure
by observing how it is employed by the most correct writers.

**The colon [:] is used when there is still less connection in the
parts of a period, than that which is indicated by the semicolon.
See note above.**

**The period [.] is used after a sentence which is complete and
independent.**

A period is also used after abbreviations ; as N. S., P. S., N. B.

**The dash [—] denotes an abrupt turn in the sentence ; or,
that a significant pause is required ; as, " Here lies the great —
false marble."   It is also used to denote the omission of letters
in a word, and of words in a sentence ; as, K — g, for king.**

**The mark of interrogation [?] is used to denote that a ques-
tion is asked.**

The mark of exclamation [!] denotes wonder or surprise.

**The parentheses ( ) are used to include an explanatory clause,
not connected in construction with the rest of the sentence.**

**The brackets, [ ] or hooks, are used to inclose an explanatory
note or word. †**

---

* A period is a sentence complete, making perfect sense, and not connect
ed in construction with what follows. — *Webster.*

† The use of other marks, such as the apostrophe ('), the double comma
(" "), caret (∧), &c., can be learned from spelling books.

Section LXIII.

467. COMPOSITION.*

Description. — *Result of Perception.*

EXERCISE I. SIGHT.

DIRECTION. — Place an object before you. Examine it carefully by your sense of sight. You must neither touch, taste nor smell it. Then write what you have learned by sight.

Model. A piece of sealing-wax.

This piece of sealing wax is about four inches long, half an inch broad, and a quarter of an inch in thickness. It is of a very bright red, and stamped with the name of the manufacturer. Its surface shines like glass, so that I suppose it is smooth, though I cannot be sure of this without touching it. One end is rough as if broken, and the other is smoked from having been in the flame of a candle.

Describe in a similar manner the following objects.

A book.	An inkstand.	A chair.
A pen-knife.	A sheet of paper.	A looking-glass.

EXERCISE II. TASTE.

DIRECTION. — Taste the object and write the result.

Model. A cup of tea.

The substance in the cup is called tea, though, properly speaking, it is only an infusion of the leaves of that plant. Its taste is peculiar, but pleasant. It is naturally somewhat bitter, but the sugar prevents it from being unpleasantly so. The flavor is aromatic and agreeable.

Objects to be described.

Onion.	Honey.	Cinnamon.
Potato.	Orange.	Strawberries.
Lemon.	Coffee.	Apples.
Vinegar.	Liquorice.	Cheese.

---

* Since the first edition of this work was published, the author has received, through the kindness of a friend, a small work on composition, published in Edinburgh, 1839, edited by W. & R. Chambers, to which he is mainly indebted for some of the following pages.

EXERCISE III. SMELL.

DIRECTION. — Exercise the sense of smell, and write the result.

Model.　A full blown rose.

This beautiful flower is called the rose. Its buds are gradually opening, and from each proceeds a most delightful odor. But the chief perfume is from the petals of the full blown flower. The essence which is extracted from the rose-leaves, forms a fragrant scent termed otto of roses.

Objects to be described.

Violet.	Lilac.	Burnt-feather.
Boxberry.	Cologne.	Tansy.
Orange.	Strawberry.	Hartshorn. .
Pine-apple.	Geranium.	Wormwood.

EXERCISE IV. FEELING.

DIRECTION. — With eyes shut, touch the object, and write the result.

Model.　An octavo volume.

I perceive by feeling, that this book is about ten inches long, six broad, and three in thickness.

The book is smooth and hard, with raised ornaments on the back. I think it has been near the fire, for it feels somewhat warm.

Objects to be described.

Door.	Hair-glove.	A shilling.
Sponge.	Marble.	
Bread.	Paper.	
A bell.	Silk.	

EXERCISE V. HEARING.

DIRECTION. — Strike the object, or listen to its
them.

Model.

Last night I listened to the wind. Sometimes it whined like a dog, then it gave a sort of a shrill whistle. That was followed by a hollow moaning, and then there was a loud rush like a waterfall. This ceased, and afterwards there was a mixture of whistling and hissing. At last, it died away in gentle murmurs.

Objects to be described.

A fife.	The sea.	Singing of birds.
A violin.	Trees.	A choir.
A trumpet.	Thunder.	Bells.
A drum.	Hail.	Sounds in a street.

W   EXERCISE VI. ALL THE SENSES.

DIRECTION. — Place the object before you, examine it carefully by your senses in turn. Then write down the information which each organ has given you. Finish what you have learned from one sense, before you proceed to the next.

Model. A pencil.

1. My eyes tell me that the pencil is about five inches long, and a quarter of an inch in thickness. Its shape is round like a pillar, quite flat at one end, and tapering to a point at the other. Its color is a beautiful light brown with dark streaks. It is at present lying on a sheet of white paper, with an old pen on one side, and a short piece of red sealing wax on the other.

2. By feeling I perceive its shape to be exactly what my eyes communicated. But I ascertain something which my eyes could not tell; namely, that the pencil is as hard as this sealing-wax. It is smooth on one side and rough on the other.

3. When I put it to my nostrils, I perceive that it has a very slight pleasant odor, like that of cedar wood.

4. The taste is sweetish. 5. It utters no sound.

Objects to be described.

A piece of money.	An apple.	A thistle.
An orange.	A shell.	A pen.
A watch.	A lemon.	A ball.
A flower.	A book.	A clock.

EXERCISE VII. STATEMENTS AND EXPERIMENTS.

DIRECTION. — Place an object before you. Try it by your own senses as before; then make experiments on it, and write down the result.

Model. A piece of India-rubber.

This piece of India-rubber, or caoutchouc, is three inches long, two broad, and one thick. It is in shape, a sort of solid oblong. Its color is nearly black, with whitish or grayish parts in the middle, while some portions of it seem somewhat brown. Its smell is strong and somewhat disagreeable. It has no peculiar taste; though some boys are fond of chewing it. I shall now make some *experiments* with it. While I hold one end, you must pull out the other. When you let go, it returns to its former shape. Then I find it is *elastic.* Next I put a small piece into the flame of a candle, and I perceive it takes fire very readily, burning with brilliant light, white at the bottom, and red at the top, emitting a considerable quantity of black smoke. I therefore ascertain that it is *inflammable.* By putting it into water, I perceive it floats, so its specific gravity must be less than that of water. I further observe that it does not diminish its bulk, from which I infer that it is *insoluble* in water. I have been informed, however, that tar will dissolve it. I have found it very useful in rubbing out pencil marks.

Things to be described.

1.   Small piece of glass.

QUALITIES, *as proved by the senses.* Size. Shape. Color. Weight. Heat. Hardness. Smell. Taste.

Experiments. By breaking, marking, &c.

2.   Coal.

QUALITIES, *as proved by the senses.* Size. Shape. Color. Weight.

Experiments. With water, with fire, with a hammer.

3.   A sheet of paper.

QUALITIES. Size. Shape, &c.

Experiments. With water, with fire, with paint, with pencil, with ink.

4.   Sealing-wax.

QUALITIES. Shape. Size. Color. Weight, &c.

Experiments. With flame, with water, &c.

EXERCISE VIII. SOURCES OF THINGS.

DIRECTION. Place an object before you. Think of its origin, or from what source it came. If you do not know, ask your teacher or consult a book. Then put down all that you have heard. You may then add an account of its appearance, qualities, &c. Your description may conclude with some experiments.

Model.   A piece of lead.

The substance before me is a metal called lead. I procured this piece at the plumber's, and he bought it of the owner of the lead works. Lead is obtained by melting the ore, which is dug out of mines by men employed for that purpose. Lead is bluish white, very bright when cut or newly melted, but it becomes dull and dim after it has been in the air for some time. It has no taste, but if you rub it, you will perceive a slight smell. It is very soft, and may be hammered into thin plates. It is easily melted, as you may prove by putting a piece into the fire.

Objects to be described.

1. A piece of bread.

Suggestions. Baker, oven, flour; *miller,* mill, stream, horses, water; *farmer,* ground, plough, harrow, horses, men, sun, rain, harvest, thrashing, winnowing; soft, white, sweet, wholesome, nutritious.

2. A coat.

Suggestions. Tailor, cloth, merchant, manufacturer, wool, dying, spinning, weaving ; wool-grower, sheep-washing, shearing. Shape, color, quality, &c.

3. Sugar.

Suggestions. Grocer, merchant, ship, sailors, oven ; West Indies, plantation, negroes, sugar-cane ; refining. Shape, color, size, smell, taste, &c.

4. Paper.

Suggestions. Stationers, paper-maker's mill, water or steam, rags, boiling, sizing, &c. ; rag-merchant, linen, flax plant, mode of preparation, &c. Shape, size, color, quality.

EXERCISE IX. USES OF THINGS.

DIRECTION. — Place the object before you, and think for what purpose it is usually employed. If you do not know, ask your teacher, or consult a book.

Model. A piece of lead.

· This metal is of very great use. Water pipes, cisterns, and roofs of houses are made of it. Chemists form two substances out of it, called red and white lead, both of which are poisonous. If we mix it with tin, the result is that useful compound·called pewter, of which some table spoons are made. When blended with antimony, it affords a composition from which printers' types are cast.

Mention the uses of the following objects.

Iron and steel.	Gold.	Sheep.
Wood.	Leather.	Silver.
Mahogany.	Cotton Cloth.	Water.
Glass.	Cows.	Steam-engine.

EXERCISE X. PARTS OF THINGS.

DIRECTION. — Place the object before you. ·Inquire how it came there, say where you bought it, whence the merchant procured it, &c. Tell whether it is natural or artificial, simple or compound, &c.

Model. A pen-knife.

There is a pen-knife on the table before me. I bought it at the cutler's. He either made it himself, or procured it of the manufacturer. It consists of two parts, each formed of a different substance. The handle is of horn, probably that of a stag. It is of a brown color, rough and hard. It has several small rivets in it for the purpose of holding its sides together. On one side there is a small plate on which the owner's name may be engraven. The second substance is steel, of which the blade is composed. Steel is an artificial

18

metal, the result of iron prepared with charcoal. It is very hard and smooth. When properly tempered, it makes very sharp blades.

Practice according to the Direction and Model.

1. A room.

Suggestions. Floor-boards, carpet-maker, pattern, color, texture, size, shape, walls, plaster, paper, color, figure, quality.

2. A book.

Suggestions. Leaves, pages, margins, title-pages, edges, plates, wood cuts, binding, author, printer, book-binder, book-seller.

3. A house.

Suggestions. Foundation, walls, roof, floors, doors, windows, stairs, chimneys, wood-work, plastering, painting, papering. What are the tradesmen employed in making a house?

4. A fire-place.   5. An ink-stand

EXERCISE XI.

The following directions may afford some aid to the learner in his efforts at composition.

1. A subject should be selected on which the writer has some definite knowledge, and which is not beyond his power of comprehension.

2. The writer should *think long* and *patiently* on his subject before attempting to compose.

3. When the subject admits of it, he should form a plan and make such divisions as will enable him to examine every part separately, something like the following example.

EXAMPLE.

Subject. — Children should render obedience and love to their parents.

1. Because they are under obligations to their parents for benefits received from them.

2. Because in this way they secure their own happiness.

3. Because God has commanded them to honor their parents.

Sometimes merely the heads of an essay or subject are presented as a skeleton of the whole; as follows:

Subject. — Independence.

1. The meaning of independence.
2. Its effect upon the character.
3. Its effect upon society.
4. The different kinds of independence.
5. The difference between independence and obstinacy.

EXERCISE XII.

Let a plan or skeleton be made out for the treatment of the following subjects.

Subjects.

Benevolence.	Industry.
Power of conscience.	The love of praise.
Integrity.	Intemperance.
The observance of the Sabbath.	Education.
A fretful temper.	The love of knowledge.

After the subject has been selected, and methodized or planned, the following directions may be observed.

1. Examine the divisions separately, and place such thoughts under each division, and no others, as properly belong to it.

2. Carefully analyze every sentence after it has been written, to see wheth er any improper or unnecessary words have been used, and whether the sentence is grammatically correct.

3. After the essay or composition has been once written, begin anew and re-write every sentence, and inquire at each, whether some different expressions would not be more clear and forcible, keeping in mind that almost every thought may be expressed in a variety of ways.

4. Attend carefully to the spelling, pointing, and capitals.*

EXERCISE XIII.　VARIETY OF EXPRESSION.

The same idea may be expressed in different ways; and it will be both useful and entertaining for the learner to practice such exercises as the following.

Model.

The soul is immortal.

The same idea may be expressed in different ways.

The soul will never die.
The soul will never cease to exist.
The soul will live forever.
The soul is destined to an endless existence.

Sentences for Practice.

A wise son maketh a glad father. A foolish son is the heaviness of (cause of sorrow to) his mother.

---

* Newman's Rhetoric. See also Parker's Aids to English Composition.

When we have finished our work, we will play.

After dinner we will walk in the field.

Intemperance is ruinous to the mind as well as to the body

A wolf let into the sheep-fold, will devour the sheep.

True religion teaches us to be gentle and affable.

My friend died last night, without a struggle or a groan.

PART V.

—

P R O S O D Y.

SECTION LXIV.

468. Prosody treats of accent, quantity, and the laws of versification.

1. *Accent* is the laying of a particular stress of voice on a certain syllable in a word; as, the syllable *ban* in a*ban*don.

2. Accent should not be confounded with Emphasis. *Emphasis* is a stress of voice on a word in a sentence, to mark its importance. *Accent* is a stress of voice on a syllable in a word.

3. The *quantity* of a syllable is the time which is required to pronounce it. A short syllable requires half the time of a long one.

VERSIFICATION.

469. *Versification* is a measured arrangement of words into poetical lines or verses.

1. A *verse* consists of a certain number of accented and unaccented syllables, arranged according to certain rules.

2. *Rhyme* is the correspondence of the last sound of one line to the last sound of another.

3. *Blank verse* is the name given to a kind of poetry written without *rhyme*.

4. A *stanza* consists of several lines, and is sometimes improperly called a verse.

5. A *couplet*, or distich, consists of two poetical lines which make complete sense.

6. A *foot* is a division of a verse consisting of two or three syllables.

7. *Scanning* is dividing a line into the feet of which it is composed.

The principal feet in English verse are the following:

FEET.

1. An Iambus, ◡
2. A Trochee, – ◡
8. An Anapæst, ◡ ◡

8. An Iambus has the first syllable unaccented, and the last accented; as, Betráy, consíst.

9. A Trochee has the first syllable accented, and the last unaccented; as, Háteful péttish.

10. An Anapæst has the first two syllables unaccented, and the last accented; as, Contravéne, acquiésce.

IAMBIC VERSE.

470. Iambic verses may be divided into several species, according to the number of feet or syllables of which they are composed.

1. The shortest form of the English Iambic consists of an Iambus, with an additional short syllable; as,

> Disdaining,
> Complaining,
> Consenting,
> Repenting.

NOTE.— We have no poem of this measure, but it may be met with in stanzas.

2. The second form of our Iambic is also too short to be continued through any great number of lines. It consists of *two* Iambuses.

18*

NOTE.—In reading Iambic verse, the accent is on the second syllable of each foot; or on the even syllables; as,

> To mé | the róse.

> What pláce | is hére!
> What scénes | appéar!

It sometimes takes, or may take an additional short syllable; as,

> . | Upón | a moúnt | ain
> Besíde a foúntain.

3. The third form consists of *three* Iambuses.

> In plá | ces fár | or neár,
> Or fá | mous ór | obscuré.

It sometimes admits of an additional short syllable; as,

> Our heárts | no lón | ger lán | guish.

4. The fourth form is made up of *four* Iambuses.

> And máy | at lást | my weá | ry áge,
> Find oút | the peáce | ful hér | mitáge.

5. The fifth species of English Iambic consists of *five* Iambuses.

> How lóv'd, | how vál | u'd ónce | aváils | thee nót,
> To whóm reláted, ór by whóm begót.

This is called the *Heroic* measure. In its simplest form it consists of five Iambuses; but by the admission of other feet, it is capable of many varieties.

6. The sixth form of our Iambic is commonly called *Alexandrine* measure. It consists of *six* Iambuses.

> For thóu | art bút | of dúst; | be húm | ble ánd | be wíse.

7. The seventh and last form of our Iambic measure is made up of *seven* Iambuses.

The Lórd | descén | ded fróm | abóve | and bów'd | the heáv | ens high.

This was anciently written in one line; but it is now broken into two; the first containing four feet, and the second three; as,

> When áll | thy mér | cies O' | my Gód!
> My rís | ing sóul | survéys.

471. TROCHAIC VERSE.

1. The shortest Trochaic verse in our language consists of one Trochee and a long syllable.

> Túmult | céase,
> Sínk to | péace.

This measure is defective in dignity, and can seldom be used on serious occasions.

2. The second English form of the Trochaic consists of *two* feet; and is likewise so brief, that it is rarely used for any very serious purpose.

> On the | móun | tain,
> Bý a | foún | tain.

NOTE.— In reading Trochaic verse, the accent is placed on the first sylla-ble of each foot, or on the odd syllables; as,

> On' the | moun'tain.

It sometimes contains two feet, or trochees, with an additional long syllable; as,

> In the | dáys of | old
> Fábles pláinly told.

3. The third species consists of *three* trochees; as,

> Whén our | heárts are | móurning.

Or of three trochees, with an additional long syllable; as,

> Réstless | mórtals | tóil for | nóught;
> Blíss in | váin from | eárth is | sóught.

4. The fourth Trochaic species consists of *four* trochees; as,

> Róund us | róars the | témpest | lóuder.

This form may take an additional long syllable, as follows:

> I'dle | áfter | dínner | ín his | chair,
> Sát a | fármer, | rúddy, | fát and | fair.

But this measure is very uncommon.

5. The fifth Trochaic species is likewise uncommon. It is composed of *five* trochees,

> All' that | wálk on | foót or | ríde in | chári | ots,
> All' that | dwéll in | pála | cés or | gárrets.

6. The sixth form of the English Trochaic consists of *six* tro-chees; as,

> On' a | móuntain, | strétch'd be | néath a | hoáry | wíllow,
> Láy a | shépherd | swáin, and | víew'd the | rólling | bíllow.

This seems to be the longest trochaic line that our language admits.

472. ANAPÆSTIC VERSE.

1. The first and simplest form of our genuine Anapæstic verse is made up of *two* Anapæsts; as,

> But his coúr | age 'gan faíl,
> For no árts | could aváil.

This form admits of an additional short syllable.

> Then his coúr | age 'gan faíl | him,
> For no árts | could aváil | him.

2. The second species consists of *three* Anapæsts.

> O ye woóds, | spread your bránch | es apáce;
> To your deépest recésses I flý;
> I would híde with the beásts of the cháse;
> I would vánish from évery eyé.

This is a very pleasing measure, and much used, both in solemn and cheerful subjects.

3. The third kind of the English Anapæstic, consists of *four* Anapæsts.

> May I góv | ern my pás | sions with áb | solute swáy;
> And gro wí | ser and bét | ter as lifé | wears awáy.

This measure will admit of a short syllable at the end; as,

> On the wárm | cheek of youíth, | smiles and ró | ses are blénd | ing.

NOTE.—In reading Anapæstic verse, the accent is placed on the third syllable of each foot; as,

> I would híde | with the beásts | of the cháse.

SECTION LXV.

POETIC LICENSE.

473. Poetry owes much of its effect to the peculiar style in which it is dressed. It indulges more freely than prose in

figurative expressions, in contractions and transpositions, in exclamations, antiquated words, and phrases, and other peculiarities.

Such licenses may be explained under what is usually termed *Figures of Etymology, Figures of Syntax,* and *Figures of Rhetoric.*

1. A figure of Etymology is the intentional deviation in the usual form of a *word.*

2. A figure of Syntax is the intentional deviation in the usual construction of a word.

8. A figure in Rhetoric is a departure from the usual application of a word.

FIGURES OF ETYMOLOGY.

474. The principal Figures of Etymology are *Elision, Synæresis, Diæresis, Paragoge, Prosthesis* and *Tmesis.*

1. ELISION is the omission of a part of a word.

This figure includes *Syncope,* or an omission in the middle of a word; as, List'ning, lov'd; *Apocope,* or the elision of a final vowel or syllable; *Aphæresis,* or the elision of a letter or syllable from the beginning of a word; as, 'gainst, for against; 'squire, for esquire.

2. SYNÆRESIS is the contraction of two syllables into one; as, *Seest,* for *see-est; drowned,* for *drown-ed.*

3. DIÆRESIS is the separation of two vowels that might form a diphthong; as *aërial,* not *ærial; coöperate,* not *cooperate.*

4. PARAGOGE is the addition of a letter or syllable to the end of a word; as, *Without-en* for *without; bound-en* for *bound.*

5. PROSTHESIS is the prefixing of an expletive letter; as, *Beloved* for *loved; a-down* for *down; y-clad* for *clad.*

6. TMESIS is the separation of a compound word, by an intervening word; as, *To-us-ward* for *toward us.*

FIGURES OF SYNTAX.

475. The principal figures of Syntax are *Ellipsis, P nasm, Enallage, Hyperbaton.*

1. ELLIPSIS is the omission of some word or words necessary to complete the construction of the sentence, but not essential to express the meaning.

Almost all compound sentences are more or less elliptical, some examples of which may be seen under the different parts of speech.

1. The ellipsis of the *article;* as, A man, woman, and child. The article *a* is omitted, by ellipsis, before woman and child.

2. The ellipsis of the *noun;* as, The laws of God and man; that is, the laws of God and the laws of man.

3. The ellipsis of the *adjective;* as, A delightful garden and orchard; that is, a delightful garden and a *delightful* orchard.

4. The ellipsis of the *pronoun;* as, I love and fear him; that is, I love *him,* &c. This is the man they love; that is, *which* they love.

5. The ellipsis of the *verb;* as, The man was old and crafty; that is, the man was old, and the man was crafty. She was young and beautiful and good; that, is, she was young, she was beautiful, and she was good. I went to see and hear him; that is, to see him, and to hear him.

6. The ellipsis of the *adverb;* as, He spoke and acted wisely; that is, He spoke wisely, and he acted wisely.

7. The ellipsis of the *preposition;* as, He went into the abbeys, halls, and public buildings; *into* is omitted before *halls,* and *public buildings.*

8. The ellipsis of the *conjunction;* as, They confess the power, wisdom, goodness, and love of the Creator; *and* is omitted, by ellipsis, before *wisdom* and *goodness.*

9. The ellipsis of the *interjection;* as, O pity and shame! that is, O pity! O shame!

2. PLEONASM is the use of more words than are necessary to express the meaning; as,

        Peace, O virtue! Peace is all thy own.

3. ENALLAGE is the use of one part of speech for another; as,

        The fearful hare limps *awkward.*
        They fall *successive* and *successive* rise.

4. HYPERBATON is the transposition of words; as,

        The muses fair, these peaceful *shades among.*
        He wanders *earth around.*

FIGURES OF RHETORIC.

476. The principal figures of Rhetoric are *Simile, Metaphor, Personification, Allegory, Metonymy, Vision, Apostrophe, Hyperbole, Synecdoche, Irony, Antithesis* and *Climax.*

1. A SIMILE is an express and formal comparison.

EXAMPLES.

The actions of princes are like those great rivers, the course of which every one beholds, but their springs have been seen by few.

> As from the wing no scar the sky retains,
> The parted wave no furrow from the keel,
> So dies in human hearts the thought of death.

2. A METAPHOR is a comparison implied in a single word.

EXAMPLES.

> I will be unto her a *wall* of fire round about.
> Thou art my *rock* and my fortress.
> Thy word is a *lamp* to my feet and a *light* to my path.

3. PERSONIFICATION OR PROSOPOPŒIA is that figure by which we attribute life and action to inanimate objects.

EXAMPLES.

Jordan was driven back!   The mountains skipped like rams, and the little hills like lambs.

> Rome for empire far renowned,
> *Tramples* on a thousand States;
> Soon her pride shall *kiss* the ground —
> Hark! the Gaul is at her gates.

4. An ALLEGORY is a continued metaphor; for examples see Ezekiel XVII. 22 — 24. and Psalms LXXX. 8—17.

5. METONYMY is substituting the name of one thing for that of another.

They crown *the wine* [cups]. They read Cowper; that is, The poetry of Cowper. *Gray hairs* should be respected.

6. VISION is a figure by which something imaginary is represented as *real*, and present to the senses.

I seem to myself to behold this city, the ornament of the earth, and the capital of all nations, suddenly involved in one conflagration. I see before me the slaughtered heaps of citizens lying unburied in the midst of their ruined country. The furious countenance of Cethegus rises to my view, while, with a savage joy, he is triumphing in your miseries.

7. APOSTROPHE is turning off from the regular course of the subject, to address some person or thing.

Soul of the Just! Companion of the Good.
O sun! thy everlasting light.

8. HYPERBOLE consists in magnifying or diminishing a thing beyond the truth.

I saw their chief, tall as a rock of ice; his spear the blasted fir; his shield the rising moon; he sat on the shore like a cloud of mist on the hill.

9. SYNECDOCHE is putting the name of the whole of any thing for a part, or a part for the whole; as the *waves* for the sea, the *roof* for the house, the *head* for the person, the *heart* for the emotions, &c.

10. IRONY is the intentional use of words in a sense contrary to that which the writer or speaker intends to convey; as,

The prophet Elijah, when he challenged the priests of Baal, "mocked them and said, Cry aloud, for he is a god; either he is talking, or he is pursuing, or is on a journey, or peradventure he sleepeth, and must be awaked."

11. ANTITHESIS is the placing of different or opposite words in contrast; as,

If you wish to enrich a person, study not to increase his stores, but to diminish his desires.

Though *poor, luxurious;* though *submissive, vain.*
Though *deep,* yet *clear;* though *gentle,* yet not *dull.*

12. CLIMAX is a figure in which the sentiment rises or sinks in regular gradation; as,

Add to your faith virtue; and to virtue knowledge; and to knowledge temperance; &c. See 2 Pet. 1: 5—7.

19

APPENDIX.

DERIVATION.

ABOUT 23,000, or five eighths, of the words in the English Language are of Anglo-Saxon origin ; the remaining part are derived from the Latin, Geek, French, and some other languages.

The following is a specimen of the orthography of the English Language about the fourteenth century :

In the days of Eroude, kyng of Judee, ther was a prest, Zacarye by name ; of the sort of Abia, and his wyf was of the doughtirs of Aaron ; and hir name was Elizabeth. Luke I. — *Wickliffe's Version, written* 1380.

The following extracts are from some of the earliest authors :

Nowe for to speak of the commune,
It is to dread of that fortune,
Which hath befalle in sondrye londes. — *Gower.*

Alas, alas ! with how defe an ere deth cruell turneth awaie fro wretches, and naieth for to close weepyng eyess. — *Chaucer.*

A knight ther was, and that a worthy man,
That fro the time that he first began
To ridin out, he lovid chevalrie,
Trouth and honour, fredome and curtesy. — *Id.*

Mine high estate, power and auctoritie,
If yene know, enserche and ye shall spie,
That richesse, worship, welth, and dignitie,
Joy, rest, and peace, and all things fynally,
That any pleasure or profit may come by,
To mannes comfort, ayde and sustinaunce,
Is all at my deuyse and ordinaunce. — *Thomas More.*

DERIVATION OF WORDS.

Words are either primitive or derivative.

A *primitive* word is one which is not derived from any other word in the language.

A *derivative* is one which is formed from some primitive word or words.

Words are derived from one another in various ways ; namely :

1. Substantives are derived from verbs.

2. Verbs are derived from substantives, adjectives, and sometimes from adverbs.

3. Adverbs are derived from substantives.

4. Substantives are derived from adjectives.

5. Adverbs are derived from adjectives.

1. *Substantives are derived from verbs ;* as, from "to love," comes "lover;" from "to visit, visitor;" from "to survive, survivor;" &c.

In the following instances, and in many others, it is difficult to determine whether the verb was deduced from the noun, or the noun from the verb ; namely : Love, to love ; hate, to hate ; fear, to fear ; sleep, to sleep ; walk, to walk ; ride, to ride ; act, to act; &c.

2. *Verbs are derived from nouns, adjectives,* and sometimes from *adverbs ;* as, from the noun *salt,* comes "to salt ;" from the adjective *warm* "to warm ;" and from the adverb *forward* "to forward." Sometimes they are formed by

lengthening the vowel, or softening the consonant; as, from *grass*, "to graze;" sometimes by adding *en*; as, from *length*, "to lengthen;" especially to adjectives; as, from *short* "to shorten;" *bright*, "to brighten."

3. *Adjectives are derived from nouns*, in the following manner; Adjectives denoting plenty are derived from nouns by adding *y*; as, from health, healthy; wealth, wealthy; might, mighty; &c.

Adjectives denoting the matter out of which any thing is made, are derived from nouns, by adding *en*; as, from Oak, oaken; wood, wooden; wool, woollen; &c.

Adjectives denoting abundance are derived from nouns, by adding *ful*; as, Joy, joyful; sin, sinful; fruit, fruitful; &c.

Adjectives denoting plenty, but with some kind of diminution, are derived from nouns by adding *some*; as, from Light, lightsome; trouble, troublesome; toil, toilsome; &c.

Adjectives denoting want are derived from nouns, by adding *less*; as, from worth, worthless; from care, careless; joy, joyless; &c.

Adjectives denoting likeness, are derived from nouns, by adding *ly*: as, from man, manly; earth, earthly; court, courtly; &c.

Some adjectives are derived from other adjectives; or from nouns, by adding *ish* to them; which termination, when added to adjectives, imports diminution, or lessening the quality; as, White, whitish; that is, somewhat white. When added to nouns, it signifies similitude or tendency to a character; as, Child, childish; thief, thievish.

Some adjectives are formed from nouns or verbs, by adding the termination *able*: and those adjectives signify capacity; as, Answer, answerable; to change, changeable

4. *Nouns are derived from adjectives* sometimes by adding the termination *ness*: as, White, whiteness; swift, swiftness; sometimes by adding *th* or *t*, and making a small change in some of the letters; as, Long, length; high, height.

5. *Adverbs of quality are derived from adjectives*, by adding *ly*, or changing *le* into *ly*: and denote the same quality as the adjectives from which they are derived; as, from *base* comes *basely*: from *slow*, *slowly*: from *able*, *ably*.

There are so many other ways of deriving words from one another, that it would be extremely difficult, and nearly impossible, to enumerate them. The primitive words of any language are very few; the derivatives form much the greater number. A few more instances only can be given here.

Some nouns are derived from other nouns, by adding the terminations *hood* or *head*, *ship*, *ery*, *wick*, *rick*, *dom*, *ian*, *ment*, and *age*.

Substantives ending in *hood* or *head*, are such as signify character or quali-s, Manhood, knighthood, falsehood, &c.

Nouns ending in *ship*, are those that signify office, employment, state, or condition ; as, Lordship, stewardship, partnership, &c. Some nouns ending in *ship*, are derived from adjectives ; as, Hard, hardship, &c.

Nouns which end in *ery*, signify action or habit; as, Slavery, foolery, prud ery, &c. Some nouns of this sort come from adjectives ; as, Brave, bravery, &c.

Nouns ending in *wick*, *rick*, and *dom*, denote dominion, jurisdiction, or con-dition ; as, Bishoprick, kingdom, dukedom, freedom, &c.

Nouns which end in *ian*, are those that signify profession ; as Physician, musician, &c. Those that end in *ment* and *age*, come generally from the French, and commonly signify the act or habit ; as, Commandment, usage.

Some nouns ending in *ard*, are derived from verbs or adjectives, and denote character or habit ; as, Drunk, drunkard ; dote, dotard.

Some nouns have the form of diminutives ; but these are not many. They are formed by adding the terminations, *kin*, *ling*, *ing*, *ock*, *el*, and the like ; as, Lamb, lambkin ; goose, gosling ; duck, duckling ; hill, hillock ; &c.

PREFIXES AND SUFFIXES.

Most of the derivative words of the English language are formed by the aid of *prefixes* and *suffixes*.

A *prefix* is a letter, syllable, or word, joined to the beginning of a word ; as, *a*shore, *re*turn.

A *suffix* is a letter or syllable annexed to the end of a word ; as, sure*ly*, content*ment*.

1. SAXON PREFIXES.

A signifies *on*, *in*, or *at* ; as, *a*shore, *a*far, *a*sleep.
BE, *upon*, *by*, *for*, &c. ; as, *be*speak, *be*tide, *be*sprinkle, *be*cause.
FOR, *from* or *against* ; as, *for*bear, *for*bid.
FORE, *before* ; as, *fore*tell, *fore*know.
MIS, *wrong*, *erroneous*, or *defective* ; as, *mis*conduct, *mis*rule.
OUT, *beyond*, *more*, or *exterior* ; as, *out*run, *out*live, *out*side.
OVER denotes *excess*, or *superiority* ; as, *over*do, *over*come.
UN, *negation*, or *privation* ; as, *un*certain, *un*bind. .
UNDER signifies *beneath*, *inferior* ; as, *under*mine, *under*go.
UP denotes *elevation*, or *subversion* ; as, *up*land, *up*set.
WITH signifies *from*, or *back* ; as, *with*stand, *with*hold.

2. LATIN PREFIXES.

A, AB, or ABS, signify *from*; as, *a*vert, *abs*tract.

AD, A, AC, AF, AG, AL, AN, AP, AR, AS, or AT, signify *to*, *at*; as, *acce*de, *al*lot, *an*nex, *ar*rest, *abs*tract, *af*fix.

ANTE, signifies *before*: as, *ante*cedent.

CIRCUM, signifies *round*: as, *circum*navigate.

CON, CO, COG, COL, COM, or COR, signify *either*, *together*: as, *co*here, *col*lect, *com*press, *cor*relative.

CONTRA signifies *against*: as, *contra*dict. This prefix is sometimes changed to *counter*; as, *counter*act.

DE signifies *from*, or *down*: as, *de*duce.

DIS generally implies *separation*, or *disunion*: as in *dis*solve. It has sometimes a negative use; as in *dis*approve. *Dis* takes also the form *di* and *dif*: as in *di*verge, *dif*fuse.

E or EX signifies *out of* or *from*: as *e*ject, to cast out; *e*vade, to escape from. This prefix takes also the forms *ec* and *ef*: as, *ec*centric, *ef*face.

EXTRA signifies *beyond* or *more than*: as, *extra*ordinary.

IN, IM, EN, IG, IL, and IR, before adjectives, have a negative signification: as, *in*active, not active. Before a verb, they signify *in*, *into*, or *against*.

INTER signifies *between* or *among*: as, *inter*vene, *inter*sperse, to scatter among.

OB, OC, OF, OP, *for*, *in the way of*: as, *ob*struct, *oc*cur.

PER, *through*, or *by*: as, *per*vade, to pass through; *per*chance, by chance.

PRE or PRÆ, *before*: as, *pre*cede, to go before.

PRO, *for*, *forth*, or *forward*: as, *pro*noun, for a noun; *pro*voke, to call forth; *pro*mote, to move forward.

RE, *again*, or *back*: as, *re*enter, *re*call.

RETRO, *backward*: as, *retro*cession.

SE, *aside*: as, *se*cede.

SINE, *without*: as, *sine*cure, without care.

SUB, SUC, SUF, SUG, SUP and SUS, signify *under*: as, *sub*scribe, to write under.

SUPER signifies *beyond*, *above*, or *over*: as, *super*natural, beyond nature; *super*vise, to oversee.

TRANS signifies *over*, or *beyond*: as, *trans*fer, to carry over.

3. GREEK PREFIXES.

1. A and AN, in Greek, denote privation; as, *A*nomalous, wanting rule; *an*onymous, wanting name; *an*archy want of government.

2. AMPHI, *both* or *two*: as, *Amphi*bious, living in *two* elements.

3. ANTI, *against*: as, *Anti*acid, against acidity; *anti*febrile, against fever; *anti*thesis, a placing against.

4. APO, APH, *from*: as, *Apo*strophe a turning from; *aph*æresis, a taking from.

5. DIA, *through*: as, *Dia*gonal, through the corners; *dia*meter, the measure through.

6. EPI, EPH, *upon*: as, *Epi*demic, upon the people; *eph*emesa, upon a day.

7. HEMI, *half*: as, *Hemi*sphere, half a sphere.

8. HYPER, *over*: as, *Hyper*critical, over-critical.

9. HYPO, *under*: as, *Hypo*thesis, supposition, or a placing under.

10. META, *beyond, over*: as, *Meta*morphose, to change to another shape.

11. PARA, *against*; as, *Para*dox, something contrary to common opinion

12. PERI, *around*: as, *Peri*phery, the circumference, or measure round

ABBREVIATIONS.

A. or *Ans.* Answer.

A. A. S. Fellow of the American Academy.

A. B. or *B. A.* Bachelor of Arts.

Abp. Archbishop.

Acct. Account.

A. C. Before Christ.

A. D. In the year of our Lord.

Adj. Adjective.

Admr. Administrator.

Adv. Adverb.

Aet. Of age.

Agt. Agent.

Ala. Alabama.

Alt. Altitude.

Am. American.

A. M. Before noon; or in the year of the world.

A. M. or *M. A.* Master of Arts.

Anon. Anonymous.

Apr. April.

Ark. Arkansas.

Art. Article.

Atty. Attorney.

Bp. Bishop.

Capt. Captain.

Chap. Chapter.

Chas. Charles.

Chron. Chronicles.

Co. Company; county.

Col. Colonel.

Coll. College.

Com. Commissioner.

Con. On the other hand.   *E. E.* Errors excepted.

Conj. Conjunction.

Const. Constable.

Cor. Corinthians.

C. P. Court of Probate.   *Eph.* Ephesians.

Cr. Credit, *or* creditor.

Ct. or *Conn.* Connecticut.

Cts. Cents.   and so on.

Cwt. Hundred weight.   *Ex.* Exodus; example.

D. A penny, *or* pence.   *Exr.* Executor.

Dan. Daniel.   *Exrx.* Executrix.

D. C. District of Columbia.   *Feb.* February.

D. D. Doctor of Divinity.   *Fig.* Figure.

Dea. Deacon.   *Fla.* Florida.

Dec. December.   *Fol.* Folio.

Deg. Degree.

Del. Delaware.

Dep. Deputy.

Deut. Deuteronomy.

Dft. Defendant.

Do. or *ditto.* The same.   *Gal.* Galatians.

Doct. or *Dr.* Doctor.   *Gall.* Gallon.

Dolls. or *$.* Dollars.   *Gen.* Genesis; general.

Doz. Dozen.   *Gent.* Gentlemen.

D. P. Doctor of Philosophy.   *Geo.* George.

Dr. Debtor; doctor.   *Gov.* Governor.

Gr. Grain.

G. R. George the King.

H. or *hr.* Hour.

H. B. M. His *or* her Britannic Majesty.

Heb. Hebrews.

Hhd. Hogshead.

H. M. His *or* Her Majesty.

Hon. Honorable.

H. S. E. Here lies buried.

Hund. Hundred.

Ia. or *Ind.* Indiana.

Ib. or *ibid.* In the same place.

id. The same.

i. e. That is.

Ill. Illinois.

Incog. Unknown.

Inst. Instant, *i. e.* present, or of this month.

Isa. Isaiah.

Jan. January.

Jas. or *Ja.* James.

Jno. John.

Jona. Jonathan.

Jos. Joseph.

Josh. Joshua.

Jr. or *Jun.* Junior.

Just. Justice.

Kt. Knight.

Ky. Kentucky.

La. Louisiana.

Maj. Major.

Mar. March.

Mass. Massachusetts.

Matt. Matthew.

M. C. Member of Congress.

Md. Maryland.

N. North ; note.

N. A. North **America.**

N. B. Take particular notice.

N. B. New **Brunswick.**

N. C. North Carolina.

N. E. New England ; north-
east.

Nem. con. No one opposing.

N. H. New Hampshire.

N. J. New Jersey.

No. Number.

N. O. New Orleans.

Nov. November.

N. S Nova Scotia ; new style.

N. T. New Testament.

Num. Numbers.

N. W. North-west.

N. Y. New York.

O. Ohio.

Obt. Obedient.

Oct. October.

O. S. Old Style.

Oxon. Oxford.

Oz. Ounce *or* ounces.

P. Page.

Pa. or *Penn.* Pennsylvania.

Per cent. By the hundred.

Pet. Peter.

Pl. Plural.

P. M. Afternoon ; Postmaster.

P. O. Post Office.

Ss. To wit; namely.

St. Saint; street.

S. T. D. Doctor of Theology.

S. T. P. Professor of Divinity.

S. W. South-west.

Tenn. Tennessee.

Theo. Theological.

Thess. Thessalonians.

Thos. Thomas.

Tim. Timothy.

Tit. Titus.

Tr. Translator; treasurer.

U. C. Upper Canada.

Ult. The last month.

U. S. United States.

U. S. M. United States Mail.

U. S. N. United States Navy.

V. or *vid.* See.

Va. Virginia.

Viz. To wit, namely.

Vol. Volume.

Vols. Volumes.

Vs. Against.

Vt. Vermont.

W. West.

W. I. West Indies.

Wk. Week.

Wm. William.

Wt. Weight.

Yd. Yard.

and so forth.

SYNOPSIS OF GRAMMATICAL RELATIONS.

Subject.	Modifiers of the Subject.	Predicate.	Modifiers of the Predicate.
The SUBJECT of a sentence may be a noun or pronoun; a verb in the infinitive; a clause; or any word or letter of which something can be affirmed.	MODIFIERS of the subject may be a noun in apposition; an adjective; a preposition with its object (adjunct;) a verb in the infinitive and rarely an adverb.	The PREDICATE o a sentence may be a verb; or the verb *be* with any word or expression connected with 1 to complete an assertion.	The MODIFIERS of the predicate may be a noun in the objective case (if the verb is transitive;) a verb in the infinitive; an adverb; a preposition with its object (adjunct;) a clause; and rarely an adjective.

The Subject, modified by one or more words, is called the MODIFIED (or ogical SUBJECT.

The predicate, modified by one or more words, is called the MODIFIED (or logical PREDICATE.

SIMPLE SENTENCES.

BJECTS.

Subject.	Modifiers of the Subject.	Predicate.	Modifiers of the Predicate.
Ferdinand,	the *king*,	held	a council at *Cordova*.
He,	the *marquis* of Cadiz,	beheld	
To die	in peace,	is the privilege	
That you hav wronged me	by your *denial*,	is evident	admission.
Evergreens	*only, among the trees*,	look	nler.
An,	called an article,	is derived	
The rose,	so *fair and beautiful* to-day,	may wither and fade	
Those	who are obliging,	may expect	ted.

MODIFICATION OF WORDS.

Noun or Pronoun.	Verb or Participle.	Adjective.	Adverb.
A noun or pronoun may be modified,	A verb or participle may be modified,	An adjective may be modified,	An adverb may be modified,
1. By a noun in apposition; as, George, the king.	1. By a noun in the objective case, if the verb is transitive; as, The sun gives *light.*	1. By an adv rb; as, *Very* rich.	1. By another adverb; as, *Most* assuredly.
2. By an adjective; as, A *tall* mast.	2. By a verb in the infinitive; as, He hopes *to return.*	2. By a verb in the infinitive; as, Pleasant *to behold.*	2. By a preposition with its object (adjunct;) as, Agreeable *to nature,* most *of all.*
3. By a preposition with its object; (adjunct;) as, A life *of toil.*	3. By a preposition with its object; as, I walk *in the grove.*	3. By a preposition with its object; as, True *to nature.*	
4. By a participle; as, The sun *rising.*	4. By a clause; as, I hope *that you are well.*	4. By another adjective: as, *Deep blue; Liverpool deep blue* earthen pitchers.	**Preposition.**
5. By a verb in the infinitive; as, A time *to die.*	5. By an adjective; as, The wind blows *fresh.*		preposition by be odified,
6. By a clause; as, I, *who speak with you.*			1. y adverb , as, *Fa* beyond.
7. Rarely by an adverb as, Not my feet *only.*			2. By a noun i ;

Analysis of Sentences.

Compound Sentences.

A compound sentence is made up of two or more clauses joined by connectives. Connectives are, 1. *Conjunctions;* 2. *Conjunctive Adverbs;* 3. *Relative words.*

The clauses of a compound sentence are, *Independent, Principal,* and *Subordinate.*

Subordinate clauses are, *Substantive, Adjective,* or *Adverbial.*

it
e

Classification of Sentences.

1. *Declarative;* as, I
2. *Interrogative;* as,
3. *Imperative;* as, B

ti
or predicate *independent;*

INDEX.

—

ABBREVIATIONS.

A. or *Ans.* Answer.

A. A. S. Fellow of the American Academy.

A. B. or *B. A.* Bachelor of Arts.

Abp. Archbishop.

Acct. Account.

A. C. Before Christ.

A. D. In the year of our Lord.

Adj. Adjective.

Admr. Administrator.

Adv. Adverb.

Aet. Of age.

Agt. Agent.

Ala. Alabama.

Alt. Altitude.

Am. American.

A. M. Before noon; or in the year of the world.

A. M. or *M. A.* Master of Arts.

Anon. Anonymous.

Apr. April.

Ark. Arkansas.

Benj. Benjamin.

Chron. Chronicles.

Co. Company; county.

Col. Colonel.

Coll. College.

Com. Commissioner.

Con. On the other hand.

Conj. Conjunction.

Const. Constable.

Cor. Corinthians.

C. P. Court of Probate.

Cr. Credit, *or* creditor.

Ct. or *Conn.* Connecticut.

Cts. Cents.

Cwt. Hundred weight.

D. A penny, *or* pence.

Dan. Daniel.

D. C. District of Columbia.

D. D. Doctor of Divinity.

Dea. Deacon.

Dec. December.

Deg. Degree.

Del. Delaware.

Dep. Deputy.

Deut. Deuteronomy.

Dft. Defendant.

Do. or *ditto.* The same.

Doct. or *Dr.* Doctor.

Dolls. or *$.* Dollars.

Doz. Dozen.

D. P. Doctor of Philosophy.

Dr. Debtor; doctor.

Dwt. Pennyweight.

and so on.

Ex. Exodus; example.

Exr. Executor.

Exrx. Executrix.

Feb. February.

Fig. Figure.

Fla. Florida.

Fol. Folio.

Royal

Gal. Galatians.

Gall. Gallon.

Gen. Genesis; general.

Gent. Gentlemen.

Geo. George.

Gov. Governor.

They crown *the wine* [cups].   They read Cowper ; that is, The poetry of Cowper.   *Gray hairs* should be respected.

6. VISION is a figure by which something imaginary is represented as *real*, and present to the senses.

I seem to myself to behold this city, the ornament of the earth, and the capital of all nations, suddenly involved in one conflagration. I see before me the slaughtered heaps of citizens lying unburied in the midst of their ruined country.   The furious countenance of Cethegus rises to my view, while, with a savage joy, he is triumphing in your miseries.

7. APOSTROPHE is turning off from the regular course of the subject, to address some person or thing.

Soul of the Just ! Companion of the Good.
O sun ! thy everlasting light.

8. HYPERBOLE consists in magnifying or diminishing a thing beyond the truth.

I saw their chief, tall as a rock of ice ; his spear the blasted fir ; his shield the rising moon ; he sat on the shore like a cloud of mist on the hill.

9. SYNECDOCHE is putting the name of the whole of any thing for a part, or a part for the whole ; as the *waves* for the sea, the *roof* for the house, the *head* for the person, the *heart* for the emotions, &c.

10. IRONY is the intentional use of words in a sense contrary to that which the writer or speaker intends to convey ; as,

The prophet Elijah, when he challenged the priests of Baal, " mocked them and said, Cry aloud, for he is a god ; either he is talking, or he is pursuing, or is on a journey, or peradventure he sleepeth, and must be awaked."

11. ANTITHESIS is the placing of different or opposite words in contrast; as,

If you wish to enrich a person, study not to increase his stores, but to diminish his desires.

> Though *poor*, *luxurious*; though *submissive*, *vain*.
> Though *deep*, yet *clear*; though *gentle*, yet not *dull*.

12. CLIMAX is a figure in which the sentiment rises or sinks in regular gradation; as,

Add to your faith virtue; and to virtue knowledge; and to knowledge temperance; &c. See 2 Pet. 1: 5 — 7.

19

When we have finished our work, we will play.

After dinner we will walk in the field.

Intemperance is ruinous to the mind as well as to the body

A wolf let into the sheep-fold, will devour the sheep.

True religion teaches us to be gentle and affable.

My friend died last night, without a struggle or a groan.

PART V.

P R O S O D Y.

Section LXIV.

468. Prosody treats of accent, quantity, and the laws of versification.

1. *Accent* is the laying of a particular stress of voice on a certain syllable in a word ; as, the syllable *ban* in a*ban*don.

2. Accent should not be confounded with Emphasis. *Emphasis* is a stress of voice on a word in a sentence, to mark its importance. *Accent* is a stress of voice on a syllable in a word.

3. The *quantity* of a syllable is the time which is required to pronounce it. A short syllable requires half the time of a long one.

VERSIFICATION.

469. *Versification* is a measured arrangement of words into poetical lines or verses.

1. A *verse* consists of a certain number of accented and unaccented syllables, arranged according to certain rules.

2. *Rhyme* is the correspondence of the last sound of one line to the last sound of another.

3. *Blank verse* is the name given to a kind of poetry written without *rhyme*.

Lightning Source UK Ltd.
Milton Keynes UK
UKOW05f1937081216
289489UK00001B/293/P